Braking the Special Interests

Braking the Special Interests

Trucking Deregulation and the Politics of Policy Reform

Dorothy Robyn

The University of Chicago Press • Chicago and London

Dorothy Robyn is assistant professor of public policy in the John F. Kennedy School of Government, Harvard University.

The University of Chicago Press, Chicago 60637
The University of Chicago Press, Ltd., London
© 1987 by The University of Chicago
All rights reserved. Published 1987
Printed in the United States of America

96 95 94 93 92 91 90 89 88 87   5 4 3 2 1

Library of Congress Cataloging-in-Publication Data

Robyn, Dorothy L.
  Braking the special interests.

  Bibliography: p.
  Includes index.
  1. Trucking—United States. 2. Trucking—Government
policy—United States. I. Title.
HE5623.R63   1987   388.3'24'0973   86-16015
ISBN 0-226-72328-3

For Lennie

Contents

Preface

In the fall of 1979, I was hit by a truck—figuratively speaking. Leonard Ross, a young Berkeley law professor who had served recently as a California public utilities commissioner, enthralled me and fellow members of a seminar in regulatory economics with tales of futile efforts to deregulate California's trucking industry. After receiving veiled threats from union members who, like the regulated carriers they worked for, preferred to keep on truckin' in the existing system, Ross and other reform commissioners began wearing specially made buttons that read, "Keep on Deregulatin'."

Would-be trucking deregulators at the national level were encountering the same fierce opposition. Eliminating the federal system of protective regulation, which kept shipping rates artificially high, would produce billions of dollars of diffuse savings to consumers. But it would mean large and visible losses for two of Washington's undisputed heavyweights—the regulated trucking industry and the Teamsters Union. Political observers said it couldn't be done.

The dilemma was familiar. As a student in Berkeley's Graduate School of Public Policy, I had encountered a range of policy problems in which the basic obstacle to reform was the same: While society as a whole would benefit (diffusely) from the change, certain highly organized, politically influential interests would lose visibly. Hence these interests, however narrow, were able to block reform.

Intrigued by the prospect of studying this policy dilemma in more detail, I went to Washington, D.C., in December 1979 to interview supporters and opponents of federal trucking deregulation—a reform favored by the Carter administration because of its anti-inflationary potential. I packed enough clothes for a month; I stayed a year. At the beginning of that year, deregulation of the trucking industry was an unlikely prospect; at year-end, it was a congressional fait accompli.

While the deregulators' victory was by no means complete—the Motor Carrier Act of 1980 stopped short of total decontrol—it was significant: The potential savings to consumers were vast (estimates ranged from $5 billion to $8 billion annually). Even more important, it represented a case where diffuse interests triumphed over fire-in-the-belly resistance from narrow economic groups.

In part this upset was due to exogenous factors—that is, to structural changes in society that altered the traditional policymaking environment. It's no coincidence that Congress deregulated airlines, air cargo, buses, financial institutions, and trucking all within the space of a few years. The economy is perhaps the single most important structural explanation for deregulators' repeated success: The persistence of double-digit inflation served to enhance the traditionally poor political "market" for efficiency-based reforms.

But structural factors such as steep inflation by no means made trucking decontrol inevitable. In part, the upset is explained by the calculated efforts—strategic behavior—of regulatory reformers. (The two explanations link up at many points, since good strategy exploits structural conditions.) That explanation—and, more generally, the political strategy involved in defeating client groups—is the focus of the following pages.

That focus makes sense if one's interest in policy is prescriptive, as mine is. To explain a political upset as the product of structural conditions is illuminating, to be sure; but one can do little to influence such conditions. The aim of this analysis of the trucking battle is more instrumental: to draw practical insights pertinent to circumventing special interests. This calls for a focus on that part of the explanation—namely, strategic action—that *can* be influenced.

The analysis draws on my own observation of the trucking contest—both on and off the battlefield—between December 1979, when President Carter put motor-carrier deregulation on his "short list" of desired reforms, and July 1980, when he signed the act. Committee hearings, markups, and floor votes provided a view of the formal process. However, far more information and insight came from my contacts with participants on both sides—through office interviews, shared subway rides, and informal conversations in Capitol Hill cafeterias and watering holes.

Particularly important as a source of information were the meetings of the ad hoc coalition supporting reform, which I attended regularly as an observer. These strategy sessions, held approximately every week, brought together lobbyists, Capitol Hill staffers, White House aides, and other representatives of the Carter administration. I was also able to observe many other, less structured get-togethers where deregulators or truckers discussed strategy.

Based on my observations, following the deregulators' victory I developed a simple formula to explain that outcome and then undertook a more systematic examination of the formula's four elements: strategic use of economic evidence and policy analysis to demonstrate the merits of deregulation; organization of a diverse coalition of firms and interest groups lobbying for reform; use of transition strategies to soften opposition to change; and strategic bargaining by the president with Congress. I interviewed at length most of the key participants—about sixty deregulators, congressional staffers, and representatives of trucking and Teamster interests. Wherever possible, I examined relevant files and records of the individuals I interviewed.

This brief description of methodology gives only a hint of the many people who contributed to the pages that follow. The list rightfully begins in Berkeley. Eugene Bardach at the Graduate School of Public Policy directed my dissertation, on which this book is based; I benefited greatly from the guidance and insight he provided through lettters, coast-to-coast phone conversations, and back-of-the-chapter critiques. Lee Friedman helped me to see where an economic perspective shed light on political strategy and where it failed to; that's been the smallest of his contributions as my teacher and friend for many years. David Kirp approached the task of advising me with his usual enthusiasm, reviewing chapters with a writer's fine eye for detail and pushing me to see their potential as a book.

I was fortunate to have capable "advisers" in Washington as well. Con Hitchcock, the coordinator of the ad hoc coalition, spent many hours educating me about airline deregulation and the nuances of interest-group politics. Four other leaders of the deregulation team were immensely helpful in allowing me to observe the process from the inside: Ron Lewis and Rick Neustadt, the two White House aides who directed the administration effort; Frank Swain, the chairman of the ad hoc coalition; and Gary Broemser, the head of DOT's Office of Regulatory Policy. Two lobbyists from the American Trucking Associations—Kent Burton and George Mead—were informative and supportive.

I am grateful to the many lobbyists, congressional staffers, and others who took time to talk with me and showed such an interest in "my paper." While I cannot list them all, I would like to acknowledge some: Joe Ayres, Lana Batts, Bill Borghesani, Chas Cadwell, Tom Callaghan, Cindy Douglass, Nancy Drabble, Pamela Garvey, Stan Hamilton, Dick Henderson, Mary Jo Jacobi, Allan Jones, Dick Klem, Sharon Nelson, Jack Pearce, Will Ris, Stan

Sender, Shelby Southard, Jay Steptoe, and Don Tepper. Dave Cawthorne was a continuing source of information and encouragement. Martin Cromartie was kind and helpful; I am one of the many people who miss him.

Financial support came from several sources. As a Ph.D. student in the public policy school, I received fellowships from the National Institute of Mental Health and the Pericles Foundation. Berkeley's Institute for Governmental Studies awarded me a small grant to study trucking deregulation. The Institute for Transportation Studies at Berkeley gave me generous support while I was writing my dissertation and paid my way for an extended return visit to Washington, D.C. The Bureau of Social Science Research provided me with office space while I was in Washington; Albert Biderman of the bureau gave me warm support and good advice. Finally, the Department of Urban Studies and Planning at MIT awarded me a postdoctoral fellowship, which allowed me to complete my research.

Harvard's Kennedy School of Government, where I have been teaching the last two years, provided a stimulating environment in which to continue thinking and writing about political strategy; two colleagues—Jim Verdier and Steve Kelman—were particularly supportive. Two members of the larger Boston academic community—Bob Fogelson of MIT and Joe Quinn of Boston College—also gave guidance. In addition, I would like to thank Richard Elmore of Michigan State University and Marc Landy of Boston College for their thorough reviews of a book draft.

Lennie Ross, who sparked the idea for my dissertation, died tragically in May 1985. He inspired me far more than he ever knew, and he continues to do so.

1

Congress and the Special Interests

There is nothing more difficult to carry out, nor more doubtful of success, nor more dangerous to handle, than to initiate a new order of things. For the reformer has enemies in all those who profit by the old order, and only lukewarm defenders in all those who would profit by the new order....
—Niccolò Machiavelli

A recent *New York Times* editorial speculated what would happen if the proposal to proclaim Thanksgiving an official holiday came before Congress today. The bill—introduced, naturally, by the Massachusetts congressman whose district embraces both Plymouth Rock and cranberry bogs—meets trouble at the Agriculture Committee hearings from goose and duck growers who denounce what they call rank favoritism for turkeys. But the outlook for Thanksgiving improves with favorable testimony from the Farm Bureau Federation, representing pumpkin and corn growers; television networks, for whom legalization would mean a three-game football day; and the greeting card industry. The House and Senate eventually pass the Thanksgiving bill in different forms, but they cut deals and compromise in conference. Even the poultry growers are appeased by pledges to promote the Long Island duck for Easter and talk up the Christmas goose.[1]

Satiric license aside, a proposal to create a new national holiday would not likely be dominated by narrow economic interest groups. It's too visible, and the impact on individual citizens too direct and widespread. Far more typical of economic interest-group domination was a fight in Congress reported in the same issue of the *Times*. The news story described how the tobacco lobby, despite its stiffest challenge ever, had preserved the federal tobacco program—a system of price supports and acreage allotments set up in the 1930s ostensibly to ensure stable prices and supply. Even if those aims were once valid, the program has become a needless subsidy to a politically potent industry. Health effects notwithstanding, the program costs taxpayers millions of dollars a year.

The tobacco lobby's victory was no fluke. Fifty thousand tobacco growers have repeatedly defeated the interests of millions of federal taxpayers because on low-visibility distributive issues, intensity overwhelms numbers in our political system. The loss to an individual grower from ending the inefficient subsidy would be considerable, whereas the gain to an individual taxpayer would be minuscule. Thus the tobacco industry is highly organized around the issue, while the public at large is not. Much of what opposition the industry did meet appeared to represent, not taxpayer representation, but rather backlash against one of tobacco's staunchest defenders, Sen. Jesse Helms (R–N.C.), whose tough stands on abortion, school busing, and food stamps angered moderates and liberals.[2]

The intensity phenomenon also explains why many desirable policy initiatives (as distinct from policy terminations) are never adopted. Whenever a proposed change promises small benefits to many at the expense of substantial losses to a few, potential losers are more informed, organized, and motivated than those who stand to gain. Thus small minorities can block programs that would serve the general welfare.

This political problem is one of the greatest obstacles to economic growth in this country. Respected economists have argued that the solutions exist to the nation's major economic problems—inflation, environmental decay, energy scarcity, overregulation. But the solutions all require that some identifiable group undergo a significant drop in its standard of living. No group wants to be the one to suffer for the general good, and our political system has difficulty forcing anyone to shoulder the burden.[3]

Special-Interest Benefits

If the strength of narrow interests is a major obstacle to solving our economic problems, it's also an initial cause of those problems. Thousands of organized elites press for favored treatment, and their demands go largely unnoticed by the dispersed majority that pays the cost. Lacking an adequate internal mechanism or incentive to force trade-offs among competing claims, Congress sequentially accommodates these elites with too little concern for overall consequences.

Special-interest benefits take many forms—acreage allotments to tobacco growers, price supports for dairy farmers, tax-exempt municipal bonds, subsidized student loans, parity prices for grain producers, restrictions on auto and motorcycle imports, home mortgage deductions, bailouts for troubled industries, tax credits for owners of wood-burning stoves, minimum-wage guarantees, public-works projects, subsidized financing for international trade, sugar price supports, charter restrictions for banks, marketing orders for oranges and lemons, the oil depletion allowance, real estate tax shelters, low-interest financing for rural electric cooperatives, postal subsidies for nonprofit organizations. While some are justified, many are not; they reduce economic efficiency with no offsetting contribution to equity, equality, or any other legitimate policy aim. "The hogs were really feeding," said OMB director David Stockman about the Reagan administration's efforts to reduce the budget in the face of interest-group opposition.[4]

Special-interest benefits such as import tariffs and price supports are inefficient in the short run. Over time, the accumulation of these short-run inefficiencies stunts the economy's growth by distorting the market's means to allocate resources and thus eliminate surpluses and shortages.

But the most important way economic interest groups impede long-term growth is by limiting the entry of competitors into the markets they control. Acreage allotments, motor carrier operating rights, airline franchises, bank charters, professional licensing requirements, closed-shop laws; these and other barriers to entry—erected by groups that proclaim the virtues of the competitive marketplace for everyone but themselves—create an "institutional sclerosis" that discourages innovation and impedes the healthy struggle for survival in an evolving economy.[5]

The inability of the majority to veto the costly demands of narrow elites is perfectly consistent with economic reasoning. By "the logic of collective action," an economic explanation of organizations and public goods, a rational individual will not voluntarily make sacrifices to help achieve the political objectives of any large group to which he belongs. His absence will not be noticed: The support or lack of support of any single individual will not affect the political outcome. Moreover, the benefits of political victory are nonexclusive, so he will receive them whether or not he pays dues to an organization or writes to his congressman.[6] Thus, while the benefits (losses not incurred) would be worth a great deal to the group as a whole, no single individual has the incentive to contribute to the costs of collective action.[7]

Most members of a large majority don't know enough even to consider collective action against a minority demand. The potential cost to any one of them is so small that it's not worth their while to be informed. Few milk consumers know how their congressman voted on dairy price supports, but every milk producer knows. Thus 200,000 producers can repeatedly defeat the interests of 200 million consumers in Congress.[8]

To a point, the political process should legitimately weigh intensity of feeling. The flaw in a purely democratic system is that an apathetic majority can defeat an intense minority to the detriment of both equity and efficiency. But basic features of our modified democracy serve to give organized minorities undue weight.

Perhaps no feature of our political process does more to generate benefits for concentrated interests than the principle of geographic representation. Under a system of geographic—as opposed to at-large—representation, legislators are foremost concerned with protecting local and regional interests. When a region's economic base is concentrated—as with manufacturing industries such as steel, textiles, or automobiles, or agricultural industries such as tobacco, sugar, or dairy products—political representatives quite rightly serve as spokesmen for that narrow economic interest. Tariffs, import quotas, crop subsidies, defense contracts, public-works projects, tax concessions to individual industries and companies—these are all policies adopted in part because of their economic impact on narrow geographic regions.[9]

In many areas of social and economic policy, such as national defense, foreign affairs, criminal justice, and welfare policy, members of Congress vote according to their (and their constituents') perception of the costs and benefits to the nation as a whole. But where policy has a strong "local imprint," congressmen engage in the "quest for local benefits."[10]

That quest is often successful because of the decentralization and specialization that characterize much congressional decision making. The committee and subcommittee are the loci of power, and assignment to those work groups is based largely on self-selection.[11] Hence, policy affecting the dairy industry is set chiefly by a Senate committee and House subcommittee that overrepresent dairy states. Even when policies have no particular geographic link, the incentive is for committee members to cater to the narrowly attentive groups. "More than mere specialization," observed Douglass Cater, "the subcommittee system permits development of tight little cadres of special interest legislators and gives them great leverage."[12]

As Richard Fenno so aptly demonstrated, "committees differ from one another."[13] Some are predominantly concerned with gaining influence within Congress, others with making good public policy, still others with ensuring members' reelection.[14] Even among the latter group, there are differences: committees that must balance a range of potentially conflicting interests are less responsive to special interests than those that deal with narrow constituencies.

Whatever their predominant concern, the absence of central leadership—a condition that has described Congress throughout most of its history—means that committees, and individual members within committees, need not compete with one another for resources, at least with respect to low-visibility issues. Rather, the members follow a policy of reciprocity or "reciprocal noninterference," whereby narrow groups form coalitions, each agreeing to support the others' claims in return for support of its own.[15] As Roger Davidson observed, issues characterized by low salience and low conflict are typically handled in subcommittee with little interference in committee or on the floor. "In the absence of incentives for widespread member involvement, legislators and staff members from the panel with original jurisdiction are the primary, and perhaps the only, cue-givers."[16]

Under other conditions, vote trading produces more efficient collective decisions than straight majority voting. When everyone has an equal stake in the outcome of the entire set of votes, logrolling is a desirable way to reflect the relative intensity of preferences on individual issues. The problem in our system is that narrow groups with a small stake in the total set of issues can trade away votes on all but the few issues that touch them and thus ensure their victory to the detriment of the general welfare.[17]

Political parties, though never very strong in this country, once forced some discipline on this process of accommodating narrow interests out of concern for their own future. But major political and technological developments—civil service, direct primary elections, and television—have usurped the parties' traditional roles in supplying patronage, slate making, and providing cues to voters. Partly in response to the decline of parties, Congress has further increased the number and autonomy of subcommittees and weakened the central leadership still more.

These and other structural adaptations on the part of Congress were a response to changing economic and political conditions. Historically, several key committees—House and Senate Appropriations, House Ways and Means, and Senate Finance—provided a brake on the expenditure demands of authorizing committees and executive agencies, in keeping with prevailing notions of balanced budgets and limited government. But as postwar public expectations legitimized an increasingly active role for the federal government in providing programs, benefits, and services for constituents, those "control committees" were weakened or otherwise changed to accommodate the new politics of distribution.[18]

Economic growth throughout the 1950s and 1960s enabled Congress to provide distributive benefits to countless organized interests without instituting redistributive policies such as tax increases. But when the 1970s brought a decline in productivity and economic expansion, Congress—which had only recently completed the adaptation to a politics of growth and distribution—could not, and still has not been able to, respond adequately.[19] These developments, according to Aaron Wildavsky, may explain a political puzzle: the increasing support shown for representatives by their constituents amid a general decline in esteem for Congress as a whole. The key may be that "constituents are in fact getting what they want from their representatives, but what they want and get on each matter does not [equal] what they want in total."[20]

Imposing Losses

Everyone's solution to this dilemma—and to our overall economic dilemma—is the same: Let someone else make the sacrifice. "Each group," wrote Lester Thurow in *Zero-Sum Society,* "wants government to use its power to protect it and to force others to do what is in the general interest."[21] Most get their wish. For the same forces that produce countless bills and amendments benefiting special interests operate even *more* reliably to protect organized groups from suffering substantial economic losses.

Human nature is one reason for this difference. People are inherently risk averse: They are more sensitive to sudden and sharp losses than to equally sudden and sharp gains.[22] Thus, an organized minority is even more intense when faced with the prospect of loss than with the prospect of gain.[23]

The political process respects this instinct. As Charles Schultze observed in *The Public Use of Private Interest,* an implicit rule of our political system is "Do no direct harm." Sometimes we make it up to those who get hurt directly by government action—either through monetary compensation or through general income redistribution. But more often, we preclude the harm in the first place.[24]

This happens automatically because the intensity-sensitive features of our political system weight the vote of organized groups according to the potential harm to them. We tacitly observe what Schultze called the principle of increasing marginal harm—the mirror image of the notion of diminishing marginal utility—whereby large costs to a few are more to be avoided than small costs to many.

This principle is rooted in the Constitution. The founding fathers feared that a popular majority would coalesce and trample the liberties of the privileged elites. To guard against a tyranny of the majority, power was parcelled out through an elaborate system of constitutional checks and balances. Over the years, other formal and informal rules for decentralizing political control—judicial review, the power of congressional committees, the Senate filibuster—have been developed and justified on the rationale of protecting minority rights.[25]

Our system has reduced the risk of majority tyranny at the expense of facilitating minority tyranny. It is a complex, fragmented system geared to grind slowly. At key stages, influential groups can often veto the alternative preferred by the majority. At the very least, they can substantially delay the harm to themselves, and the power to delay is often the power to decide.

The principle of increasing marginal harm makes sense to a degree. To restate an earlier point, from an economic standpoint, collective action should reflect intensity of feeling. If a proposed change will cost five people $1,000 each but only save 1,000 people $4 each, the change is not efficient. Yet a system of majority rule would adopt it overwhelmingly. Our system errs in the other direction, however, so that efficient changes—ones where the gains outweigh the losses—can often be blocked by the losers.

Of course there is nothing sacred about efficiency, as Schultze reminds us: "Dealing with the problem of losses, which an emphasis on efficiency necessarily raises, is one of the stickiest social issues. There is absolutely nothing in either economic or political theory to argue that efficiency considerations should always take precedence."[26] But Schultze, like many other people, believes that "we place far too much stress on eschewing efficient solutions, and far too little on compensation and general income-redistribution measures. Over time, the cumulative consequences are likely to be a much smaller social pie for everyone."[27] Stated differently, by compensating losers out of the gains from an efficient change, no one need be made worse off. We can have our pie and eat it too.

Some would argue that it is preferable to settle for a smaller social pie overall in return for the assurance that no one will lose part of his or her share. Even if the government could simultaneously guarantee a larger pie and assure protection of those who would lose in the process, this would not be sufficient; the objection is not to the potentially unequal outcomes but to the unjust process.

But if greater economic equality is the goal, a political system that caters to organized interests is hardly the way to achieve it. As E. E. Schattschneider wrote many years ago in response to the popular view that the plurality of special-interest groups reflects *all* interests: "The flaw in the pluralist heaven is that the heavenly chorus sings with a strongly upper-class accent."[28]

The accent—still distinctly upper class—has faded somewhat. The War on Poverty and the Great Society programs, while not primarily a response to organized pressure, created their own focused constituencies. Disadvantaged groups such as blacks, women, the poor, and the handicapped have become more militant, in part with the aid of federal funds.

The politicization of the have-nots is one reason that it's becoming even harder to find solutions to our economic problems, all of which require that there be losers. Groups that once shouldered much of the burden will no longer tolerate their plight, and our system is paralyzed in the face of their (as well as any other) organized resistance. Economist Lester Thurow calls for major income redistribution as the solution—equitable in its own right—to the political stalemate.[29]

Thurow cites other reasons that it is increasingly difficult to make efficient (loss-imposing) changes. Industrialization is one. Whereas economic destruction is unavoidable in agrarian societies, which are at the mercy of weather and agricultural blight, in industrial societies destruction results from identifiable human actions. Because economic loss is avoidable, it's become intolerable. Another product of industrialization—the growth of large economic institutions—also forces government to intervene as a protector. While "the doctrine of failure" is at the heart of capitalism, government can't afford the failure of major economic institutions like Lockheed, Chrysler, and New York City. And when one major institution is bailed out, others demand the same treatment.[30]

Changes in our legal and political system have also added to the difficulty of imposing concentrated losses. The courts now provide a way for organized groups to delay that which they oppose. Often the cost of the delay and uncertainty forces both government and private industry to cancel projects that would otherwise be profitable. Also important is the decline of political parties, which could be held accountable for the economic problems resulting from *not* imposing losses. "When no one can be held responsible for failure," observes Thurow, "it becomes possible for everyone who contributed to the failure to be reelected time after time."[31]

Withdrawing Benefits

One *can* point to significant policy initiatives that were enacted in recent years despite the resistance of highly organized groups. Medicare—opposed by the powerful medical lobby—is one. Laws regulating auto safety, environmental pollution, and workplace hazards are others. Leaving aside the controversy over whether the benefits of such regulation outweigh the costs, those costs—at least directly—fall narrowly on the regulated industries.

In the cases of Medicare and health and safety regulation, the losses were imposed as the result of initiating a new policy rather than terminating some existing, special-interest subsidy. Even if that distinction is irrelevant in economic terms, it's very important politically. For the most ambitious of all loss-imposing policy reforms are those that seek to deny or reduce special-interest benefits once they are granted.

A client group has all the advantages of a political system set up to protect the rights of organized minorities, and then some. The reform proposal is sent to a specialized subcommittee with strong ties to the group, based on familiarity and a history of goodwill and campaign contributions. A promising reform proposal might get support from another subcommittee looking for a good issue, but generally legislative entrepreneurs find it more rewarding to create than to terminate.

If the proposal gets a hearing, the witness list is typically stacked. Experienced interest-group spokesmen testify that to terminate the program will jeopardize the public interest—something many of them sincerely believe—and they offer well-packaged evidence to support their claims. Skeptics face the risk of electoral damage made credible by a "snowdown" of letters and Mailgrams, as well as numerous telephone calls and personal visits, all coordinated by a well-heeled professional organization whose existence may well depend on the continuation of the government policy in question. Group members, confronted by a clear and visible threat from the outside, become more cohesive and integrated than ever.

The client group has also gained a powerful ally in the time since Congress initially accommodated its interests. Much has been written about the "iron triangle"—the symbiotic link between the committee (or subcommittee) that legislates, the outside group that benefits, and the agency that administers. In addition to sympathetic ties to the client group, a bureaucratic agency develops an enormous stake in administering per se. James Q. Wilson has observed that the "special interests" that regulatory agencies serve are often really the judges, consultants, business lobbyists, and others involved in the regulatory process itself.[32]

Terminating any government undertaking is hard, be it a tariff to protect industry, the U.S. Army Horse Cavalry, or the Vietnam War. A public program inevitably builds up a constituency of direct and indirect beneficiaries who will fight for its survival. Their fight is made easier by the fact that government programs, like national monuments, are built to last. As Robert Biller observed, examples of policy termination are so rare because we have "taken persistence and continuity to be in general what we want to produce. . . . [We] assume that our investments in policies and organizations are . . . to be amortized through their future 'rightness'. . . ."[33]

Battles to terminate political programs take on a special cast because of their moral element as well. Eugene Bardach concluded that the "peculiar strength of most anti-termination coalitions lies, first, in the general moral repugnance Americans . . . feel towards the deliberate disruption of arrangements which people have learned to rely on for a significant portion of their livelihoods or careers."[34] Jerry Wilson, chief of the Washington, D.C., police department, said it another way in describing his (ultimately successful) struggle to abolish the city's motorcycle squad: "It's hard to get people to do things that will hurt somebody."[35]

In sum, in any battle to eliminate government benefits, the defenders have powerful forces on their side, and their leaders are highly skilled at marshalling these forces. "Power is contingent," said a dismayed David Stockman. "The client groups know how to make themselves heard. The problem is, unorganized groups can't play in this game."[36]

Trucking Regulation

Until recently, few examples illustrated the power of client groups better than federal regulation of the trucking industry. Interstate Commerce Commission controls on rates and entry resulted in a gigantic subsidy to regulated trucking firms. Consumers unwittingly paid the cost.

By a generous interpretation of history, motor carrier regulation may have served a valid purpose when it was instituted in the days of bread lines and soup kitchens. Many policymakers lost faith in the market during the Depression and feared that excessive competition would destroy struggling industries. Banks and airlines were regulated partly for the same reason: Congress feared they would compete to the death under Depression conditions. But Congress was encouraged in its thinking by established members of those industries—businessmen who preferred the security of regulation to the discipline and uncertainty of the marketplace.

Even if government protection of the trucking industry once served the public's interest, it ceased to years ago. By limiting the number of firms that could compete, and by allowing those firms to collude in setting prices, regulation kept shipping rates above the competitive level. So profitable was the regulated trucking business that individual firms sold their operating authorities for millions of dollars.

Recognizing its stake in preserving regulation, the trucking industry developed one of the strongest lobbies in the country. The industry's political strength knew no geographic boundaries, since there is at least one trucking firm in nearly every congressional district in the country. Moreover, the industry had a powerful ally in the giant International Brotherhood of Teamsters union, whose members received the trickle-down benefits of the truckers' cartel.

Essential to the regulated industry's continued prosperity was the active support of the ICC. Whatever the intent of the Depression legislation, the commission came to see its role as that of protecting the regulated industry. This protection cost consumers billions of dollars annually. But transportation charges are small and hidden enough in the cost of individual items that the prospect of eliminating regulatory controls inspired little enthusiasm on the part of those who would benefit. Harry Truman was the first of several presidents who tried unsuccessfully in Congress to reform trucking regulation.

Jimmy Carter finally succeeded. Despite the all-out opposition of the trucking industry and the Teamsters Union—two of Washington's undisputed heavyweights—Congress passed a bill in 1980 to substantially deregulate trucking. How that reform came about—in seeming violation of all the established rules—is the subject of this book.

The following chapters attempt to analyze this political upset in a way that will prove useful to others with an interest in policy reform. Hence the focus is on strategy—which is subject to reformers' control—more than structure. Trucking was only one of several industries that Congress partially or substantially deregulated in the late 1970s and early 1980s. Clearly major structural changes in the economic and political order helped to produce this unusual outcome, and three of them—a highly inflationary economy, greater intellectual acceptance of the competitive-market ideal, and the rise of a consumer movement followed by the mobilization of business interests—receive considerable attention in the following chapters. But my major interest is in what trucking reformers did—given a climate that was favorable to deregulation—to bring it about and in what one can say about strategy more generally based on their experience.

I posit a four-part recipe for deregulators' political success and then examine the four "ingredients" as they operated in the trucking battle: (1) strategic use of economic evidence and analysis to demonstrate the merits of the case for reform; (2) formation and maintenance of an ad hoc coalition to lobby actively; (3) use of transition strategies to soften the opposition to change; and (4) strategic bargaining by the president to gain sheer political leverage. The concluding chapter generalizes from that battle to other contests where the aim is to terminate a client-group policy.

2

The Trucking Industry
and Its Regulation

*If we stick with the [NRA] Code or can get some [ICC] regulation
with enough of the Code features to at least make possible organization of the industry, we can ... begin to get results that will
mean dollars and cents in the pockets of trucking operators like
yourself.*
—Trucking Industry Leader, March 1935

Origins of Trucking Regulation

Like an understudy who outshines the absent star, the trucking industry established itself during a temporary "absence" of railroads, and the
railroads never regained the spotlight. During World War I, when the rails
were nationalized to assure speedy transport of military troops and sup-
plies, they were often forced to suspend shipment of other freight. Motor
carriers took up the slack. The railroads returned to private control in 1920,
but by then, trucks were an accepted form of transportation, and their use
quickly expanded.[1]

The railroads campaigned for state controls that would limit the
competitive advantage of the trucking industry. The railroad industry had
itself been regulated for many years—both by state commissions and by the
Interstate Commerce Commission, established in 1887 for that purpose.
Maximum-rate controls shielded merchants and farmers from monopolistic
pricing. Even more important as a historical explanation for regulation,

minimum-rate controls protected the railroads from one another. But the same regulation that restrained rate cutting within the rail industry left railroads vulnerable to competition from outside.

The state commissions that oversaw railroads also sought controls on trucking, as a way both to ease the decline of railroads and to expand their own influence. Pennsylvania was the first state to adopt trucking controls, in 1914. Thirty-five states had followed suit by 1925. These controls—modeled after regulation of railroads and public utilities—restricted entry into the trucking industry and limited maximum and minimum rates that truckers could charge.

The first proposal for federal regulation of motor carriers took shape in 1925, in response to Supreme Court decisions that upset the informal practice of states controlling interstate trucking on the grounds that the practice invaded a field reserved by the Commerce Clause of the Constitution for federal regulation.[2] The bill—drafted by the National Association of Regulatory Utility Commissioners—called for national controls that would be administered by boards of state commissioners, with the ICC—which had shown little interest in trucking regulation—to intervene only in the event of an appeal. The railroads solidly supported the proposal. Opponents included most truckers, representatives of labor, and shipper groups. But Congress delayed action with respect to trucks and focused instead on regulation of buses, since railroads were still primarily concerned with the decline in passenger traffic and revenue.[3]

When the depression settled in several years later, the railroads were extremely hard hit, and the pressure for trucking regulation increased. One vocal proponent was the Security Owners' Association—a politically powerful group of investors in railroad securities that included more than 1,500 national and state banks, trust companies, mutual savings banks, and life insurance companies. In 1932, the SOA established the National Transportation Commission, with former president Calvin Coolidge as its chairman, and the following year the commission recommended regulation of trucking.[4]

The railroads' plight also attracted the support of many politicians, most notably Franklin Roosevelt. In a widely publicized campaign speech in 1932, presidential candidate Roosevelt called for elimination of the "unfair competitive advantages" of the trucking industry. Once elected, Roosevelt announced "plans for the regulation of all forms of transportation."[5]

The depression also served to eliminate the trucking industry's resistance to regulation, as Ellis Hawley describes:

> With the coming of the depression, the drastic drop in demand, and the resulting struggle for available markets, the attitude of some of the larger

trucking firms began to change. Their position, they felt, was seriously threatened by the appearance of cut-rate, "fly-by-night" operators, who, with the aid of truck dealers and manufacturers, managed to get a truck on credit, to eke out a living on cut rates until they lost it, and in the process to force down wages and disrupt the whole rate structure. Under the circumstances, there was growing support in trucking, bus, and teamster circles for some type of regulation, some system that would establish minimum rates and wages and eliminate irresponsible operators.[6]

Thus, in 1933, many trucking firms welcomed the establishment of a price and wage code under the National Industrial Recovery Act. Most truckers continued to prefer the code to legislation that would give regulatory control to the rail-minded ICC—the alternative favored by railroads, state rail commissions, and Roosevelt's federal coordinator of transportation. The motor carrier industry—represented by the newly formed American Trucking Associations (ATA)—was joined in its opposition to legislation by shippers and by auto manufacturers concerned with maintaining the growing market for trucks.[7]

Fearful that Congress would not renew the National Recovery Administration codes when they expired in 1935, the ATA modified its stance on a regulatory bill and testified that the industry was "willing to be controlled by the Federal Government" under a reorganized ICC. But when the Supreme Court declared the NRA unconstitutional in May of 1935, the ATA dropped its opposition to a regulatory bill altogether and became an active sponsor of federal controls.[8]

With the major source of resistance now gone, legislation passed Congress with relative ease. The Motor Carrier Act of 1935 gave the ICC broad regulatory powers over most interstate motor carriers with respect to entry and rates, as well as labor practices, safety, and the issuance of trucking securities. Exempted from regulation were shippers who transported their own goods and carriers hauling unprocessed agricultural commodities—a testament to the political clout of "private carriers" and farmers. (In addition, intrastate trucking remained subject solely to state regulation.) With its domain only slightly narrowed by these exemptions, the ICC set out to reduce competitive disturbances both within the trucking industry and between trucking and rail.[9]

The following years saw dramatic changes in the ICC and the industries it oversaw. Once regarded suspiciously by the trucking industry, the commission gradually adopted an attitude toward motor carriers that was strongly protectionist. The regulated trucking industry changed too—from a struggling infant to a mature, prosperous adult. State highway construction, responding to the flood of new cars bought following World War II, made trucking faster and cheaper. But the real boon was construction of the interstate highway system, which permitted truckers to compete seriously with railroads for long-distance freight. With the highways began a movement of industry away from rail sites and into suburban and rural areas serviceable by trucks. The industrialization of the South, which had few railroads to start with, also benefited trucking as it hurt the rails.[10]

The highway network, combined with significant increases in standard truck size (from twenty-seven feet in the late 1940s to forty-five feet thirty years later), and the inherent advantage of being able to offer door-to-door delivery, produced a rate of growth in motor carriage far greater than that of the economy itself. By 1980, interstate trucking earned $67 billion a year, accounting for over 70 percent of interstate freight revenues.[11] In 1979, the average family spent $800 a year for interstate truck transportation, which is a hidden cost in virtually every product the consumer buys. Of that, about 46 percent—$31 billion total—went to motor carriers regulated by the ICC.

The following section describes the basic regulatory system that shaped the growth of the entire industry. Many of the policies described were modified or eliminated in the late 1970s by the ICC; the Motor Carrier Act of 1980 essentially codified changes made by a commission that became increasingly reform minded as the prospect of legislative deregulation increased. Other aspects of the system were preserved; the 1980 act reduced regulatory controls on the trucking industry, but it did not eliminate them altogether.

The System

I used to say that if you drew an organization chart of the ATA, there would be a dotted line leading to a box labeled "ICC".
—ATA lobbyist, July 1980

Entry

ICC controls on trucking (like the earlier state controls) were modeled after classical public-utility regulation. The traditional rationale for such regulation is that certain enterprises—like the telephone industry, railroads, and electric utilities—are "natural monopolies." The technology of these industries is (or once was) such that it would be wasteful to society to have more than one company take on the enormous cost of stringing phone lines or laying track. Since the average cost per connection goes down as the network expands, one competitor will inevitably emerge as the sole provider—or "natural monopolist." In return for protecting the naturally monopolistic industry from competition, regulation requires that it provide service to all who desire it—what's known as the common-carrier obligation. Thus the phone company can't refuse to connect lines to a new home just because it's out of the way.

The motor carrier industry was regulated as a public utility, even though it did not fit the description of a natural monopoly and that was not the rationale for the 1935 act. The ICC granted trucking firms near-exclusive operating rights to carry certain commodities on certain routes. In principle, these firms performed a common-carrier obligation in return.

The great majority of common-carrier operating rights held even in the late 1970s were issued under the "grandfather clause" of the Motor Carrier Act. Given automatically to (18,000) trucking companies that were in business in 1935, the grandfather rights authorized them to maintain their existing routes and service. Later, operating rights became much more difficult to obtain.

New operating authority required a showing of "public convenience and necessity," the watchwords of the 1935 act. An applicant had the burden of proving that existing firms weren't already providing a needed service and that they wouldn't be financially damaged by the additional competition. That a new carrier promised to offer an existing service at a lower cost was by law not relevant to the ICC.

Entry applications were open to challenge by established carriers, and requests for significant operating authority were almost always litigated—a process that could take up to two or more years and $250,000.[12] As a result, applicants often struck deals with would-be competitors, narrowing the scope of their request in return for withdrawal of the legal challenge. Other requests were narrowly drawn to begin with so as to avoid litigation. Thus while the ICC technically granted a very high percentage of all applications for operating rights, the effect on competition was negligible.[13] Most amounted to insubstantial requests, and from existing carriers at that. (Because operating rights were so narrowly defined, carriers had to apply continually for new authority to meet changing freight demands resulting from, for example, construction of a new factory or warehouse.)

Since entry was so tightly restricted, trucking firms typically acquired rights by buying them from an existing carrier. Operating certificates, like broadcast licenses and taxicab medallions, had a market value. For many companies, these certificates were their most valuable asset, and banks routinely accepted them as collateral on loans.

Most coveted were the "general commodity, regular route" certificates, which represented common-carrier authority to truck all but legally exempt goods over designated ("regular") routes. Those licenses were so lucrative that, in 1977, the eight largest trucking companies—all of which held them—earned a rate of return on equity twice that of the average Fortune 500 company.[14]

General commodity carriers engage in "less-than-truckload" operations—the heart of the motor carrier business. An LTL operation involves diverse cargoes of packaged freight and requires large terminals with loading docks where the cargo can be assembled for shipment or reassigned to local fleets for final delivery. LTL service makes transportation of many small shipments economically feasible—a service no other form of surface transportation can duplicate. Only 1,000 of the 17,000 trucking companies that were regulated in 1979 were general commodity carriers, but they accounted for two-thirds of total regulated trucking revenue.[15] Each of the three largest general commodity carriers—Roadway Express, Consolidated Freightway, and Yellow Freight System—earned close to a billion dollars in 1979.[16]

Most of the remaining firms regulated by the ICC were specialized, irregular route common carriers. These firms, which rely heavily on owner-operators to perform the actual transportation, haul truckload (TL) shipments of a homogeneous cargo using specially tailored equipment such as refrigerated trucks ("reefers"), armored cars, or automobile trailers. Specialized carrier rights—less valued than LTL rights because of competition from railroads for TL shipments—allowed considerable flexibility with respect to routes but authorized only a narrow range of specified commodities.

This system of assigning rights produced some bizarre restrictions. A specialized carrier, for example, might be allowed to carry exposed film but not unexposed film, or lead pipe but not plastic pipe. General freight carriers were often forced to take long, roundabout routes because their authority represented a "tacking" together of operating rights acquired through purchase and merger. Many operating rights contained only one-way authority; thus carriers were legally barred from carrying a load on their return trip (backhaul), even if cargo was readily available to be shipped.

Overall, the ICC's system of route and commodity restrictions served to divide the market into thousands of segments, each served by only a few carriers. For shipments between large cities that were well-served in 1935, when grandfather rights were issued, there might have been as many as 12 carriers to choose from. In geographic areas of the country that developed after 1935, the choice was likely between only two or three.[17] Long-distance shipments often had to be "interlined" between two or more carriers with adjacent routes.

In addition to general commodity and specialized common carriers, ICC regulation governed contract carriage—service to individual shippers on a long-term contract basis, often using specialized equipment. In recent years, some 3,000 contract carriers, operating under ICC permits that had negligible market value, hauled approximately 7 percent of the total regulated tonnage.[18] During the 1920s and early 1930s, state-regulated common carriers perceived the contract hauler as a threat because he could attract lucrative freight by undercutting their published rates—rates that in theory reflected the added cost of the common-carrier obligation. To prevent what common carriers argued was cream-skimming, the 1935 act provided for setting a floor on contract carriage rates. The ICC also limited severely the number of shippers a contract carrier could serve.

Rates

In addition to restricting entry, the ICC was authorized to regulate trucking rates. The need to control excessive rates is apparent, since a shipper often had little choice as to which carrier could haul his goods to a given destination. But the major objective of ICC controls was to prevent rates from being set too low to maintain an acceptable level of profits and service in the industry. The system that developed—collective ratemaking—was well suited to that objective.

Collective ratemaking in the (regulated) motor carrier industry was performed, much as it had been historically in the railroad industry, by private "rate bureaus." These bureaus—regional organizations run by a full-time staff and financed by dues from participating carriers—established rates that were applied uniformly throughout a designated geographic area. Ten rate bureaus composed of general commodity carriers controlled the vast majority of trucking shipments within and between regions of the country.[19]

Rate bureaus operated much like cartels. Carriers held open meetings at which shippers could testify but then voted in secret on proposed rates. While this is price-fixing pure and simple, it was exempted from antitrust action by the Reed-Bulwinkle Act of 1948—passed by Congress over the veto of President Truman.[20]

By law, all bureau-set rates had to be approved by the ICC. But over the years, the commission was extremely sympathetic to the industry and protective of its health. What's more, the magnitude of the task—several thousand rates were filed every day—left the ICC little choice but to rubber-stamp rate-bureau decisions. In 1977, the commission rejected fewer than 1 percent of the trucking rates filed.[21]

In theory, any regulated firm was free to undercut the collectively fixed rate, but few did since the local rate bureau or a rival carrier was sure to protest. Protests were often filed automatically, regardless of whether the challengers were directly affected. The most notorious example involved an exasperated carrier who filed a rate to carry yak fat from Omaha to Chicago. Even though yak fat was an imaginary product, thirteen different carriers challenged the rate![22]

Rate bureaus traditionally served other functions besides providing a forum in which carriers could meet to discuss and set rates. None was more important than the periodic filing of "general rate increase" proposals, designed to raise every bureau-published rate by a fixed percentage in response to higher costs. These proposals, based on average carrier costs, were routinely approved by the ICC. Unlike most regulated utilities, the trucking industry was not held to a maximum rate of return, and the average return on equity for regulated truckers was well above that for other industries.[23]

Unregulated Trucking

A substantial sector of the trucking industry was unregulated, technically speaking. Though not of major size in 1935, this sector accounted for 60 percent of total industry revenue in 1979 and was growing rapidly. Unregulated trucking companies—primarily private carriers and haulers of exempt products—did not need ICC approval to operate, but their services were severely restricted by the ICC nonetheless.

Private carriers are actually shippers who choose to haul their own goods. In 1935, only a small percentage of industry freight went by private truck; by 1978, that share of tonnage had grown to 40 percent.[24] Some of the largest private carriers—Sears Roebuck, for example—have fleets of more than 1,000 trucks.

The dramatic growth in private trucking came about despite ICC regulations. In general, private carriers were barred from soliciting freight on a commercial basis. (The major rationale was the potential for a private carrier to subsidize his transportation operations out of his nontransportation operations and thus gain a competitive advantage.) Since the normal flow of goods for an individual shipper is in only one direction, private carriers' backhauls were generally empty.

Empty backhauls were also a chronic problem for the 100,000 or more owner-operators who made a living hauling unprocessed food—the other major form of unregulated trucking. An exempt trucker who carried tomatoes to a cannery could not haul canned tomatoes—a regulated commodity—back to the growing area. To avoid "deadheading," many independent truckers carried nonexempt goods on the return haul under temporary contract to a (specialized) regulated carrier—a practice known as trip-leasing. (Also common was the hauling of "hot" freight.)

Other owner-operators worked under permanent contract to regulated carriers. Under this system—much as with trip-leasing—the certified carrier provided operating rights plus managerial services in return for a 20 to 30 percent commission. (Critics of regulation termed this practice "share-cropping.") Many specialized commodities—such as household goods and steel—were carried almost exclusively by owner-operators working under long-term contract.

Economic Objections to Regulation

[A common] view is that regulated firms naturally abhor regulation and would prefer their "freedom." But the regulated firms in the trucking industry are the very last to want freedom . . . In this sense, regulation is topsy-turvy. Rather than protecting consumers from the vices of "unbridled enterprise," regulation is protecting regulated enterprises from the discipline of the marketplace.
—James C. Miller III

Economists criticized the idea of regulating the trucking industry almost from the beginning. Their basic theoretical argument can be simply stated: Trucking is an inherently competitive industry which, when allowed to operate by free-market rules, does an efficient job of allocating and pricing trucking services. The industry possesses neither of the characteristics of a natural monopoly—high capital costs (or other natural barriers to entry) and large economies of scale. Only in LTL operations, which require expensive terminals and a large volume of shipments to run efficiently, might one find significant concentration, but even there, the economies of scale are exhausted far short of monopoly control. And the truck-load sector—made up of tens of thousands of small firms, many of them operating just a single rig—is almost a textbook example of a competitive industry.

Regulation's defenders often counter that the trucking industry should be sheltered from competition because, like a public utility, motor common carriers have an obligation to provide service. The economist's first response is that such an argument puts the cart before the horse. The common-carrier obligation is the necessary result of a regulated system in which consumers have no alternative supplier, not the justification for it.[25] Second, there is no evidence that ICC-regulated common carriers actually honor that obligation, which is impossible to enforce anyway; trucking firms serve out-of-the-way places, but only when it's profitable to do so.

While trucking was regulated as if it were a natural monopoly, the rationale for the 1935 act—aside from protection of railroads—was that the industry was *too* competitive, with alleged results—chaos, cutthroat pricing, excess capacity—that were destructive to the trucking industry, shippers, and ultimately the public. Even if that rationale was valid during the Depression, it ceased to be long ago.

Destructive competition is a "theoretical novelty" about which economists have argued for years, according to James Miller:

> It is still not clear whether even in theory destructive competition is feasible (assuming that firms in the industry are rational profit maximizers). But if it is, the requirements are that the industry have substantial fixed costs and that demand be either quite unstable or secularly declining. The interstate trucking industry simply does not fit these requirements. Although there are some fixed costs, the vast majority of costs are variable. As a matter of fact, the ICC uses a rule of thumb that 90 percent of all trucking costs are variable. Also, though demand fluctuates, with seasonal peaks in various areas of the country and for different commodities, its overall pattern is fairly predictable. Finally, as is well known, the demand for trucking has grown rather steadily over time.[26]

That growth in trucking demand came partly at the expense of railroads, and one argument for continued regulation of trucking—echoing the concerns of the 1930s—was the need to prevent further diversion of freight from rails. This raises considerations related to the theory of the second-best, which states that when distortions exist in one part of the economy (e.g., certain aspects of railroad regulation), it is not necessarily efficient to correct distortions in other parts (e.g., trucking regulation).[27] However economists have also shown that second-best considerations do not hold insofar as the distortions are the source of excessive costs of operation. It is always desirable to correct imperfections that lead to smaller output.[28]

In sum, the major arguments for treating the trucking industry like a public utility—to prevent industry concentration, assure service to out-of-the-way places, and hinder destructive competition—have little basis in theory and scant empirical support, as chapter 4 will further discuss. (Another justification for regulation—highway safety—is also discussed in chapter 4.) Nor are second-best considerations with respect to railroads compelling. What theory and evidence point to, rather, is a system that produces monopoly profits, excessive costs, inefficient price-service options, and discriminatory rates—in short, a system that benefits the regulated industry at great cost to the public.

Monopoly Profits

Regulation provided the two conditions necessary for cartelization: barriers to entry and a means of price fixing. Rate bureaus could set prices well above cost without fear of being undercut by new firms. As a result, regulated carriers received monopoly "rents."

The clearest evidence of monopoly profits is the value the market placed on operating certificates granted free by the ICC. If profits were normal, no one would pay for the right to enter the industry.

Various estimates placed the total value of operating certificates prior to deregulation at several billion dollars. In 1974, the ATA reported that in recent acquisitions, operating rights had generally sold for amounts equal to 15 to 20 percent of the revenue produced by those rights.[29] Using ATA figures, the White House Council on Wage and Price Stability estimated that industry rights were worth $3 billion to $4 billion.[30] In an independent study of twenty-three attempts to purchase certificates, Thomas Gale Moore confirmed the ATA's judgment: Buyers on average paid about 15 percent of the expected annual revenue for the rights they purchased. Based on that figure, Moore estimated that large and medium-sized carriers owned rights worth between $2.1 billion and $3 billion.[31]

Other evidence of monopoly profits comes from the 1950s, when unusual circumstances produced a virtual controlled experiment. A series of court decisions forced the ICC to broaden the exemption of unprocessed agricultural goods to include fresh and frozen poultry and frozen fruits and vegetables. The U.S. Department of Agriculture conducted "before" and "after" studies in different markets and concluded that deregulation led to both lower rates *and* improved service. Shipping rates for fresh poultry fell by 12 to 53 percent, for an average of 33 percent. For frozen poultry the average decline was 36 percent. (Averages for poultry are unweighted.) Rates for frozen fruits and vegetables declined by 19 percent on average. After Congress reregulated frozen fruits and vegetables in 1958, shipping rates rose.[32]

Variations on intrastate trucking controls have also enabled economists to conduct crude natural experiments. Trucking within the state of New Jersey is unregulated. Rates there were found to be 10 to 25 percent lower than for comparable interstate shipments.[33] In Maryland, where intrastate household-goods moving is unregulated, rates were found to be 27 to 87 percent below those of interstate movers.[34] International comparisons also found that trucking rates in countries with little or no regulation were substantially lower than those in regulated countries.[35]

Still other evidence of monopoly profits comes from a comparison of brokerage commissions in the regulated and unregulated sectors. Regulated carriers typically claimed 20 to 30 percent of the revenues earned by owner-operators working under a leasing arrangement. This commission paid for services—insurance, marketing, management—and rental of operating rights. In the exempt sector, agricultural brokers charged 7 to 10 percent for the same services. The difference in commission rates would seem to represent a monopoly rent on ICC certificates.

Excessive Costs

ICC controls enabled carriers to set rates above cost, but they also raised the cost of operation itself—for both regulated and unregulated truckers.[36] The evidence here is more qualitative, as analysts have been hard put to quantify the economic effects.

Route and commodity restrictions are one likely source of inefficiency, leading to unnecessary circuitry, low load factors, and excessive interlining (i.e., transfer of cargo between shippers), all of which consume gasoline and labor. Various studies have reported finding high rates of empty backhauling, particularly among exempt and private carriers, but it's hard to say how much of total industry underutilization was caused by ICC restrictions.[37]

The ICC's system of rate regulation was another source of excessive costs. Particularly in the LTL sector—where general rate increases were based on *average* industry costs—the system protected less efficient firms. That protection was limited, however, in areas where (LTL) carriers could compete on the basis of service.

The general rate-increase mechanism also led to higher labor costs. Since over 60 percent of motor carrier operating expenses go for labor, a rise in Teamster wages was usually sufficient to trigger an across-the-board increase in bureau-set rates. Regulated carriers had less incentive to resist union demands, knowing they could pass the cost along to their customers automatically.[38] Any single firm had an incentive to reduce its costs, but the industry as a collective bargainer faced no such incentive. (While high wages are treated here as an "excessive cost" of operation, they more accurately represent a monopoly rent to organized labor.)

Regulation tends to increase wages through another effect as well. It strengthens union power by preventing nonunion firms from entering the industry and competing for traffic carried by unionized firms. Based on an empirical study of these two effects, Moore estimated that regulation-unionization produced gains to Teamsters employed in the trucking industry of between $1 billion and $1.3 billion in 1972.[39]

Inefficient Price-Service Options

In the same way banks offered depositors free checking accounts and other bonuses to get around federal ceilings on interest rates, many regulated truckers offered better service—such as more frequent pickup or rush-hour delivery—in place of cheaper rates. When regulation restricts rival firms from lowering prices, they will inevitably compete by offering customers better service. Additional service raises operating costs. While this is not intrinsically bad, service competition is inefficient because customers generally don't value the additional service at what it costs to provide it. On the plus side, the service *is* worth something to customers, and it serves to reduce monopoly rents as it restores consumer surplus.

While regulated carriers found limited ways to circumvent ICC controls, shippers were still faced with inflexible and inefficient rate-service (price-quality) choices. Some shippers would have preferred less service at a lower rate. Others would have gladly paid a premium for still better service.[40] Collective ratemaking precluded this, however, and thus distorted shippers' decisions about such things as where to locate, when to schedule production, and how large an inventory to maintain.

Discriminatory Rates

Other distortions resulted from the rate structure for regulated trucking. To prevent individual shippers from being arbitrarily advantaged by preferential treatment or efficiency differences between carriers, the ICC required regulated firms to charge "equal rates for equal miles" to shippers moving similar freight. But when costs varied, some shippers were overcharged and others were subsidized.

For example, regulated carriers charged the same rates for backhaul (the direction with the light load) as for prime haul, even though backhaul costs are lower because of the additional capacity. This affected shippers' locational decisions and discriminated against certain regions, because traffic to an area tends to be either predominantly prime haul or predominantly backhaul. The "equal rates for equal miles" rule also precluded peak-load pricing. Thus shippers had no incentive to take advantage of off-season months, when carrier costs are lower.[41]

Another form of price discrimination resulted from regulated truckers' policy of charging more for high-value goods than for low-value goods that cost the same to transport. The greater the market value of a product relative to its transportation costs, carriers reasoned, the less concerned shippers would be with freight prices. Thus truckers charged twice as much to haul nylon as cotton hosiery out of South Carolina. The shipping rate for champagne was considerably higher than that for ginger ale.

This system of price discrimination eventually proved counterproductive as certain shippers resorted to more expensive (to society) alternatives such as private carriage or air freight. The loss of "good freight"—freight assigned rates that were especially high relative to cost—

eventually became one of the most serious problems faced by the regulated trucking industry.[42]

In sum, ICC regulation produced monopoly profits, excessive costs, and other inefficiencies resulting from inflexible price-quality choices and rate discrimination. The price tag to consumers, by many estimates, was billions of dollars annually.[43]

Who benefited from this system? Most directly, the owners of ICC certificates did. But only the original owners, oddly enough. Those who bought certificates earned no more than a competitive rate of return when the cost of the certificates was taken into account. As with any asset, the value of future earnings made possible by ownership gets capitalized into its price.

Labor was the other major beneficiary of ICC regulation. Teamsters, like certificate owners, earned economic rents in that cartelization of the industry, combined with unionization, resulted in wages higher than would have been necessary to entice them to work. Moore estimated that between 74 and 97 percent of the cost to consumers of ICC regulation ($3.4 billion in 1972 by his calculations) was rent to capital and labor.[44]

Trucking regulation had other, less direct beneficiaries. Among them were the 3,500 attorneys who comprised the ICC Practitioners' Association. Employees of the ATA, member conferences, state trucking associations, and rate bureaus also benefited. These individuals were evidence for the argument that a large portion of monopoly rents will often be spent on trying to protect the monopoly.

The arguments for and against regulation set out above will appear again—though in different garb—in chapter 4. That chapter looks at how both sides debated the merits before an audience of self-interested congressmen with a limited knowledge of economics. To put that debate in context, chapter 3 describes the political battle for trucking deregulation.

3

The Political Battle for Trucking Deregulation

This is like the French Revolution in terms of the intensity of feeling on both sides.
—ICC Staffer, January 14, 1980

W hen Congress overrode Truman's veto of the Reed-Bulwinkle Act, he became the first of several presidents whose efforts to reduce trucking regulation proved no match for powerful vested interests. Twenty-five years later, Richard Nixon backed off from planned legislation when he met strong Teamster resistance. Gerald Ford sent Congress a sweeping reform proposal on trucking. But during the final weeks of the 1976 campaign, pressure from truckers and Teamsters caused Ford to beat a hasty retreat.

Ford's opponent, candidate Jimmy Carter, spoke out for regulatory reform but then feigned support for trucking controls in response to the same political heat. Carter sent his close friend Bert Lance to address a high-level gathering of trucking executives late in the campaign. Lance analogized motor carrier operating rights to government allotments to grow peanuts and convinced the truckers that Jimmy Carter, the Georgia peanut farmer, was sympathetic to their position.

Carter was decidedly not sympathetic, and his true colors began to show through soon after he took office. In March 1977, at a Massachusetts town meeting, Carter responded to a disgruntled owner-operator by promising to push for "substantial deregulation." The following month he elevated to ICC chairman the agency's youngest commissioner, a lawyer with a reputation as a progressive. A. Daniel O'Neal, forty, had been transportation counsel to the Senate Committee on Commerce, Science, and Transportation before joining the ICC in 1973. Initially one of the agency's defenders, O'Neal had become critical of the ICC's "institutional inertia" and supportive of regulatory reform short of "deregulation."

With a progressive ICC chairman in place, political observers expected that Carter would send trucking-reform legislation to Capitol Hill. But the White House hoped to score a quick hit by championing the Cannon-Kennedy airline-deregulation bill then before Congress. Administration aides feared that a second regulatory reform initiative would jeopardize passage of the airline bill. They decided to concentrate White House energies on defeating the airline industry and, if they succeeded there, to challenge the more politically powerful trucking industry then.

Airline Deregulation

The Cannon-Kennedy airline-reform bill, which the Carter administration strongly supported, was the culmination of months of hearings and careful spadework by its two sponsors, particularly Edward Kennedy. That Howard Cannon's name appeared first on the bill was significant; having invaded Cannon's jurisdictional turf, Kennedy sought to mollify the powerful Nevada senator in order to gain his cooperation. That Cannon's name appeared at all was even more significant; only months earlier, he was regarded as an opponent of airline decontrol.

The issue of airline regulatory reform was first "discovered" by Senator Kennedy, in late 1973. In search of a topic on which the Judiciary Subcommittee on Administrative Practice and Procedure he chaired could hold hearings, Kennedy consulted Stephen Breyer, a Harvard Law School professor specializing in economic regulation and administrative law. Breyer recommended holding oversight hearings on the Civil Aeronautics Board, the independent federal agency responsible for regulating pricing and entry in the airline industry.*

---

*Airline regulation was a response to conditions similar to those that spawned the Motor Carrier Act of 1935. The appearance of small, "hungry" carriers, combined with economic problems brought on by the Depression, threatened the security of the larger, established air carriers. These carriers formed a trade association and demanded legislative protection from the "financial starvation" they predicted would lead to industry chaos and competition so intense as to sacrifice safety. Congress established the CAB and gave it the authority to restrict entry into the airline industry and to control industry pricing.

Breyer envisioned Kennedy's subcommittee investigating not only CAB procedure but also whether the strongly protectionist agency should allow more competition in the airline industry. The issue of airline regulatory reform had no outside constituency, and several well-organized groups—namely industry and labor, which had grown comfortable in the regulatory environment—were sure to oppose it vehemently. But the reform issue had at least the potential of attracting support from consumer groups concerned with lowering air fares and from ideological groups interested in reducing government interference in the marketplace.

The hearings that Kennedy subsequently held were carefully staged (under the supervision of Breyer, by then on leave from Harvard), to push the academic case for airline reform into the political arena. A number of economists testified, along with officials from the Ford administration. By far the most persuasive evidence presented came from a few well-studied states—California and Texas—where intrastate airlines were unregulated. Not only had competition not been "ruinous," as the regulated industry was predicting, but fares were substantially lower than for comparable air service in other parts of the country, and the unregulated markets were characterized by constant innovation, intensive advertising, and dramatic growth.

The Kennedy hearings gave the issue of airline reform sudden visibility in Congress. They also created considerable friction between Kennedy and Howard Cannon who, as chairman of the Aviation Subcommittee of the Senate Commerce Committee, had jurisdiction over the CAB. The clash was largely over turf, though substantive differences were also a factor. Cannon, an aviation buff, was generally perceived to be a close friend of the airline industry. Moreover, Sen. Warren Magnuson, the Commerce Committee chairman, opposed decontrol seemingly for fear it would harm Boeing Company, the major employer in his home state of Washington.

In an effort to reclaim the aviation subcommittee's territory, Cannon convened his own set of hearings on airline regulation in April 1976. As the hearings progressed, he became increasingly skeptical of industry arguments for maintaining the status quo. Particularly convincing to Cannon was the testimony of John Robson, recently appointed chairman of the CAB. Robson testified that CAB regulation not only had encouraged inefficiency and higher fares but might ultimately destroy the financial health of the industry. Robson called for reform legislation that would significantly reduce the agency's control over pricing and entry.

Persuaded that reform was necessary, Cannon nevertheless favored a much milder, more gradual reduction of CAB controls than did Kennedy. Opponents hoped this disagreement would be sufficient to stall the efforts at a reform bill altogether. But Cannon and Kennedy teamed up, and in

February 1977, they introduced legislation that represented a compromise between their previous positions.

Even as the Senate was holding hearings on the Cannon-Kennedy bill, Robson was instituting CAB reforms under the agency's own authority. The pace of administrative reform picked up considerably when Robson was succeeded by Carter appointee Alfred Kahn, a Cornell University economics professor who had served as head of the New York State Public Service Commission from 1974 to 1977. Under Kahn's direction, the CAB began giving domestic carriers latitude to lower fares without agency approval and at the same time relaxing controls on who could enter the airline industry.[1]

Thirty-nine Recommendations

As Kahn orchestrated a major rollback of controls at the CAB, across town at the ICC, a campaign for less sweeping regulatory reform got underway. In July 1977, a task force appointed by Chairman O'Neal issued thirty-nine recommendations for improving ICC regulation. The task force did not call for major deregulation but rather proposed more moderate steps the commission could take—from simplifying the application process to exempting more commodities from regulation.

O'Neal had asked for the task force report in part to defuse any effort by Carter or the Congress to impose deregulation through legislation. However, as he traveled the country to chair hearings on the thirty-nine recommendations, he met with strong opposition by truckers and Teamsters to all but the mildest proposals. One industry spokesman told O'Neal that small carriers would be hit especially hard by deregulation: "What is at stake here is not just the future of many marginally financed trucking companies, we are talking about defending an ideal...."[2]

As O'Neal continued his public hearings in an effort to stave off legislative deregulation, another Washington figure convened hearings in the hopes of accomplishing just that end. In October 1977, three years to the week after he opened his celebrated hearings on the airline industry, Edward Kennedy began a similar investigation into deficiencies in trucking regulation. The focus was nominally on rate bureaus, in keeping with Kennedy's new Judiciary Committee jurisdiction—chairman of the prestigious Subcommittee on Antitrust and Monopoly.

Much of the initial, quite technical testimony received little notice. However, things perked up when ICC auditors testified that truckers and railroads spent up to $1.5 billion a year on gifts to shipping agents and government officials and then passed the cost along to consumers. The auditors maintained that paid vacations to Las Vegas and the Caribbean, hunting trips, and other gifts—most of them illegal—were "common practice" in the truck and rail industries, which couldn't compete on prices because of federal regulation.[3] One witness—an Ohio air freight carrier—suffered extensive losses when his firm was bombed four weeks after he testified about the misuse of ICC route authorities.[4]

The Kennedy hearings lasted twelve days over the course of ten months and produced more than 1,700 pages of testimony and evidence. Though less dramatic than the proceedings on CAB reform, the rate bureau hearings drew considerable attention to the issue of trucking deregulation. That visibility put new pressure for reform on the ICC and the White House. The week Kennedy's investigation closed, O'Neal announced that his staff would undertake a major review of truck regulatory policy.

The hearings also worked to smoke out a senator who would be key to any legislation dealing with transportation—Howard Cannon, who had recently replaced Warren Magnuson as chairman of the Senate Commerce, Science, and Transportation Committee. In a June 1978 speech to the Executive Committee of the American Trucking Associations (ATA)—the industry's powerful trade group—Cannon predicted that legislation to loosen trucking regulation would be introduced in the Senate that session. But he emphasized that any such legislation should be handled solely by the Commerce Committee—a reference to speculation that Kennedy would try to seize the lead from Cannon and use his antitrust subcommittee as the forum for a deregulation bill. The Nevada Democrat also told the truckers that if motor carrier regulation needed a congressional overhaul, "then the appropriate response should be action to eliminate the weaknesses, not to throw everything out the window in the process."[5]

Dissension in the Administration

Cannon's speech only confirmed what proponents of reform already felt—that the powerful Commerce Committee chairman—a Democrat from a state where the Teamsters had considerable sway—was no fan of trucking deregulation, despite his support for airline decontrol. But they expected even more resistance from the leadership of the House Committee on Public Works and Transportation, which would have jurisdiction over any legislation affecting ICC regulation. Opposition from that committee had proved a major obstacle to deregulators' efforts at airline reform.

The makeup of the congressional committees led to general agreement within the Carter administration that Congress would not pass any proposal calling for substantial trucking deregulation and that opposition by labor and industry might be strong enough to kill any reform measure.[6] But beyond that, there was little consensus. When an interagency task force set out to draft trucking legislation in early 1977, the group bogged down because of sharp differences over how, and how much, to reduce motor carrier regulation.

The controversy pitted the Justice Department's Antitrust Division, which favored a "substantial legislative initiative," against the Department of Transportation, which felt that Carter should work through the ICC to make changes within the existing law. Rival options papers proposed in the summer of 1977 contained differences so sharp that even the fallback positions of Justice called for more cuts in federal controls than DOT's primary position.[7]

DOT's stance was partly a reflection of its leadership. Secretary Brock Adams, formerly chairman of the House Surface Transportation Subcommittee, made no secret of his opposition to trucking deregulation. But even reform supporters within the agency believed an ambitious legislative initiative would be counterproductive. Justice gave less heed to pragmatic considerations on the explicit rationale that it was one agency that should be above politics.

Early in 1978, Brock Adams and James McIntyre, acting director of the White House Office of Management and Budget, submitted an options paper that reflected considerable compromise between DOT and Justice. The memo was the work of a DOT-organized task force that represented the Departments of Agriculture, Commerce, Justice, and Transportation; OMB; the White House Domestic Policy Staff; the Council of Economic Advisers; and the Council on Wage and Price Stability. In blunt terms, the memo said that trucking regulatory reform was difficult to explain to the public, had no large constituency in its favor, and, "in short, [was] a tough issue bringing with it little if any political benefit, at least in the short run." The memo urged that Carter "nudge the ICC along" toward administrative reform, while proposing limited legislation to encourage competition.[8]

The options paper was never given to Carter, and the administration did not develop legislation. White House advisers feared that even raising the trucking issue would jeopardize the airline bill, which was meeting continued resistance in a House Public Works subcommittee. Eight months later, Congress finally approved an airline-deregulation bill—one that went much farther than regulatory reformers had expected—and administration aides began preparing a second, more detailed memo describing the options on trucking reform and outlining recommended legislation.

"Open-Heart Surgery—Blindfolded"

Even before Congress approved the airline bill, the effects of deregulation by the CAB were being felt. "Laissez-faire and half-fare" is how one observer described it. In an effort to compete, airline companies began offering a rash of discount fares—with names like "chickenfeed" and "peanutsfare"—much to the delight of the public.

Borrowing a page from Alfred Kahn's best-seller, ICC chairman O'Neal proposed a plan for significant reduction of motor carrier regulation. O'Neal told commission members that the apparent success of airline deregulation had created sudden interest in trucking reform, and that the ICC was under pressure to begin its own regulatory rollback lest Senator Kennedy, the White House, or the Justice Department seize the initiative.

O'Neal had by then conceded that legislation was ultimately needed; a year after the task force issued its report, the commission had adopted only thirteen of thirty-nine recommendations. But O'Neal proposed to undertake widespread reform administratively even before Congress acted— much as the ICC had done.

Stimulated partly by the administration's legislative plan, O'Neal's proposal called for eliminating most regulation of specialized trucking, including the public convenience and necessity test for gaining entry and antitrust immunity to set rates collectively. O'Neal said there was little reason to continue regulating the fifteen thousand (specialized) carriers who hauled full truckloads, since free competition wouldn't likely lead to concentration in fewer firms.[9]

For general commodity carriers, O'Neal proposed two major changes. The first would shift the burden of proof in entry proceedings from the applicant to the protestant; an existing carrier who protested an application would have to demonstrate that the new authority wasn't warranted. The second change would allow individual truckers to lower or raise their rates within a specified zone without having to get approval from the ICC or from their trucking competitors.

The trucking industry reacted angrily. "We're seriously thinking of suing the ICC for trying to deregulate without benefit of law," said one industry member, reflecting the discussions that followed O'Neal's action at an industry convention.[10] In addition, representatives of over fifty of the largest trucking firms and related businesses—including shippers, and bankers who provided financing for much of the industry—met in Chicago to develop a counterstrategy. They formed a group called Assure Competitive Trucking (ACT) and promptly circulated a petition calling for O'Neal's resignation.

At about the same time, the ATA began circulating among its executive board members a draft of compromise regulatory-reform legislation— legislation the industry trade group had developed in the hopes of heading off efforts at the ICC and on Capitol Hill toward more substantial reform. "The purpose of our proposal is to bring forth a positive position of the trucking industry that [will] answer many of the critics and at the same time alleviate the misconception that the ATA and its members are only in favor of the status quo," said C. James McCormick, a former ATA chairman. "We want to preserve the system through modernization."[11]

Despite a decidedly lukewarm reaction to O'Neal's proposals by fellow commissioners, within the month the ICC approved two other significant reforms. By a five-to-one vote, the commission abolished a forty-year-old rule barring companies that hauled their own goods—Safeway, for example—from transporting goods for other shippers. "The new policy will provide for increased efficiency in the transportation system by filling up otherwise empty backhauls," said the ruling. While the Private Carrier Conference of the ATA applauded the commission, the ATA itself assailed the decision as "arbitrary, capricious and unreasonable."[12]

Even more disturbing to the regulated industry was a unanimous ICC ruling that truckers would thereafter be held to freight-rate increases that generated no more than a 14 percent rate of return on stockholders' equity—the average return for all manufacturing industries. The decision against the Southern Motor Carriers Rate Conference (SMCRC) meant that regulated firms—whose average return on equity was above 20 percent—would have to settle for considerably smaller rate increases than they were accustomed to getting from the ICC.[13]

Trucking stocks tumbled following the SMCRC decision. ATA president Bennett Whitlock, Jr., accused the ICC of having "performed open-heart surgery—blindfolded."[14] Trucking executives said the action threatened the financial stability of the industry and began urging members of Congress to rein in the commission. But to add salt to the wound, the ICC tentatively approved still another significant reform that would shift the burden of proof from applicants for new authority to existing carriers.

In response to industry pressure, key congressional leaders sought to halt further ICC reforms, but with only embarrassing results. In a letter to O'Neal, House Public Works Committee chairman Harold (Bizz) Johnson (D-Cal.) and Surface Transportation Subcommittee chairman James Howard (D-N.J.) warned the commission to stop adopting new regulatory policies and let Congress look at the issue first.

To the surprise of many, O'Neal refused to defer. The ICC had acted within its discretion as an independent agency, he told the two congressmen, and he intended for it to continue to act.[15] At the same time, a *New York Times* editorial rebuked the two House members:

> If the House Public Works and Transportation Committee were more interested in serving the public and less in serving its trucking industry friends, the committee would be applauding the about-face at the [ICC] instead of challenging the agency's independence.[16]

Taken off guard, Johnson and Howard backed off from their earlier demand with a conciliatory response, which led one industry newsletter to characterize the exchange as follows:

Johnson and Howard:	*Stop that!*
O'Neal:	*No I won't!*
Johnson and Howard:	*Thank you, please continue.*

The Referral Fight

The second options memo on trucking reform that administration aides prepared, following passage of the airline bill, never reached Carter's desk either. Another legislative goal—railroad deregulation—was accorded first priority. Partly to put pressure on the White House, Senator Kennedy held a crowded press conference in January 1979 to announce legislation to repeal the 1948 law giving truckers immunity from antitrust laws. Kennedy made the announcement surrounded by supporters from opposite ends of the political spectrum. The group included consumerist Ralph Nader, newly appointed White House inflation fighter Alfred Kahn, Carter's consumer adviser Esther Peterson, and representatives from Common Cause, the National Association of Manufacturers, the American Conservative Union, the Independent Truckers Association, and the Contract Carrier Conference of the ATA.[17] Only one other cause—airline deregulation—had previously brought such erstwhile adversaries together.

The press conference caught the administration in an embarrassing position. The morning of the event, Carter had summoned top trucking-industry executives to the White House and assured them he had not yet made up his mind on trucking-deregulation legislation. The president's special trade representative, Robert Strauss, and domestic policy chief, Stuart Eizenstat, specifically told the assembled group that the administration would take no position on the Kennedy bill. Hours later at the press conference, Kennedy announced that he had administration backing, and Kahn told assembled reporters he regarded the bill as an "important plank in the president's campaign to fight inflation."[18]

The White House tried to gloss over the contradictory statements but with little success. A group of trucking-industry executives subsequently wrote Carter that the inconsistent positions represented either "a complete lack of understanding of the import of Senator Kennedy's legislation by some of your advisers or a complete breach of faith with the statements which you and your advisers made to us at our meeting."[19]

The press conference itself touched off a bitter, two-month jurisdictional tug-of-war between the Judiciary Committee, of which Kennedy had recently become chairman, and the Commerce Committee. To many people it seemed that the outcome of the parliamentary fight would decide the fate of trucking regulation itself. Stung by allegations that he was seeking jurisdiction over the trucking legislation in order quietly to bury it, Cannon denied any favoritism. "I have not lost sight of the implication that we won't move on trucking," the Commerce Committee chairman said. "But that's not so; I still have an open mind on this, although Mr. Kennedy appears fully decided."[20]

The referral fight was reported widely by the press. Editorial support for Kennedy was near unanimous, for much the reason given by the *Boston Globe*:

> The public may get an early reading this year on exactly how committed the U.S. Senate is to stemming inflation when that inflation benefits powerful private interests. . . . A decision by the Senate to refer the legislation exclusively to the Commerce Committee would be a sign that the Senate is not anxious to make the fight to restore competition to the trucking industry.[21]

But when it came to sheer political clout, Cannon proved the stronger. The Commerce Committee chairman enlisted the help of the truckers and Teamsters in his fight—though they needed little prodding—which only confirmed suspicions that he was friendly to regulated interests. Some Senate offices reported receiving more than 4,000 pieces of mail from union and industry members. Kennedy got support from consumer and shipper groups, but it was no match.

Cannon refused to compromise on joint referral and threatened to take the matter to the Senate floor. After considerable stalling—in part to draw attention to the issue—Kennedy conceded exclusive jurisdiction to Commerce in exchange for sequential referral—the right to review antitrust provisions and offer amendments on the Senate floor—and Cannon's commitment to "diligently and thoroughly" consider Kennedy's bill during that session.

That consideration got underway almost immediately. In an effort to dispel fears that he would bury reform legislation, Cannon had earlier scheduled a day of hearings for the end of March. The jurisdictional dispute wasn't settled until a few days before the scheduled date. Cannon convened the hearing on March 28 and called Kennedy as the lead-off witness.

The Teamster Talks

Noticeably absent from the hearing was a spokesman for the White House. It was no secret that the administration deliberately stayed out of the referral fight and offered no legislation of its own so as not to offend the Teamsters as the March 31 (1979) expiration date for their master-freight contract approached. For months, financial observers had been predicting that the outcome of the negotiations for a new Teamster contract would be the test of Carter's wage-and-price guidelines.

In mid-March, in response to a guideline-busting wage demand by the Teamsters, Alfred Kahn announced that the Carter administration would move swiftly for sweeping deregulation of the trucking industry if the labor union won a new contract "substantially" beyond the president's guidelines. Kahn also told reporters that while the White House remained committed to reducing trucking controls, "political realities" would lead to "more modest" legislative proposals if the guidelines were observed.[22]

The administration was criticized from all sides for its carrot-and-stick strategy toward the labor talks. Senate Majority Leader Robert Byrd (D-W.Va.) said that it was not within the president's domain to use legislation as a bargaining chip. Similar comments from Capitol Hill reflected the shaky status of any trucking-reform bill in Congress.[23] Supporters of reform, like the *New York Times,* were also miffed: "The Administration made a serious mistake by establishing an ambiguous link between the outcome of the [negotiations] and its plan to deregulate trucking. . . . Trucking deregulation is too important to the long-term fight against inflation to be bargained away for such a contract."[24]

Following a ten-day strike that idled several hundred thousand auto workers when parts weren't delivered, the trucking industry and the Teamsters agreed on a contract. The settlement added up to less in percentage terms than the 35 percent increase the Teamsters had won three years earlier, but by any rational standards it far exceeded the 22.5 percent increase allowed by the president's guidelines. In an effort to keep its wage-and-price program alive, the administration employed creative arithmetic to "clarify" the settlement and declare it in compliance. ("One more damn clarification and we'd have been in the poorhouse,"said the trucking industry's top negotiator.) But *U.S. News & World Report* called the pay hike a "body blow" for the Carter guidelines. Combined with ICC efforts to reduce truckers' rates of return, the new contract also had serious implications for the ability of unionized firms to compete and seemed almost certain to cause some bankruptcies, mergers, and loss of business to private trucking fleets and other non-Teamster carriers.[25]

Everything but "Motherhood and Apple Pie"

With the contract talks out of the way, regulatory reformers looked to the White House for its long-awaited initiative on trucking. Cannon scheduled two days in June for hearings and dedicated the first to "specific legislative proposals" in an effort to smoke out the administration. To put added pressure on the White House, and to prevent Carter from excluding Kennedy from the reform effort, Kennedy's staff circulated the draft of a trucking-deregulation bill to supporters and to the press.

The Kennedy proposal was the most sweeping piece of trucking reform legislation ever submitted. It called for an end to antitrust immunity for both single- and joint-line collective ratemaking in 1981, virtual open entry by 1983, and termination in 1985 of the ICC's role in regulating the trucking industry, with the Departments of Justice and Transportation and the Securities and Exchange Commission to assume former responsibilities relating to mergers, data collection, and securities transactions. (Single-line rates apply to shipments that are handled by a single carrier; joint-line rates apply to interlined shipments—shipments handled by two or more carriers. Many reformers argued that even if there were a justification for the collective setting of joint-line rates, which involve more than one carrier, no such justification existed for single-line ratesetting.) The ATA immediately denounced the Kennedy proposal as "irresponsible and ill-informed" and warned members that Kennedy was attempting "to keep pressure on President Carter to follow through on his promise to submit his own deregulation proposal."[26]

Several weeks later, one day before the Teamsters ratified their master-freight contract, the White House began quietly to circulate its own proposal on Capitol Hill. The administration's sweeping reform plan was contained in a summary paper rather than legislation, indicating a willingness to be flexible on some provisions in order to gain the sponsorship of Kennedy and other congressional supporters of reform. "We think it's a good shot," said a Kennedy aide of the administration proposal. "It's a very, very great contribution."[27]

In early June, after months of goading the White House to act on the trucking issue, Kennedy phoned President Carter to suggest that they team up and introduce a joint reform bill. Staffers from the Judiciary Committee, DOT, and the White House spent the next week ironing out the few differences between the two men's proposals—primarily over the fate of the ICC: Carter was reluctant to go as far as Kennedy and set a date for abolishing ICC authority over the trucking industry.

On the first day of summer, President Carter held a White House press conference with Kennedy at his side. The two men unveiled a proposal for the gradual dismantling of most—but not all—ICC controls on interstate trucking. Surrounded by a large group of deregulation supporters, President Carter said "unnecessary and sometimes absolutely nonsensical" regulations had added billions of dollars in transportation costs to almost every item Americans bought. Alfred Kahn said the bill was being put forward in the name of anti-inflation efforts, energy conservation, competition, regulatory reform, and free enterprise. "Motherhood and apple pie are being taken care of in other legislation," he joked.[28]

The ATA called the bill a "radical approach" and admonished Carter for having "bowed to political pressure from Senator Kennedy."[29] So as not to appear completely negative in its approach, the industry group had earlier announced its own bill, which had been months in the making. "Our bill is not a reaction to Kennedy or the administration," ATA president Whitlock told the press. "We've been working up a piece of legislation to benefit the system and the consumer."[30] Whitlock said the bill represented a partial compromise from earlier ATA positions, particularly in that it established a zone of pricing freedom. But the key provisions on entry, rate bureaus, and commodity restrictions led some industry members to refer privately to their proposal as the "Avon bill" because it embraced purely cosmetic changes.

More Hearings

When Carter and Kennedy introduced their bill, S. 1400, Cannon said he saw "an awful lot of problems" getting such a controversial measure through Congress. But he promised to give it "thorough and fair" consideration—recent press reports cited Cannon aides as saying the senator was now open-minded on the subject of reform—and within the week Cannon held two days of hearings on trucking reform.[31]

This time the administration was out in full force. Alfred Kahn, Council of Economic Advisers Chairman Charles Schultze, and even Brock Adams testified in strong support of S. 1400. Kahn told Commerce Committee members that a 10 percent savings in transportation costs that could result from trucking deregulation might reduce the Consumer Price Index for food by 1 percent. "I would easily shed blood for 1 percent on the food CPI," said Kahn.[32]

In his testimony, ATA spokesman C. James McCormick cited the strike of independent truckers that had begun the previous week—largely the result of rising diesel fuel prices and a severe shortage of fuel. McCormick said the strike provided a "frightening preview" of what deregulation would lead to. "The present crisis in the transportation of fresh fruits and vegetables emphasizes what will happen. . . . The exempt area today is the only area of motor carrier transportation where there is rate instability and uncertainty of service."[33]

Teamster president Frank Fitzsimmons testified that deregulation would reduce highway safety by flooding the roads with thousands of heavy-footed independent truckers. He cited a study which showed that the average independent truck driver was an overworked, financially pressed thirty-eight-year-old man who drove fifteen hours a day, six days a week; who used a citizens-band radio to avoid the police and drove "with his foot clear down on the accelerator." "Even if there were some solid basis for deregulation," Fitzsimmons said, "the risk to the lives and livelihood of our members and, for that matter, the lives of anyone using the intercity highways, is so great that deregulation should be rejected."[34]

The ICC's Gauntlet

The Commerce Committee held six more days of hearings on trucking deregulation in the late summer and fall, including three sessions in San Francisco, Reno, and Fallon, Nevada. Representative Howard also chaired hearings before his Public Works subcommittee at locations around the country. The field hearings focused especially on the likely effects of regulatory reform on service to small communities, a major concern of committee members.

But the most significant action in the battle over deregulation occurred on the administrative front, with the appointment of three new commissioners to the ICC: Marcus Alexis, chairman of the Economics Department at Northwestern University in Evanston, Illinois; Darius Gaskins, Jr., formerly chief economist at the Civil Aeronautics Board under Alfred Kahn; and Thomas Trantum, a Wall Street transportation financial analyst. The White House had nominated the three men the previous February, along with James Gray, secretary of the executive cabinet of Kentucky governor Julian Carroll. But Gray, who was backed by the Teamsters Union, withdrew from consideration in March.

The three nominees appeared before the Senate Commerce Committee in late June at a confirmation hearing. Alexis gave little clue as to how he would vote on major deregulation issues. But Trantum told the committee that he believed "free markets are the most efficient and desirable way to allocate goods and services," and Gaskins said his experience with airline deregulation had indicated "that there may be substantial advantages to relying on competition."[35] Gaskins was questioned closely by Sen. John Warner (R-Va.), who said fleet operators and Teamster representatives had expressed strong misgivings to him about Gaskins's nomination.

Despite the ATA's opposition, the three nominees were confirmed by the committee—and later, pro forma, by the full Senate. Gaskins, the most controversial nominee, received a ten-to-three committee vote; Trantum and Alexis were both approved fourteen to one.[36]

In early September, the public got its first look at the new commissioners in action. At a special meeting called to discuss a staff task force report, a majority of the eight commissioners—including Alexis, Gaskins, and Trantum—endorsed sweeping reform proposals that had received only O'Neal's support when he first outlined them a year earlier. Demonstrating his commitment to change, Gaskins said the staff's ambitious entry proposal—which called for removing virtually all controls over twelve specialized segments of the industry—"may not go far enough."[37]

Chairman O'Neal all but laid down the gauntlet when Robert Gresham, one of two commissioners who opposed the proposed reforms (a third was noncommittal), said Congress, not the ICC, should properly consider such actions. "The commission has wide discretion written into the Interstate Commerce Act," O'Neal replied. "If Congress doesn't like the direction we're taking, they can let us know."[38]

Bennett Whitlock immediately issued a statement saying the ICC proposals "far exceed the commission's statutory authority." "This back-door approach to deregulation shows contempt for the congressional process," Whitlock said, adding that the ATA would sue the commission if it proceeded with its unlawful proposals.[39]

The ATA's threat had little impact, however, and in mid-October, the commission adopted a policy making it considerably easier for new firms to enter the trucking industry. The action did away with a forty-three-year-old test requiring an applicant for operating rights to prove that the proposed new service couldn't be performed as well by existing carriers.[40]

Within days, Congress picked up the ICC's gauntlet. At an ICC-sponsored workshop in Reston, Virginia, Senator Cannon complained that independent regulatory agencies were ignoring Congress and going their own way. "We're mad as hell," said Cannon, "and we aren't going to take it any more. It is time that the agencies began to listen to the Congress." Cannon urged the commission to forego making "irreversible" changes in trucking regulation until Congress had been given a chance to act. He set a deadline of June 1, 1980, to have legislation on President Carter's desk "expressing the will of Congress."[41]

Both O'Neal, who had announced his plan to leave the commission at year's end, and Darius Gaskins, whom Carter had designated to succeed O'Neal as chairman, said later that Cannon's request would at least delay final commission action in some matters. Gaskins singled out commission proceedings aimed at limiting the ability of rate bureaus to set rates collectively and at issuing "master certificates"—across-the-board entry approval for entire classes of truckers. "We can . . . gather the information, make it available to Congress and for our own uses, and if Congress doesn't act, we could go through with a final rule," said Gaskins.[42]

Several days later, the Senate Appropriations Committee backed up Cannon by directing the ICC not to implement any new regulations easing entry into the trucking industry until Congress had been given an opportunity to pass legislation. The committee's directive actually represented a softening of language it had adopted a few days earlier ordering the commission not to initiate any new trucking regulations.[43] The House and Senate Appropriations committees also denied the ICC's request for $2.5 million to study the effects of deregulation.[44]

Following Cannon's speech, O'Neal and Gaskins wrote to the senator promising him to delay major regulatory reforms until Congress had passed legislation or until June 1. Nevertheless, in early December, the ICC proposed a significant regulatory change that would allow trucking companies to begin serving all intermediate points on their authorized routes on a temporary basis. The proposal was designed to save fuel during the winter months when energy demand was greatest and to assure transportation service during the ongoing fuel shortage.

Industry reaction was predictably strong. "This will kill us," said a spokesman for the ATA's Local and Short Haul Carriers Conference. "The bigger carriers will pick up the most profitable loads, taking away business from our fellows. This could be the deciding factor in putting a lot of people out of business."[45]

But the *Washington Post* sided with the ICC in an editorial that said the potential fuel saving was "adequate justification for putting the change into effect immediately": "The opportunities for energy conservation and cost reduction in this notoriously inefficient industry are vast. Not all of them should be held back until Congress gets done trying to work out a better regulatory system for companies and a union that like things the way they are."[46]

While Congress remained silent in that debate, ten days later, Cannon used a letter to the president of the Teamsters to warn the ICC against another step it was reportedly about to take—granting master certificates to carriers hauling shipments for the federal government. In their letter to Cannon, O'Neal and Gaskins had singled out the government-shipment proceeding as one they felt they could go ahead with even as Congress debated major legislation. While Cannon never answered their letter, he did tell a meeting of minority truckers—whom the reform was primarily intended to benefit—that "the liberalization of entry into government traffic is the kind of limited rule-making that need not come to a halt while Congress is considering legislation." Cannon's letter to Fitzsimmons in December represented an apparent turnaround. Conceding that he had publicly stated his support for less restrictive entry in the government transportation sector, Cannon wrote to Fitzsimmons that "I am, however, not certain that the master-certificate approach is the best way to achieve that reform."[47]

S. 2245: An "Unexpectedly Tough" Proposal

Committee aides and others close to Cannon had seen the senator become increasingly sympathetic to the need for deregulation during the summer and fall, even as he took seemingly antagonistic actions. But to the trucking industry, Teamsters, supporters of decontrol, and the press, it came as a surprise when Cannon, together with Sen. Robert Packwood of Oregon, the ranking Republican on the Commerce Committee, introduced a strong reform bill. Packwood's position was no secret. He called the bill "a move" toward the sharp deregulation that he favored, though he added, "It isn't as much of a move as I want to see."[48]

The *Washington Post* described the Cannon-Packwood bill as an "unexpectedly tough legislative proposal."[49] Most unexpected was the strong provision on rate bureaus. Much to the industry's abhorrence, it called for elimination of antitrust immunity for single-line ratemaking as of 1983. To provide for immediate rate flexibility, the bill created a 10 percent zone of pricing freedom. The bill also shifted the burden of proof for entering the industry, though it barred the ICC from issuing master certificates. In other provisions, the bill called for substantial elimination of route restrictions, expanded the list of commodities exempt from regulation—most significantly to include bananas and red meat—and gave owner-operators authority to carry regulated goods on the backhaul.

Labor and industry were predictably upset with the Cannon-Packwood proposal. Teamster president Fitzsimmons telegrammed Cannon that the bill was "completely unacceptable" and that the union would "expend all [its] effort to have this measure changed." "If enacted into law," Fitzsimmons continued, "the proposal will result in complete destruction of qualified motor carriers who now employ over 500,000 of our members." The ATA had a more measured response, reflecting the industry's belief that some legislation was necessary to prevent independent deregulation by the ICC. "While the trucking industry adamantly opposes some of the provisions of the Senate Commerce Committee [bill] and has grave reservations concerning others, we pledge our support for Congress's effort to give specific directives to the [ICC] as to its intent for future truck regulatory policy."[50]

The Public Works Committee introduced a bill days later that diverged from the Senate proposal on the key provisions of entry and rate bureaus. It preserved antitrust immunity for single- and joint-line ratemaking and placed the burden of proof for entry on the applicant rather than the protestant, thus negating the ICC's reforms in that area. Not surprisingly, the ATA said it could "live with" the House proposal.

"Operation Pendorf"

Five days after Cannon introduced S. 2245, the *New York Times* reported that the Federal Bureau of Investigation had been secretly investigating the Nevada senator to determine whether he "was illegally influenced in handling trucking deregulation legislation. . . ." Specifically, the FBI suspected that Chicago businessman Allen Dorfman, a Teamsters crony with alleged ties to organized crime, had found a way to reward Cannon for steering trucking deregulation legislation into his committee.[51]

Dorfman, convicted in 1972 on a federal charge of conspiring to facilitate a loan from the Teamsters' Central States pension fund in return for a $55,000 kickback, had been under secret federal investigation since approximately 1978. The FBI's "Operation Pendorf"—referring to the pension fund and Dorfman—was one of a dozen specialized operations within a broad federal inquiry into organized crime and political corruption. The *New York Times* had published accounts of another of those operations— "Abscam"—just three days before the Cannon story. That sting operation, in which FBI agents posed as wealthy Arab sheiks, implicated Sen. Harrison Williams (D-N.J.) and seven other members of Congress.

The one-year, highly secret investigation of Cannon's ties to Dorfman was set off in early 1979 when FBI agents, monitoring a court-authorized wiretap of Dorfman's phones, overheard a conversation between him and Cannon. The conversation apparently concerned Cannon's efforts to acquire some Nevada land that was owned by a Teamsters Union pension fund. Cannon was leading his successful fight to take over jurisdiction of trucking deregulation legislation when the call was intercepted.

Cannon denied any wrongdoing or any awareness of the inquiry. He acknowledged that he had talked with Dorfman in 1979, when he and some of his neighbors banded together to prevent the sale of some Teamster-owned land to developers with plans for high-rise units. Cannon said he got in touch with Dorfman to ask who he should contact about buying the land. (The 5.8-acre plot of land, which bordered the Las Vegas Country Club and a luxury housing development where Cannon lived, was eventually sold to a buyer other than the homeowners' group.) But as to any connection between the land deal and his efforts on deregulation, Cannon said, "I've never heard anything more absurd in my life." Noting the deregulation proposal he had introduced days earlier, he said "the Teamsters have threatened to defeat any member of Congress who votes for this bill."[52]

Masterpiece Theater

Two weeks later, when the Senate Commerce Committee began three days of hearings on S. 2245, Cannon, whose face was slightly bandaged, joked about the publicity in his opening statement:

> Despite my appearance today, I was not mugged by a group of Teamsters or the ATA. . . .
> However, I must say that during the past few days, I have felt ambushed by certain journalists in search of a sensational story without much concern for the facts. . . .
> After my experience with the news media in the past couple of weeks, I am reluctant to even mention the fact that I have had minor surgery on my face, for fear of seeing it reported on ABC tonight that I had a lobotomy over the weekend free of charge from the American Medical Association.[53]

The Senate hearings, as well as their House counterpart, which Representative Howard held simultaneously, were essentially a replay of earlier committee hearings on trucking deregulation, as Cannon jokingly reminded the audience at the start of the second day:

> At the beginning of each of these hearings, I feel like Alistair Cooke when he's introducing the latest episode of Masterpiece Theater. To refresh your memory, when the series first began last March, we heard testimony from the administration in the form of strong reform measures; we heard from the Teamsters in opposition to any degree of deregulation; and we heard from the National Industrial Traffic League in favor of a middle position.
> Much has happened since then. In today's episode, I understand we will nave the administration in favor of strong reform measures; the Teamsters in opposition to any degree of deregulation; and the NIT League in favor of a middle position.[54]

However, one aspect of the dual hearings did make newspaper headlines. In testimony before the Howard subcommittee, Neil Goldschmidt, the new secretary of DOT, had harsh criticism for the Public Works bill: "[H.R. 6418] doesn't do enough to open up entry, it allows price-fixing to continue indefinitely, and, in light of these weaknesses, it offers too much pricing flexibility to carriers, to the detriment of shippers and consumers. The end result of this combination may well be inflationary." Goldschmidt said the administration was "extremely disturbed" that the bill would not lift anti-trust immunity, and that it was "essential that this committee develop legislation which will phase out price-fixing."[55]

Goldschmidt conveyed to the committee the same message President Carter had hinted at several weeks earlier in his State of the Union address to Congress and through his aides in two meetings they'd had with ATA representatives—namely, that Carter would veto (or let die) a regressive trucking bill and let the ICC proceed to deregulate on its own. By contrast, Goldschmidt praised the Senate bill as a "very positive step."[56]

In addition to the administration, more than fifty groups testified for and against deregulation on behalf of shippers, consumers, labor, regulated carriers, owner-operators, motor carrier lawyers, regulatory utility commissioners, port authorities, and others. They ranged from giant umbrella organizations, such as the National Association of Manufacturers, to highly specialized groups like the National Lime Association.

The weeks before and immediately after the hearings saw intensive lobbying by many of these groups, including the administration. Most of the lobbying effort focused on the Senate Commerce Committee, which was scheduled to "mark up" (amend) its bill in early March. Committee members—particularly those who were regarded as swing votes—were visited by scores of lobbyists and influential constituents flown in by lobby groups. In addition, they received hundreds of telephone calls, letters, and Mailgrams from their home states. The administration lobbied actively, and President Carter even telephoned several senators on the Commerce Committee personally, a display of commitment that provoked the ATA to sarcasm: "I am sure you derive the same comfort I do," wrote Whitlock to industry members, "in realizing that the continued imprisonment of Americans in Iran, the Russian invasion of Afghanistan, and the deteriorating economy are not of great enough consequence to cause Mr. Carter to alter his priorities."[57]

Markup—Day One

On Thursday, March 6, less than five weeks after the bill was introduced, the Commerce Committee began its markup of S. 2245. While Cannon had set aside two days for the committee to amend the bill, both sides felt that the initial votes would determine its fate. "If we lose on those," said one lobbyist supporting deregulation, "we will see [debilitating] amendments coming in like pigeons at the end of the day in Farragut Square."[58]

It was not a day for pigeons. The first critical vote came on the issue of entry. Warren Magnuson, who had chaired the Commerce Committee for thirty years before resigning to take over the Appropriations Committee, proposed to alter the entry standard in S. 2245 so as to shift the burden of proof back to the applicant, consistent with the Public Works bill. Packwood argued firmly that "Maggie's" amendment would "reverse the major thrust of the bill." When Magnuson said that under the traditional system "we don't deny right of entry," Packwood responded, "No, we just make it impossible." "Well, we're going to have chaos," said the seventy-four-year-old Magnuson weakly, but the committee disagreed and rejected his amendment ten to seven.[59]

The truckers won a few, less critical skirmishes. The committee scuttled the section of S. 2245 that would have permitted owner-operators to carry regulated goods on their return haul and weakened the provision allowing private carriers to transport for-hire for their subsidiaries (the committee leadership privately agreed to the weakening amendment to get a needed vote on another provision).

The truckers narrowly avoided another defeat, but the amendment was destined to come up again. Adlai Stevenson of Illinois proposed to expand the list of exempt commodities to include all food products as well as agricultural inputs such as fertilizer. To illustrate the seeming absurdity of exempting some commodities but not others, Stevenson regaled the audience by reading aloud from the ICC's guide to exempt commodities, "Can They Do That?":

> Hay is exempt, but hay containing 3 percent molasses is not; manure is exempt, but fermented manure "with additives such as yeast and molds, producing a rich liquor which in water solution is used for soil enrichment" is not; and "shelled, unpopped popcorn weighing ten or more ounces accompanied by a separate package of seasoning consisting of monosodium glutamate, butter flavor, cottonseed oil, and artificial color and flavor weighing approximately ¾ ounce" is exempt, while "shelled, unpopped popcorn with cooking fat or oil (one part to 2½ parts popcorn)" is not.

An opponent of the amendment, Sen. Donald Riegle (D-Mich.), asked the committee staff what market share of transported goods Stevenson's amendment would affect, and the session paused briefly while staff members conferred. (During the pause, the sound of choir music wafted into the committee room from the hallway. Sen. Harrison Schmitt (R-N.Mex.), an ardent deregulator, said "This must be an excellent amendment. I hear the voices of angels.") However, the staff couldn't supply an exact statistic, and Riegle said he thought there was a "pressing need" for such a figure. Echoing Riegle's skepticism, Sen. John Danforth (R-Mo.) asked why the staff didn't include this seemingly drastic change in the rules in the committee bill if it was such a good idea. William (Will) Ris, the staff counsel and primary author of S. 2245, responded tactfully that the provision wasn't included because the bill was a compromise. Packwood smiled and said, "Translated, that means we didn't know if we had the votes."

Packwood's doubts proved justified; the subsequent vote on Stevenson's amendment was eight to eight. Since a tie vote would have defeated the proposed change, Stevenson changed his vote to nay in order to be on the prevailing side and moved for reconsideration on day two of markup.

While the Stevenson amendment was discussed at length, another equally significant amendment slipped through without any discussion. Senator Schmitt, the Harvard Ph.D. geologist-turned-astronaut-turned-politician, offered an amendment to allow virtually automatic entry for carriers serving "small" communities. The innocuous-sounding proposal was adopted by voice vote before the pro-industry committee members realized that Schmitt's definition of a "small" community was so generous as to include the majority of all applications to the ICC.

If one of the very first votes—on Magnuson's entry amendment—signaled deregulators' surprising strength, then the last vote of the day confirmed it. Ernest Hollings (D-S.C.), who had emerged as the most outspoken opponent of deregulation, proposed to remove the provision of S. 2245 that would bar truckers from setting single-line rates collectively. In a lively debate, Hollings described himself as a "born-again regulator" because of the loss of airline service to his state following deregulation of that industry. Packwood argued that the antitrust provision was the most crucial section of the bill, and Cannon said that, "contrary to what many people think, this is not a radical proposal. . . ."

There was high tension in the packed room as Cannon polled the committee members, and both sides heard senators they thought were with them vote the other way. The biggest surprise of all came when Sen. John Warner, on whom the ATA had counted, voted nay. The final tally was nine to eight against the amendment, but Hollings maneuvered for a reconsideration—to be taken up on day two of markup the following week—so the truckers stayed alive on that, their most important issue.

Deregulators were elated when the first day of markup ended. Goldschmidt praised the committee members for having "successfully resisted efforts so far to water [S. 2245] down." Cannon and White House officials said that their nine votes on the Hollings amendment were firm, but they braced for a weekend of intense lobbying by both sides before the final votes would take place.[60]

The truckers were surprised by their setback but hopeful they could recoup their losses the following week. When asked his reaction to the day's events, the head of the Oregon Truckers' Association said, "At the end of the first round, the score is Christians 2, Lions 10."[61]

Markup—Day Two

"I can't remember more intensive lobbying," said a twenty-five-year Capitol Hill veteran at the weekend's close. Letters and telegrams flooded committee members' offices following the first markup session. Some Senate staffers reported receiving 500 pieces of mail, mostly from critics of deregulation hoping to reverse the close vote lifting antitrust immunity. Industry supporters crowded the halls of the Senate office buildings; 150 representatives of trucking companies visited the office of Kentucky Democrat Wendell Ford, considered a possible swing vote. Some Senate staff members stopped answering the telephone at their homes and offices due to the barrage of calls.[62]

While deregulators didn't match the sheer volume of letters and calls by opponents of reform, they brought out several high-powered weapons of their own. President Carter called John Warner to ask him to hold his position on the antitrust vote. And both the *New York Times* and the *Washington Post* published editorials calling for a strong bill. The *Post* editorial, which appeared the morning of the second markup session, turned the spotlight directly on one critical senator: "Industry lobbyists have tried hard to change the minds of some members of the Commerce Committee, in particular that of Sen. John Warner of Virginia, before the final vote, which is scheduled for today."[63]

A standing-room-only crowd jammed the committee room to witness the results of the weekend lobbying. At the day's end, deregulators had largely held their ground and even gained some. But the final, thirteen-to-four vote to approve the bill did not reflect the heated debate and dramatic, last-minute maneuvers.

The committee first reconsidered the Hollings amendment on antitrust immunity. In response to Hollings's arguments, Packwood said he saw "no reason why we should be controlling capitalistic acts by consenting adults." The committee agreed with him by a nine-to-seven vote. Sen. Russell Long (D-La.), who had supported Hollings on the earlier, nine-to-eight vote, was absent. However, deregulators received his proxy vote on subsequent amendments as the result of negotiations minutes before markup began.

Cannon and Packwood more narrowly rebuffed another attack on the antitrust provision when the committee defeated nine to eight an amendment offered by Nancy Landon Kassebaum (R-Kan.) to make the phase-out of immunity subject to a one-house legislative veto. The key vote against

Kassebaum's amendment—which would have effectively gutted the anti-trust provision of S. 2245—came by proxy from Senator Ford, who had previously supported the truckers on that issue.

A maneuver by Cannon's chief of staff, Aubrey Sarvis, accounted for Ford's seeming turnaround. Shortly before the session began, when Sarvis learned of the amendment Kassebaum was to offer, he recalled that Ford was strongly opposed to the legislative veto. Last-minute calls to Ford's staff moved the Kentucky senator's vote to the reform column.

In addition to preserving the ban on antitrust immunity, the committee added several strengthening amendments to the bill. A milder version of Stevenson's earlier proposal passed by a hefty ten-to-five vote, despite Hollings's contention that it would divert $4.5 billion of business from regulated carriers. The resulting amendment exempted processed food (the original amendment also included nonhazardous chemicals, fertilizers and farm machinery)—a severe blow to the specialized carriers within the regulated industry.

Deregulators lost ground on only two, secondary provisions during the final markup session. After an hour-long debate, committee members voted nine to five to strike the amendment by Schmitt that would have allowed virtual free entry for carriers serving "small" communities. More significant, the committee accepted an amendment by Danforth to index the zone of pricing freedom so as to factor inflation into rate increases. As a compromise to Cannon and others who feared that the indexing proposal would "take the lid off" trucking prices, Danforth agreed that the provision would not take effect before July 1, 1983, the date for revoking antitrust immunity.

Responses to the committee's action were immediate. Carter issued a statement praising committee members for a "first rate . . . reform bill" that would "save consumers millions of dollars." Goldschmidt called it "exceptional." ATA's Whitlock said "the only winners are inflation and increased fuel use."[64] Whitlock's subsequent message to ATA members was equally dour: "It is obvious that S. 2245 as it came out of the Commerce Committee cuts the heart out of regulation. It is just that simple."[65]

"Shredded Bark, and 300 Other Items"

When his committee approved S. 2245, Cannon optimistically pre-dicted rapid and favorable action by the full Senate. He and other reform supporters hoped to have the Senate vote on the bill before its Easter recess, when members would return home to their districts and confront grass-roots opposition to trucking deregulation. For the same reason, industry supporters preferred to delay the vote. The ATA had other concerns as well, however, which led the group to call Cannon the week after markup and propose a procedural compromise.

The ATA offered to go along with early floor action in return for limiting the agenda of votes. The industry group hoped to avoid a Senate record vote on some issues that might be defeated—particularly antitrust immunity. "I'm a realist," Whitlock told reporters. "I don't believe in butting my head against the wall. I'd rather go to conference without a mandate from the Senate."[66] Moreover, ATA lobbyists wanted to focus their efforts on defeating a few critical provisions—in particular the expanded food exemption. Because that provision hit a major segment of the industry very directly, it threatened to divide the ATA from within.

Cannon found the offer to deregulators' advantage as well, but he encountered certain obstacles to accepting it. Packwood and Schmitt both wanted to propose floor amendments. In addition, Kennedy was considering a floor amendment to eliminate joint-line antitrust immunity. Eventually, both sides worked out an acceptable "time agreement" which allowed certain amendments and precluded others. By the time the agreement was reached, Senate action was unavoidably delayed until after Easter recess. But both sides used the additional two weeks to lobby intensively. As the climax to its effort, the ATA block-booked 500 hotel rooms and arranged to have trucking executives from all across the country arrive in Washington in time to lobby their senators before the vote.

When the Senate returned from Easter recess on Tuesday, April 15, the trucking bill was the first item to be considered. The Democratic leadership moved it a day ahead of schedule partly to avoid the expected onslaught of truckers. Nevertheless, 400 to 600 industry representatives were in town, and many of them watched the six-hour debate from the Senate gallery.[67]

A single vote was all-important. In the five weeks following markup, the ATA had put nearly all its effort into defeating the Stevenson provision. (The group placed a full-page ad in the *Washington Post* the day of the Senate vote designed to show "just . . . what a bargain regulated truck transportation is for . . . processed foods.") Thus, that issue was destined to decide the fate of the entire bill. A drafting error made the debate even more dramatic than either side expected.

Ernest Hollings offered the amendment to strike the expanded exemption. The South Carolina senator charged that "if we take this 202 million tons of business out of the regulated system and hand it over to [the] extremely unstable and undependable [unregulated] sector of transportation, we will in effect destroy the regulated system's ability to operate." Hollings called it "an invitation to tragedy . . . for the sole purpose of satisfying a blind dedication to the ideology of deregulation."[68]

In a spirited defense of regulation, Hollings responded with sarcasm to Stevenson's "great to-do about the bureaucratic niggling" over what is exempt and what is not:

> [Senator Stevenson] presents us with the definition of three commodities. The first two are hay, which is exempt unless it contains 3 percent of molasses by weight, and manure, which is exempt unless it is fermented in a "rich liquor."
>
> Now I can only speak for myself, but my taste in food does not run to hay or manure, no matter how rich the liquor. Perhaps the Senator has been approached by a special interest group representing the dietary tastes of horses and soybeans.[69]

Two punches caught Hollings off guard. Cannon threw the first—in response to Hollings's oft-made charge that airline decontrol had severely hurt his own South Carolina and other heavily rural states, and that trucking reform would do the same. Cannon produced a recent letter from the governor of South Carolina to the chairman of the CAB applauding the opportunity presented that state by airline deregulation.

The second punch was more serious. Senators Stevenson, Cannon, and Packwood all noted individually that Hollings's amendment, as drafted, not only would remove processed foods from the exemption but would actually regulate unprocessed food. Cannon was indignant:

> After finally seeing this amendment I am appalled to learn that this would actually lead to the regulation of commodities that are not now regulated. Thus the amendment not only eliminates a reform, but would turn the clock back 25 years. . . .
>
> Here are the commodities that would be reregulated . . . : Cooked fish, dressed poultry, frozen poultry, cream cheese, butter, ginned cotton, rail ties, shredded bark, and 300 other items.[70]

Cannon allowed as how the mistake was made "perhaps inadvertently," but the suggestion of trickery was unavoidable.

Hollings, who had earlier brushed off attempts by Commerce Committee staffers to tell him of the drafting flaw, stridently denied that his amendment reregulated anything. But the damage was done. The Senate rejected Hollings's amendment in a dramatic forty-seven-to-thirty-nine vote. Advance vote counts by both sides had loosely predicted that the amendment would lose narrowly; nevertheless, ATA lobbyists could name several senators whose votes were lost because of the disagreement.

The remainder of the debate on S. 2245 was anticlimactic. An amendment by Magnuson to gut the entry provision was defeated fifty-six to thirty-four following Cannon's blunt appraisal of that reform: "If there is one single provision that must remain intact in this legislation, in my view, it is the entry section. It is on this section that all . . . other provisions of the bill rest."[71] The sure-to-lose amendment to eliminate all antitrust immunity was never offered. Its chief proponent, Edward Kennedy, was in Pennsylvania campaigning for the Democratic presidential nomination. By a lopsided count of seventy to twenty, the Senate approved the final bill, thus voting to relax forty-five years of government regulation.

When the vote ended, administration officials emerged beaming from the vice-president's office in the Senate, where they had been following the floor debate. A joyous Alfred Kahn ran to greet the staff counsel, Will Ris, as he came out of the Senate chamber. At a press conference with Packwood, Kahn, and Goldschmidt, Cannon was careful to describe his legislation as a "compromise, not a deregulation bill." But Secretary Goldschmidt spoke for the administration when he called it a "magnificent effort."[72]

While the truckers had ample cause for gloom, they could take heart in the response of another group to the Senate's action: The day after the vote, House Public Works staff members sent their counterparts on the Senate Commerce Committee a large, dressed turkey wearing the tag "S. 2245."

Cutting the Deal

Even before the Senate Commerce Committee had completed its markup of the trucking bill in early March, Rep. Jim Howard announced that he might propose legislation calling for "total deregulation." "There doesn't seem to be a need for that much regulation," Howard said. "Maybe we ought to look through the other end of the telescope."[73]

Howard's announcement came immediately after an editorial in the *New York Times* described the Public Works bill as "so limp that even opponents of deregulation tacitly support it." Howard's aides insisted he was sincere, but supporters of reform, who themselves opposed "total deregulation" without a substantial transition period, suspected that he was setting up a straw man to knock down with a bill more acceptable to the trucking industry.

Howard quickly abandoned his plan for total deregulation under pressure from both regulatory reformers and the ATA, which feared it would backfire. Shortly after the full Senate approved S. 2245, Howard told a reporter that using that bill as the vehicle for markup in his subcommittee "may be the way to go." He said the Senate had gone far in removing federal regulation, but "not so far as to create chaos" in the trucking industry.[74]

Pressure from the ATA helped convince Howard that using S. 2245 was not "the way to go." Instead, he proposed an industry-backed compromise between the House bill and S. 2245, in the hopes that Public Works could come up with a bill that the Senate would agree to accept without change. That unusual result would avoid a House-Senate conference and, among other things, eliminate the danger that conferees would deadlock and leave the ICC free to act independently. Further commission reforms, and the prospect of broad-scale ICC deregulation after June 1 absent legislation, made compromise suddenly desirable to the ATA.

The next four weeks saw intense negotiations, primarily between the Public Works Committee leadership and the administration and Senate Commerce Committee leaders. President Carter conferred personally with Representatives Johnson and Howard in the White House at a point when the discussions appeared to be deadlocked. In early May, the Public Works staff issued a draft bill, and the negotiations intensified around that document as the scheduled date for subcommittee markup—May 20—approached. Shortly before markup, Public Works leaders reached a compromise with the Senate Commerce Committee and the administration. Cannon and Packwood agreed to recommend that the Senate accept the compromise without a conference if it was passed by the House without substantial change.

The heart of the compromise was a trade-off of the expanded agricultural exemption for antitrust immunity. The Public Works bill retained the provision eliminating immunity for single-line ratemaking, but with a six-month delay in the phaseout. In exchange, the Stevenson exemption of processed food was replaced with a provision allowing owner-operators to haul processed food subject to certain restrictions: The owner-operator had to be the actual driver, which limited the provision to one-truck operations; and processed food could account for no more than 50 percent of his annual haul. The entry standards in S. 2245 were modified in the compromise bill, and the indexing provision was altered so as to take effect before, rather than simultaneously with, the elimination of single-line immunity. In most other respects, the compromise bill was identical to S. 2245.

Many shipper and consumer groups were disappointed in the compromise, fearing that the revised entry standard was dangerously ambiguous. Moreover, the indexing provision was a concern to shippers, who thought it would be inflationary. But administration officials contended that the compromise entry standard was no worse, and possibly even better, than the Senate's provision. Overall, they—and many other deregulators—regarded the compromise as "a bill with real substance, real gain."[75]

The "Delicate Balance"

At the subcommittee markup on May 20, the compromise bill was accepted without substantive change. Repeated efforts to amend the bill were defeated after key committee members—Representative Howard, ranking minority member William Harsha (R-Ohio), and Bud Shuster (R-Pa.)—opposed them on the grounds that, however meritorious, they would upset the "delicate balance." "I've never felt that so many people agreed with me in principle but voted against me," said one committee member when his amendment was summarily defeated. After Allen Ertel (D-Pa.), an ardent deregulator, suffered the same fate, he said in exasperation, "This is not a conference committee. . . . Are we going to legislate here a bad bill so we don't have to go to conference?"[76]

The full committee markup two days later was also "greased." The "fragile compromise" proved so solid that one Public Works member remarked it was the first time he had seen a bill pass conference and be signed by the president before it emerged from committee. The only significant amendment added agricultural limestone, soil conditioners, and fertilizers to the list of exempt commodities—a change worked out the previous day during a marathon negotiation session in order to appease major farm groups.

Most of the debate centered around a provision in the bill tangential to the deregulation compromise that allowed grocery stores to negotiate with food manufacturers for lower prices if the stores picked up the food themselves at the manufacturer's dock. The provision, supported by the Food Marketing Institute, was retained despite opposition by the powerful Grocery Manufacturers Association.[77]

Also controversial was an unsuccessful attempt by Rep. Elliott Levitas (D-Ga.) to add a legislative veto provision that would allow one chamber of Congress to overturn ICC regulations. Levitas, a strong proponent of the legislative veto, noted that "our distinguished colleagues across the Capitol are no longer virgins on this," referring to the Senate's recent approval of a two-chamber veto over Federal Trade Commission regulations. Representative Harsha said the administration and Senate would oppose any compromise bill that contained such a provision. "Just because they yielded on one occasion doesn't mean they're willing to give birth to quintuplets," Harsha retorted.[78]

The committee's action brought immediate praise from all sides. Goldschmidt said the bill would "inject a new competitive spirit in the trucking industry that will lead to lower transportation costs and better service."[79] And Bennett Whitlock congratulated the committee for the "balanced approach" it had taken in the bill. "We will, of course, resist any further substantive changes in the bill," he added.[80]

Preserving the "Fragile Compromise"

As the trucking bill moved to the full House, the administration and the Senate Commerce Committee found themselves on the same side as the ATA in resisting substantive changes that would unravel the compromise and require a House-Senate conference committee. Both sides hoped to take the bill to the House floor in early June. "Every day that goes by gives someone an opportunity to think of something new," said Representative Howard, referring to the potential for damaging amendments. But House Speaker Thomas O'Neill (D-Mass.) sidetracked most substantive legislation until Congress had resolved a major budget dispute and passed needed appropriations bills.[81]

Three possible amendments by groups not part of the "delicate balance" threatened to upset the compromise. The Teamsters hoped to amend the bill on the floor of the House so as to give drivers laid off because of deregulation the right of first hire by other firms and to set up a $100 million fund to pay dislocation benefits. The ATA, representing many nonunion firms, said it would oppose any bill that contained such a provision.

Consumer, shipper, and farm groups—led by the American Farm Bureau Federation—sought to restore the exemption of processed food through a floor fight. (The Farm Bureau had earlier agreed to the compromise, but a planned committee amendment on another issue freed the group to seek changes on the House floor.) While administration members and Commerce Committee leaders supported the effort in principle, they were bound by their agreement with Public Works to oppose it.

But the most serious threat to the compromise was Levitas's planned amendment to provide for a legislative veto. The House had never defeated a provision for a one-chamber veto, and the principle was at stake, even though the practical effect would have been to slow ICC deregulation rather than inhibit new regulation—Congress's usual objective with the veto.

When the trucking bill finally came before the full House for action, on Thursday, June 19, none of the efforts at amendment proved a match for the "delicate balance." The Teamsters' proposal, offered by a first-term congressman, was defeated by voice vote. Congresswoman Millicent Fenwick (R-N.J.) led the fight to restore the Stevenson food provision. Her amendment was easily defeated—287 to 113. In the only dramatic vote, the House rejected the Levitas amendment 192 to 189.

The House passed the final bill by a lopsided 267-to-13 vote. Twenty-four hours later, a Senate working late on a Friday night approved the House changes in less than two minutes by voice vote. Only the festivities remained.

"Historic Legislation"

On a cloudless morning—the first day of July—President Carter signed the Motor Carrier Act of 1980 in the Rose Garden. Carter was flanked by key congressional supporters of the bill, including his campaign rival, Edward Kennedy. Several hundred invited guests—lobbyists, Capitol Hill staffers, and others—watched the ceremony from chairs set up on the grass.

The occasion was ripe for humor about the rivalry between Carter and Kennedy. Before the president joined the assembled group, Kennedy stood directly behind a chair provided for Carter to use while signing the bill. When he spotted some of the reporters who had been covering his presidential campaign, Kennedy caressed the back of the chair with the hint of a smile. After Carter introduced Kennedy with strong words of praise, the senator began with a quip. "Well, there's no debate on trucking deregulation," Kennedy said, referring to his unsuccessful efforts to get Carter to "come out of the Rose Garden" and debate him on television.[82]

"This is historic legislation," Carter told the group. "There is no other nation on earth that depends as much on motor carrier transportation for its economic life's blood." Carter said Congress's action would "bring the trucking industry into the free-market system where it belongs," and he predicted that the legislation would reduce consumer costs by as much as $8 billion a year and save hundreds of millions of gallons of gasoline annually.[83]

But Carter also looked backward. "A year ago at the White House, I proposed broad changes in the regulations that deal with the trucking industry. People said then that it was impossible to pass a trucking deregulation bill because of the powerful political forces involved and the controversial nature of this kind of legislation. That I'm signing this bill into law today . . . is a tremendous credit to all those who worked so closely with me in devising and in passing this legislation."[84]

4

Demonstrating the Merits:
Strategic Use of Analysis

*People think Congress pays no heed to substance. That's not so.
Some of my colleagues turn to the merits whenever they're in
doubt.*
    —Member of Congress to Berkeley law professor
    Lawrence Sullivan

The traditional view of Congress-watchers is that the merits don't count
for much. Our system is a "scramble of self-interestedness," wrote
columnist George Will. "Hence, politics involves few appeals to reason and
public spiritedness; little reliance on statesmanlike rhetoric that appeals to
what Lincoln called 'the better angels of our nature.' "[1]

However, to defeat a client group in a scramble for the public's
interest, reformers must appeal heavily to reason. Only a strong case on the
merits will attract the attention and support of those institutions that can
effectively advocate the interest of the unorganized majority before Congress—namely, the presidency and the press. More directly, a strong showing on the merits is necessary to persuade Congress itself—especially key
committee leaders—to terminate an existing special-interest policy. For
legislators who are vulnerable to pressure from the client group, no amount
of objective evidence may be sufficient. But for those who can afford to be
"in doubt," support will hinge on what they find when they "turn to the
merits."

In our system of law, the accused is presumed innocent until proven guilty. Similarly, in our political system, the burden of proof is on those who advocate major change, especially when that change risks disruption and dislocation. To meet this burden, a case to Congress on the merits must satisfy three conditions.

First, it must establish that something is seriously wrong with the existing system.[2] Unlike accused criminals, proposed policy reforms are not guaranteed a speedy trial, or any trial for that matter, on Capitol Hill. Reformers must convince one or more key committee leaders that there is a serious problem in order to gain a place on Congress's severely limited docket. Once in "court," they must be able to demonstrate a strong need for change, since members of Congress will not likely undo established policy just for marginal gains.

The fact that an existing policy is economically inefficient has not traditionally been seen as a serious problem on Capitol Hill. Elected officials generally don't care about misallocation of resources, according to political observers, only about who wins and who loses.[3] When the costs of an inefficient policy are diffusely spread, it's hard to make a dramatic case for reform.

Because of the nature of their professional training, economists are often cast in the role of "partisan efficiency advocates" in the policy debate.[4] But a former member of the Council of Economic Advisers, George Eads, has observed that the way economists look at inefficient policies is itself inefficient, politically speaking. Since arguments about misallocation of resources rarely carry the day, what's needed is evidence on the inequity of such policies—specifically regulation—where it exists:

> While economists tend to believe that inefficiency is bad per se, the bulk of the population seems willing to tolerate inefficiencies from regulation because they believe that in return they are obtaining "fair treatment" or "equity." It does economists little good to observe . . . that what may appear to the public to be "equity" indeed may be highly inequitable. Economists have not, in general, been willing to perform the studies that would allow us to back up such claims. Most of us have contented ourselves with analyses that measure such esoteric concepts (esoteric to the general public, at least) as "deadweight loss." By doing so, we have failed absolutely to undermine the strongest support for regulation among the general public.[5]

Bradley Behrman came to a similar conclusion after studying the initial, unsuccessful efforts of airline regulatory reformers: "Only if deregulation can be converted from a technical case promising improved economic efficiency to a moral case promising an end to monopoly profits and privilege will it ever arouse sufficient . . . support."[6]

Most congressmen, like most people, prefer a devil they know to a devil they don't know. Even if the existing system is seriously flawed, undoing it could be worse. Thus, a convincing case on the merits must not only demonstrate a serious problem, it must reduce uncertainty about possible ill effects of the proposed change (condition two).

Idiosyncratic evidence is what's called for according to Stephen Breyer who, as special counsel to the Senate Judiciary Subcommittee on Administrative Practice and Procedure, played a central role in achieving airline deregulation. Breyer concluded that detailed empirical investigation of the industry or policy in question is necessary in part because there may be light years between the state of the academic art and what's needed for implementation of a specific reform proposal.[7] Breyer also found that qualitative, anecdotal evidence has impressionistic value because it assures members of Congress that the researcher has been out in the field.[8]

In order to demonstrate a serious problem and reduce uncertainty about change, a case on the merits must be understandable to politicians and sensitive to political factors (condition three). As advice for would-be policy reformers, that's hardly profound. But the observations of a veteran Washington lobbyist suggest that it's not always heeded. Complexity of evidence is one problem: "The government tells you far too much on the subject. That's because it's being done by some guy who's trying to impress his boss. . . . It's useful only to the extent they make it intelligible to people who don't have time to get a Ph.D. on the subject."

Sterility is another: "The [substantive] stuff is good if you put it in human terms. But in the form the government puts it out, it's often un-digestible. You have to have a human angle."

These and other problems with analysis used in a strategic setting result from still a third problem—the distance of the analyst from the political battlefield: "A lot of the government's stuff is turned out by people who don't get any closer to the Hill than their own desk. But it's no different than with the guy who designs a Springfield rifle. You need to send him out to the field every now and then to see if it really kills any game."[9]

The following chapter looks at how trucking deregulators went about "killing their game." The first section describes the volleying that took place between the two sides before an audience of congressmen with little knowledge of economics. The second section analyzes what deregulators did right and what—if anything—their opponents did wrong in making their case on the merits. The chapter also looks at the incentives to make soft analysis and crude estimates appear precise in the heat of debate, and at the type of economic arguments that don't play well on Capitol Hill. The conclusion points up the improved market for efficiency-based policy reforms in an era of high inflation and examines other reasons that economic arguments played a bigger role in the trucking and airline battles than they generally do.

Deregulators' Burden

In late 1978, when the Carter administration turned its attention from airlines to trucking reform, Congress looked on trucking deregulation as only a half-crazy idea. Several events had lent credence to the once-heretical notion. Senator Kennedy had held lengthy hearings critical of truckers' immunity from antitrust laws. The ICC had initiated moderate administrative reform—partly in response to unfavorable publicity from Kennedy's hearings. Even more important, airline deregulation was proving extremely popular in most areas.

The airline precedent meant that trucking deregulators didn't have to break new ground, prove that they weren't kooks. But there were differences between the two transportation industries, which the truckers were quick to point out. Unlike airlines, regulated trucking was generally a healthy and prosperous industry (too prosperous, reformers would argue), hence the ATA's antideregulation theme—"If it ain't broke, don't fix it." Trucking is also the transportation mode most vital to the nation's economy. The industry's motto, "If you got it, a truck brought it," is not far off. And while lower prices brought on by deregulation meant considerably more business for airlines, shippers' demand for trucking is less price elastic.

Where airline deregulation had caused seeming problems, truckers were quick to draw parallels between the two industries. The temporary loss of air service to some communities following deregulation played smack into the hands of the trucking industry, which had long maintained that ICC regulation was the only thing that kept trucks traveling to and from rural areas. That became the single greatest obstacle for proponents of trucking deregulation to overcome. The trucking industry also made hay of the rise in air *cargo* rates that followed decontrol of that industry in 1977. Economically, such a rise was warranted; the CAB had kept cargo rates artificially low. Politically, it was damaging to trucking reformers' case.

In short, the proposal to decontrol trucking was no longer viewed as fuzzy theory on Capitol Hill, but the substantive case had yet to be made. The burden of proof on those proposing policy termination was particularly heavy here, where a regulatory system had been in place for nearly forty years and where an industry vital to the nation's economy had grown and thrived under it. Reformers had to show not only that the system was "broke," but also that deregulation would "fix it"—and do so without significant disruption. The last requirement was key. Election-conscious legislators are understandably shortsighted; the prospect of long-term social benefits may pale next to the threat of near-term disruptions.

The System Is "Broke"

[This is] the most insane network of regulation that could conceivably have been devised by a paranoid.
—Alfred Kahn

From the economist's list of malfunction symptoms (chapter 2)—monopoly profits, excessive costs, inefficient price-service options, and discriminatory rates—evolved the major themes of deregulators' case to Congress on the merits: ICC regulation of trucking produces excessive rates, fuel waste, and senseless restrictions. Stated differently, regulation contributes to three of the country's most pressing problems—inflation, the energy shortage, and unnecessary government interference.

Excessive Rates

Trucking rates are excessive, said deregulators, largely because regulation suppresses competition that would otherwise drive prices down. Consumers ultimately bear this cost. Deregulators had no smoking gun— no single piece of evidence as persuasive as the studies of (unregulated) intrastate air service in Texas and California had been in that policy battle. What they had was a long list of smoking sling shots that were convincing in the aggregate:

- When certain agricultural commodities—frozen poultry, frozen fruits and vegetables—were exempted from regulation in the 1950s, rates fell 19 to 36 percent; rates rose back when some of those products were reregulated.
- In New Jersey, where intrastate trucking is unregulated, rates are 10 to 25 percent lower than for comparable interstate shipments; household-goods moving within Maryland is unregulated, and rates are 27 to 87 percent below those of interstate movers.
- Regulated carriers commonly "lease" their operating rights to independent truckers in return for 20 to 30 percent of the revenue from hauling the regulated goods. The fact that independents enter into such an arrangement indicates that revenues well below the regulated level are still profitable.

- Operating rights, granted free by the ICC, have market value—an indication that regulated carriers are able to earn higher-than-competitive rates.
- In recent years, the trucking industry's profits have consistently been among the highest of any industry.[10]

Moreover, deregulators had a very large "bottom-line" figure for what excessive rates cost consumers. The Council on Wage and Price Stability (COWPS) estimated the cost at $5 billion. The Congressional Budget Office (CBO) estimate, released days before the critical Senate floor vote, predicted that trucking deregulation would save consumers $5.3 to $8 billion annually by 1985.* That's equal to $70 to $105 per household, 0.3 to 0.45 percentage points on the Consumer Price Index (CPI).[11]

The ATA countered that regulation had actually served to keep prices down, as evidenced by the fact that trucking rates per ton-mile had risen less rapidly over the last decade than the CPI. The industry group estimated annual savings at several billion dollars.

As a logical proposition, the ATA's statistical comparison was not persuasive. "The rates [were] unnecessarily high to begin with," testified a Nader attorney. "The change between the [designated] years, or in any period, does not prove anything. . . ."[12]

The CPI comparison was also misleading. It ignored productivity improvements (better loading equipment, improved roads) and changes in average shipment weight—specifically, a trend by shippers toward consolidation of small shipments into larger ones, which move at vastly cheaper rates. The Department of Transportation recalculated the comparison, taking this trend into account, and found that regulated rates had risen slightly faster than the price index.

Fearing that this counter to the ATA's claim was overly technical for harried congressmen and their staffs, DOT analysts worked out another, more simplistic refutation that turned the industry's argument on its head. They computed two separate indexes—one for the less-than-truckload (LTL) sector and another for the truckload (TL) sector of the industry. DOT Secretary Neil Goldschmidt explained the results in a letter to Senator Cannon:

---

*"Deregulation Could Trim Transportation Costs by $8 Billion, CBO Claims in Study," read the *Washington Post* headline, on page one of the business news (March 31, 1980). In fact, CBO had done no "study" of its own, merely reviewed existing ones as discussed later in the chapter.

CBO's report was leaked to the *Washington Post* by a high-level deregulator in the Department of Transportation. The leak was carefully timed so that the story would appear on a Monday—normally a slow news day—and hence receive maximum exposure.

> If regulation *were* successful in holding rates down, then rates would tend to rise more slowly in the LTL sector of the industry, which is heavily regulated, than in the TL sector, where rates are more competitively determined. In fact, the findings . . . show just the opposite: *Rates on LTL shipments increased by 13.0 percent per year—over half again as fast as the CPI and almost double the 6.8 percent per year of the TL sector.*[13]

Even more commonsensical was reformers' responding query: If regulation keeps trucking rates low, why aren't carriers clamoring for deregulation? (The ATA's reply: fear of cannibalization within the industry.)[14]

Fuel Waste

Deregulators argued that regulation needlessly wastes precious fuel by requiring trucks to take indirect routes to their destination and travel many miles empty, even though freight is available to be moved. They cited estimates that nearly one-fourth of all truck miles are traveled empty and that removal of backhaul restrictions would alone save 220–320 million gallons of fuel each year.[15] They also described concrete examples of seemingly blatant waste: the regulated carrier who could travel between Omaha and Denver, 540 miles total, but only by way of Cheyenne, Wyoming, a 260-mile detour; or the carrier who had to serve the traffic between Pittsburgh and Frederick, Maryland, by way of southern New Jersey, adding 216 miles to what should be a 188-mile trip.

The trucking industry said energy waste was a phony issue: 97 percent of all empty backhauls were the unavoidable result of either natural traffic imbalances—for example, between producing and consuming regions—or use of specialized equipment designed to carry only one type of freight. Moreover, "one man's backhaul is another man's fronthaul," meaning there's no way to fill one empty truck without creating another.

What's more, argued the industry, by easing entry restrictions, deregulation would mean *more* trucks on the road and hence additional fuel consumption. Applying that logic, industry supporters amended the Senate bill so as to make the goal of the legislation "efficiency and competition" rather than just "competition." They reasoned that they could fight a liberal ICC interpretation of the entry provision on the grounds of its potential energy inefficiency.

The ATA lacked any hard numbers to back up its energy consumption claims, however. An analysis commissioned by the Federal Energy Administration in 1975 had concluded that trucking deregulation would increase fuel consumption slightly, because trucks would divert traffic from railroads, which use far less fuel. Ironically that finding (challenged by an independent DOT-sponsored analysis) was of little use to the ATA, since the lobby group steadfastly maintained that deregulation would not produce any new demand for the industry's services (the "trucking-is-not-like-airlines" argument).

Senseless Restrictions

Livestock are exempt from regulation—unless you're taking them to a show; then they're not; unless it's a 4-H show; then they are. Raisins are exempt if they're coated with honey, cinnamon, or sugar, but not if they're covered with chocolate.

Administration staff people combed the Federal Register daily for examples of seemingly absurd ICC restrictions and nitpicking rules. Reform proponents had made a conscious decision years earlier to play up these senseless-sounding distinctions; hopefully that would help offset the fact that good data on the industry—the kind the CAB had collected on airlines—didn't exist at the ICC.

Deregulation supporters studded their speeches with the examples. President Carter described as "defy[ing] human imagination" rules that permitted some truckers to carry milk but not butter, cream but not cheese, paint in two-gallon but not five-gallon cans. He ridiculed ICC regulations that prohibited the same trucker who had delivered tomatoes to the soup factory from hauling away canned soup, or that required a trucking company to go from Denver to Albuquerque by way of Salt Lake City, a detour of 300 miles.

The press loved these seeming absurdities. Many an editorial began with the case of the trucker who could carry empty gingerale bottles but not empty cola or root beer bottles, or the rule allowing exempt carriers to haul frozen TV dinners unless they contained chicken or seafood. "The Byzantine World of Trucking . . ." read the headline for a *Washington Post* article describing the regulated industry.

The examples were used to illustrate dramatically the lengths to which businessmen would go just to get around the regulatory system: the piano manufacturer who purchased refrigerated trucks so that he could carry (exempt) agricultural produce on the backhaul. The story of the trucker whose request to carry (nonexistent) yak fat received thirteen challenges pointed up the extremes carriers went to just to preserve their regulated turf. The appeal was not to a less-government-is-good ideology but to a more universal disdain for paperwork and mindless bureaucracy: "It takes 2,000 ICC bureaucrats just to keep track of the 7,000 pages of rate filings the commission receives every day."

Most of the illustrations of absurdity were based on the ICC's distinction between unprocessed (exempt) and processed (nonexempt) agricultural goods. Ironically, that was the major feature of regulation that the trucking industry successfully preserved (though it was weakened somewhat). So in a direct sense, reformers' efforts were wasted. But indirectly, the colorful depiction of regulation as "byzantine," "mindboggling," "nit-picking," and "insane" was effective because there was so little the ATA could say in defense.

Industry spokesmen argued that they were the victims of a shell game—a political ploy by faltering liberals to distract public attention from the real issue of social or environmental regulation. The ATA warned that businessmen and conservative groups had been fooled into confusing the two, even though the difference between social regulation and trucking regulation was, in Mark Twain's words, the difference between lightning and lightning bugs.

More generally, the industry appealed to the flip side of reformers' charge of mind-boggling regulation—by portraying trucking as a highly complex industry that could be destroyed in no time by the blind tinkering of naive outsiders. Truckers went for the Achilles' heel—fear of the unknown: The industry has functioned smoothly for forty-five years under regulation to provide the finest transportation system in the world; now some ivory-tower economists who have never seen the inside of a truck terminal want to rush in and dismantle it. That was their general message. Specifically, they warned that deregulation would lead to chaos, followed in time by industry concentration; in addition, safety would suffer and, most important, small communities would lose service. Discrediting these dire predictions was deregulators' greatest challenge.

". . . Don't Fix It" (Or Else)

Government operates according to the old theory which states, "If you think the problem is bad now, just wait till we've solved it."
—Bennett Whitlock, ATA president

Chaos

History will repeat itself, warned industry spokesmen as they recalled the conditions prior to the 1935 Motor Carrier Act, "when the trucking business was a cutthroat game. . . and companies went in and out of business before the ink on the letterhead could dry." (One industry consultant advised them to forget their appeal to "pre-1935 chaos." "Americans as a whole are not notably history minded," he told them. "The attitude still is widespread that 'history is bunk'.") Projecting, they described a scenario under deregulation with carriers engaged in predatory price wars, shippers facing a bewildering array of ever changing rates, rampant excess capacity, and scores of bankruptcies.

Deregulation proponents argued on theoretical grounds that destructive competition would occur only if an industry had heavy fixed costs and chronic excess capacity with little or no alternative use for its assets; neither of these two conditions described trucking.

More important, they pointed to the existence of, and experience from, unregulated trucking sectors as evidence of the lack of chaos: Department of Agriculture studies showing that bankruptcy rates for independent truckers were about equal to those for other small retail firms;[16] a recent DOT investigation of (unregulated) intrastate trucking in New Jersey that found no evidence of destructive competition;[17] a study of motor carrier deregulation in Great Britain that found there was no flood of new firms into the industry, and shippers judged service quality to be as good after deregulation as before.[18] The generally positive experience following deregulation of airline rates and entry also contradicted predictions of chaos.

On most issues, the substantive disagreement between proponents and opponents of deregulation was over questions of fact: Would additional competition cause rates to rise or fall? (An ATA official began a speech denouncing deregulators by recalling a *New Yorker* cartoon that showed a filing cabinet with drawers labeled "Our Facts," "Their Facts," and "The Real Facts.") But on certain issues—rate stability was one, "discrimination" (cross-subsidy) was another—the disagreement went to philosophy and values.

Both sides agreed that regulation served to keep rates more stable than they otherwise would be; they clashed over whether or not that was desirable. The ATA argued that the benefits of stable rates were self-evident: Shippers know what they're going to be charged, and they can plan accordingly; that's not the case in the exempt agricultural market, where rates swing widely. Proponents of deregulation portrayed variable rates as a sign of a healthy market: They represent seasonal fluctuations in demand and hence provide an efficient mechanism for allocating trucking services.

Concentration

Following a period of destructive competition, the ATA warned, the industry would go through a "shaking out" phase, after which time the "big firms with the heaviest financial and managerial guns" would dominate the field. "In the brave new world of deregulated trucking only a select few— and not necessarily the fittest—will survive."[19]

The thrust of deregulators' defense was that two conditions must hold for monopoly to result. Large trucking firms must have inherent cost advantages over small ones—that is, there must be economies of scale. And once the large firms have competed all of the others out of existence, there must be barriers to entry by new competitors. Both are absent in the trucking industry, said deregulators.

The economies-of-scale issue was particularly sticky. Several academic studies from the 1950s and 1960s had concluded that there were cost advantages to size in trucking. DOT spent considerable resources studying that issue (both internally and by funding academic research) using more refined methodologies. Most persuasive was the work of Ann Friedlaender, a Massachusetts Institute of Technology economics professor, which found that existing economies of scale were exhausted by quite small firms, after which point diseconomies of size set in.[20]

If there was ever a case where economists and industry practitioners spoke two different languages, it was on the issue of scale economies. This may account for the sincere belief of some industry members that the economic evidence on this point was naive and counterfactual. In one enlightening exchange, a major trucking-company executive challenged the remarks of a government economist who, based on his own and others' research, denied there were scale economies in the motor carrier industry: "I was the chief financial officer of the largest trucking merger that has ever been. . . . I know a lot about economies of scale, because there were tremendous [ones], but tremendous problems of management and labor . . . more than offset the economies of scale and have consistently driven down that company."[21]

The economist responded with glee, saying he had for the first time realized that what (some) businessmen mean by economies of scale is simply not what an economist means; in economic terms the notion includes management and labor as well as the physical attributes of a trucking firm.

In addition to shooting holes in the ATA's prediction of monopoly, deregulation proponents went on the offensive, charging that the industry was already heavily concentrated *as a result of* regulation. The ATA had always maintained that deregulation wasn't necessary to bring about competition in an industry that had 17,000 (regulated) firms. But of course, aggregate numbers don't tell the real story. The test is how much competition exists on individual routes.

The ICC didn't have the data to answer that question. Only the industry rate bureaus did, in the form of Continuing Traffic Study (CTS) tapes—a sophisticated data base used for collective ratemaking and for justifying

general rate increases. The ICC had tried unsuccessfully to get the CTS tapes
for years. Kennedy's Subcommittee on Antitrust and Monopoly finally
obtained them under threat of subpoena, with the promise that proprietary
information would remain confidential.

Kennedy's staff, assisted by DOT experts, analyzed the CTS data extensively. The senator unveiled the results, with a flurry of tables and charts, at
the opening day of hearings on the Carter-Kennedy deregulation bill. The
findings showed that the trucking industry was highly concentrated in
individual city-pair markets: The four largest firms had an average market
share of over 60 percent. The evidence also suggested that concentration
was due to ICC regulation: Concentration levels were much lower in the
East and Midwest—where many firms received grandfather rights in 1935—
and much higher in the West and Southwest—which experienced their
growth after 1935, when the ICC tightly restricted entry.[22]

The ATA was unable to respond to the Judiciary Committee results
because the trade group itself couldn't get the CTS tapes from the rate
bureaus. The bureaus apparently feared that the data would show which
markets had heavy freight flows and thereby encourage entry into those
markets. Much blood was spilt over that issue within the industry.

Safety

The scenario for chaos depicted by those opposing deregulation
included the sobering spectre of truckers deferring maintenance, driving
on hot tires, popping pills—in general, safety falling by the wayside under
the cost-cutting pressure of decontrol. Since motor vehicle accidents take
nearly 100,000 American lives each year—with trucks involved in many of
those accidents—the issue was highly emotional. Giving the industry's
claims credibility was a study by Harvard Business School professor
D. Daryl Wyckoff which showed that regulated carriers had a consistently
better safety record than unregulated owner-operators.[23]

Deregulators countered that certain measurement problems discredited Wyckoff's findings: He measured things that might be associated with
accident rates, rather than accident rates themselves, and these by self-
reporting (Do you pop bennies? Do you drive beyond the ten-hour limit?).
There was also some indication that regulated trucking companies had
advised their drivers how to answer the questionnaire (the study was
partially funded by the Teamsters and ATA).[24]

The administration put forth its own numbers as well. Statistics from
DOT's Bureau of Motor Carrier Safety, which regulates truck safety, showed
no appreciable differences between the accident levels of regulated and

exempt carriers.[25] (The ATA countered that *fatality* rates for exempt carriers were double those for regulated carriers.)

Numbers aside, said deregulators, economic regulation is an inappropriate way to improve truck safety. The solution to this serious (underlined) problem is better safety regulation. Reformers also proposed that a deregulation bill address the problem by setting insurance requirements—a proposal that came back to haunt them when the industry pushed through high insurance minimums intended to serve as barriers to entry.

Small-Town Service

"So long, Escanaba." That was the message contained in "Small Town Blues," the ATA's report on what deregulation would mean for Escanaba, Michigan, and other small communities across the country. Service to small towns was often uneconomical, the industry warned. The regulated carriers provided it, through a cross-subsidy from their more lucrative routes, only because of their common-carrier obligation. Absent regulation, many communities would lose service altogether or have to pay dearly for it.

The industry offered surprisingly little in the way of hard evidence to bolster its claims. "Small Town Blues" contained the results of a four-question survey of 900 regulated carriers conducted in 1976. In response to a highly leading query, 62 percent of the carriers said they would suspend service to one or more points if it were not required by regulation. It was not a persuasive piece of social science. Aside from loaded questions, there was virtually no explanation of sampling methodology, and the entire survey was published on three pages in the middle of a public-relations tract. The ATA's only other statistical ammunition was a survey of shippers and carriers in Virginia, conducted by that state's regulatory commission, with results so mixed that deregulation proponents liked to cite them as well.[26]

The assignment of convincing the public that deregulation threatened small-community service fell largely to Hill and Knowlton, a prestigious public-relations firm that the ATA hired for a multimillion-dollar sum. Hill and Knowlton developed a media campaign, aimed at small towns themselves, using slogans like "The Truck Stops Here." The ads warned that children in outlying communities might not get Halloween candy or Christmas toys if Congress deregulated the trucking industry.

The trucking industry's best argument, at least for a while, was the disruption in air service that followed deregulation of that industry. ATA President Whitlock joked with groups like the Fort Wayne, Indiana, Chamber of Commerce about the "ultimate in supersavers"—"United's Disappearing Service." He left them with the clear message that the folks "who brought you this situation—the free-market economists, the theorists, the bureaucrats," would do the same thing to trucking service.

The disruption in air service generated plenty of political heat even without the ATA around to fan the flames. Several congressmen proclaimed themselves "born-again regulators" over the loss of service to their districts. Others withheld judgment of trucking deregulation, waiting to hear what the debate would say about small-community service. Even this reaction was a boon to the ATA, since these "agnostics" tended to be from rural, conservative districts—in all other respects a natural constituency for a less-government-is-good issue like deregulation.[27]

The trucking industry's most visible attempt to exploit the airline experience was a near full-page ad in the *Washington Post* and the *Wall Street Journal* proclaiming that "Deregulation has shot down more planes than the Red Baron" and listing twenty-five communities that had allegedly lost all certificated service. (By coincidence, directly opposite the *Post* ad was an equally large advertisement for TWA family bargain fares.) The CAB chairman held a press conference to refute the Red Baron ad, and DOT compiled a thick document showing airline service changes at certificated airports in every state.

DOT's compilation was actually one of the last of a long line of documents produced by deregulation proponents to dispel the loss-of-service-to-small-communities charge. From the start, they had rightly feared this as the greatest obstacle to decontrol. When DOT began its research effort on trucking reform in the early 1970s, one of the first tasks involved sending a team of summer interns out to small towns to question shippers about trucking service.

Given what they knew, deregulators had no reason to believe that the trucking industry was serving small communities at a loss and hence would terminate service under relaxed ICC control. The commission had never once revoked a carrier's authority for failing to serve small towns. The industry argued that the mere threat of ICC reprisal was sufficient inducement but could never document the claim. Moreover, the ICC had received almost no requests to discontinue small-town service, whereas application by even the largest firms to serve small towns was not a rarity. In short, since the common-carrier obligation was effectively unenforceable, regulated carriers must be serving small communities because it was profitable to do so.

Early informal evidence indicated, moreover, that precisely because they could avoid serving small communities if they chose, regulated carriers provided little of the trucking service that went to these areas. Most of it came from private carriers, exempt agricultural haulers, and United Parcel

Service. Thus, even if deregulation did lead regulated carriers to seek more lucrative markets, the impact on small towns would be minimal.

But how to convince Congress that the small-communities problem was a red herring? Some reform proponents predicted that no amount of scientific evidence could defuse such an emotional issue.

The first test of that prediction came when the Senate Commerce Committee released a study it had commissioned from a Boston consulting firm, Policy and Management Associates, Inc. (PMA) on the impact of deregulation on small communities.[28] Using sophisticated sampling methodology, PMA surveyed shippers and carriers in several hundred towns throughout the country. The study concluded that "service to small communities would not deteriorate and might, in fact, improve under deregulation."

The ATA lambasted the study on several counts. Reform proponents were also somewhat critical, primarily of PMA's omission of towns under 1,000 population. To resolve these objections, the Commerce Committee asked the Congressional Budget Office for an independent analysis of the PMA study. CBO looked at several other studies as well and concluded that deregulation would have a negligible effect on service and rates in small communities, since there was no evidence of a significant cross-subsidy and since carriers could at present avoid serving small towns if they wished.[29] That conclusion, unencumbered by the doubt cast on the PMA study, was generally persuasive.

Deregulators' trump card, however, was a set of DOT surveys of sixteen small communities in six states. The six states corresponded to members of the Senate Commerce Committee who were concerned about the small-communities issue. It was custom-tailored research; the six senators even selected the towns to be surveyed in their own states.

A team of DOT researchers interviewed a dozen or so businessmen in each of the communities. The published reports documented each interview in folksy detail:

> Bud's Husky (McGill, Nevada) is a general service gas station that has been in business 10 years. Bud's is the only gas station in McGill; up until 5 years ago, there were three.

> Bud Ingle, the station's owner, said he receives shipments from Twin Falls, Idaho; Salt Lake City; Elko; Reno and Ely.

> [His] shipments are mainly brought in on the suppliers' private trucks. His gasoline is shipped in by Husky; Pyroil products (fan belts, clamps, bolts, windshield wipers, antifreeze, etc.) are shipped in by Packapart in

Elko, a general auto concern, and Wynn's TBA in Idaho brings in
tune up parts.

Mr. Ingle receives good service from each of the carriers. He felt, however,
that rates are too high overall. "If you're trying to figure freight prices, they're
too high, I'll tell you that."[30]

The findings were consistent across communities: Shippers were by and
large satisfied with the service they received, but that service came largely
from UPS and exempt carriers. ICC-regulated general freight carriers did
not play a major role in providing small-town service, and much of the
service they did provide was perceived as infrequent, slow, and costly. DOT
secretary Goldschmidt summed up the findings to a Capitol Hill audience:
Regulated common carriage "is not small town America's lifeline . . . [it is
her] last resort."[31]

Other DOT and ICC studies echoed these findings, as did a survey by
the California Public Utilities Commission (PUC) on trucking service in
three small communities in that state.[32] (One of the California towns fell just
outside the district represented by Bizz Johnson, chairman of the all-
important House Public Works Committee. DOT tried to get the commission to select a community located within Johnson's district, but the PUC
had its own political agenda to serve.)

The small-communities studies, particularly DOT's six state surveys,
had visible impact. DOT officials presented the preliminary findings from
the Nevada survey at a Commerce Committee hearing in Fallon, Nevada.
Howard Cannon's tepid support of deregulation warmed noticeably after
that. Sen. Harrison Schmitt of New Mexico, a conservative Republican and
natural ally, had withheld support out of fear that his state's experience
following airline deregulation would be repeated (among other things, one
air carrier pulled out suddenly during the Christmas holidays). When DOT
reported on its survey of Taos and Truth or Consequences—towns that
Schmitt picked in consultation with the New Mexico Trucking Association—
he became one of the Senate's most committed supporters of deregulation.

Overall, the small-communities issue was laid to rest more quickly
and soundly than deregulation proponents (and the ATA) expected. By the
time the action on the bill shifted from the Senate to the House, it was no
longer a major obstacle.[33]

Persuading on the Merits

Reformers' effort to make trucking deregulation substantively acceptable
accomplished its immediate goal—persuading the Senate Commerce Com-

mittee leadership. The trucking industry had always considered Howard Cannon sympathetic to its side; thus it came as a surprise when, shortly before the Commerce Committee hearings were to begin, the Nevada senator delivered a keynote speech to the ATA in which he offered his nominations for the "five worst arguments against changes in the regulatory structure."

> The winner for the most ineffective argument is the bareboned assertion that, "Deregulation will result in complete chaos." . . .
>
> In second place, but a very close runner-up, is the argument that, "We have the finest surface transportation system in the world, so why change it?"[34]

Cannon also told the truckers it was "obvious" that their industry was not a natural monopoly, but that if there were substantial economies of scale, as the industry maintained, then perhaps regulation was stifling efficiency through underconcentration.

As an old-fashioned Democrat from a state where Teamsters are a significant power, Cannon was not expected to become a fierce advocate for deregulation no matter how compelling the evidence. But he did at least become sufficiently convinced of the merits to conduct the hearings and proceed in an evenhanded way. That he fought for such a strong bill is probably due more to other factors, including the influence of Sen. Robert Packwood, the Commerce Committee's minority leader. After thoroughly steeping himself in the evidence on both sides, the Oregon senator became a passionate believer in trucking deregulation. The sophisticated understanding of the industry he acquired, plus his fluency with the economic arguments all around, made Packwood a persuasive spokesman for reform.

The substantive case for deregulation hit its mark with more than just the leadership. The battle in the Senate—both in committee and on the floor—was won largely on "the merits," as chapter 5 will discuss. The merits had far less direct impact in the House of Representatives, where the parties worked out a deal in advance and presented it to the Public Works Committee and the full House for pro forma ratification. But they were critical in the Senate.

That is not to say that economic data and analysis per se were all-important. They're only one measure of the merits of a bill. The other is the age-old political barometer—who's for it and who's agin it. The two measures work hand in hand, assuming they give consistent readings (a subject of the next chapter). But even that barometer was somewhat sensitive to economists' case for reform. In a few instances, analysis persuaded neutral or opposing groups that deregulation was, after all, in their interest.[35] More commonly, the price tag economists attached to ICC regulation served to elevate trucking reform on the legislative agendas of sympathetic interest groups and elected officials—most notably Jimmy Carter.[36]

The weight of evidence also contributed to the considerable attention and support deregulators received from the press. In 1979, more than 400 editorials supporting trucking reform appeared throughout the country; unfavorable or neutral editorials totalled only 22.[37] The typical editorial began with an example of seemingly mindless ICC regulation (birdseed is exempt, hamster food is not), then went on to recite the major substantive arguments on both sides, and ended with a ringing endorsement of deregulation couched in a warning that political muscle rather than common sense would likely dictate Congress's decision.

Common sense may not have dictated the ultimately favorable vote of Congress, but it certainly entered into the calculation. And economic analysis had both a direct effect on that vote—most visibly through the small-communities studies—and an indirect effect—by helping to gain the attention and support of interest groups, the media, and the White House.

What Deregulators Did Right

The twenty-to-one ratio of favorable to all other editorials is a good indication of just how persuasively reformers made their substantive case for trucking deregulation to a relatively impartial jury. That the merits themselves were so strong is a part, but not all, of the explanation. It's not hard to think of examples where meritorious arguments fell on deaf or disbelieving ears.

Substantial industry-specific data. To begin with, there was a substantial body of quantitative and qualitative data specific to the trucking industry. Lacking that, deregulation would probably not have gotten on Congress's agenda, much less passed. A 1977 memo from a senior lawyer in DOT described the problem: "We [still] don't know as much about trucking as we do about airlines and we probably never will. In trucking, it's very difficult to point to concrete examples, and you have to rely on theory. Theory is not that useful in passing legislation."

The case for trucking reform that was ultimately passed by the Ninety-sixth Congress represented years of research and analysis by various government agencies, in particular DOT. DOT's research program on trucking regulatory reform began in 1973 and continued virtually nonstop, despite significant political obstacles. This effort built on early academic studies and later funded much of the continued scholarly research on motor carrier regulation.

The government's research effort was for years the heart of the trucking reform movement, moreover, not an academic backwater to the larger political contest. Deregulation was an idea born of economists; they nursed and nurtured it when no one else would.

The intense commitment that many economists felt to the cause of trucking reform is ironic in light of the profession's view of individual behavior as narrowly self-interested. One strong believer, a DOT careerist, even risked being fired by a superior who opposed airline and trucking decontrol. The superior was Brock Adams, Carter's first transportation secretary. Unaware of Adams's stand on deregulation, the DOT economist-administrator briefed the new secretary on the research effort underway. Adams nodded with seeming approval. However, he soon made it known that anyone working on deregulation research would be fired, and the administrator was exiled from DOT's policy circle. Adams reluctantly embraced airline decontrol within the month, and trucking deregulation a year or so later, when Carter's all-out commitment to these reforms became clear. Meanwhile the DOT deregulator had carried on with the agency's research on trucking, contracting much of the work out to DOT's Cambridge, Massachusetts, research center.[38]

Political obstacles aside, the case for trucking deregulation was substantively more difficult to make than the one for airlines. Airplanes move a single, undifferentiated product—passengers—between a limited number of points. Moreover, the CAB had good and readily accessible data on the airline industry. "Small communities" for airlines referred to a finite number of locations, and one could quickly determine who had been serving these communities, for how long, whether service had ever been terminated, and if so, when.

The trucking industry is vastly more complex. Thousands of products move between thousands of points at billions of different rates. Not surprisingly, the ICC simply didn't know what carriers had authority to serve which towns and whether they were actually using it. Precisely because of the lack of ICC data, scholars had not studied trucking as closely as airline regulation. Thus there was not the reservoir of academic research on which to draw.

Despite these problems, the amount of analysis eventually produced on trucking regulatory reform was substantial. Most of it came out of DOT's Office of Regulatory Policy, with additional contributions from the ICC, Departments of Justice, Agriculture, and Energy, the Council of Economic Advisers, Office of Management and Budget, Council on Wage and Price Stability, Congressional Budget Office, and the Senate Commerce and Judiciary committees.

There were analytic questions that deregulators never found a way to address. All the research on economies of scale looked at production-cost advantages of size; none of it answered the question of whether size gave trucking companies marketing advantages. Another question that reformers never satisfactorily answered was why operating rights were so valuable: Rates were regulated by the ICC, but competition on the basis of service was not. Why, then, didn't service rivalry compete away the value of operating certificates?

These gaps in knowledge were not critical to the case, however, and they went unnoticed in the political debate. Given the large amount of evidence deregulators had amassed and the unanimity among experts, it was hard for any congressman to accuse reformers of not having done their homework, or to table an unpopular vote with a call for further study—a favorite ploy. "Symbolically, it was important to be able to say [that] study after study had shown [the benefits of deregulation]," observed a trade association lobbyist. "Most congressmen had piles of studies in their office. There's always some skepticism [toward studies], but here there were so many and they were so consistent."

Analysis informed by strategy. The effort to go well beyond theory reflected reformers' sensitivity to the legislative environment. But in much more subtle ways, the substantive case for trucking deregulation was informed by political strategy. DOT was never without a plan for strategic use of analysis. Spreadsheets, frequently updated, laid out the relevant information in neat columns: Desired Effects, Arguments Against, Research Completed, Research Underway, Research Needed.

Implicit in this plan was the aim of reducing the uncertainty associated with trucking deregulation. "We knew we had to have an answer to [the question], 'What will happen if we deregulate?'," said one congressional committee aide. "If you go back to your senator and say we're not sure what will happen, then forget it."

In this respect, the case for deregulating a healthy industry like trucking was harder to make than the case for decontrolling the airline industry, which had been in poor financial health for years. One legislative staffer recalled a common reaction of senators to trucking-reform proposals: "Bah! The [regulated] system works well. It may cost a little more, but we know it works."

Given Congress's fear of the unknown, perhaps the single most politically effective argument for deregulation of any kind is the existence of identical services provided side by side, one regulated and the other not.[39] Reformers capitalized on that fact extensively with studies of the exempt agricultural sector, intrastate trucking in New Jersey and household-goods transport in Maryland, both of which are unregulated, and motor carrier service in unregulated foreign countries.

To bring it closer to home, there was extensive analysis tailored to the specifics of a realistic regulatory reform bill. This was a necessary complement to academic studies, which tended to view deregulation in the absolute (How much would society save if the trucking industry were perfectly competitive?) rather than as a product of political compromise (What would be the effect of abolishing antitrust immunity *just* for single-line rate-making?).

Another complement to the more scholarly studies was evidence gained from "tromping the real estate"—that is, from venturing out into the field. This was helpful when the ATA tried to paint deregulators as ivory-tower types who had never set foot inside a truck terminal. Criticized for the narrowness of DOT's small-communities studies, Goldschmidt liked to say that analysts hadn't mailed out thousands of impersonal questionnaires because they "wanted to get out and talk to the people."

The small-communities surveys were politically tailored research at its utmost. A waffling senator effectively commissioned his own study. Even for senators and congressmen already convinced that the small-communities issue was a red herring, the studies provided "something to hang their hats on" when perturbed constituents came knocking.

Strategy informed not only the data that deregulators gathered but the way they presented it. Sophisticated economic arguments were conveyed in identifiable and understandable ways (though the basic argument against barriers to entry and, to a lesser extent, antitrust immunity had intuitive appeal). The examples of seemingly mindless rules and restrictions were important here. Moreover, deregulators used a simple measure of the public benefits from reform—the multibillion-dollar savings to consumers.[40]

While estimates of the potential savings ranged from $900 million to $12 billion, reformers almost always cited the COWPS figure of $5 billion; later on they used CBO's more authoritative estimate of $5 billion to $8 billion. (That figure was typically disaggregated as well and expressed as a savings per household of around $100 per year.) They played down other higher and lower figures, fearing that congressmen would react to wide-ranging statistical estimates by dismissing them altogether.

This push to quantify the potential savings to consumers from trucking reform went contrary to the (one-time) advice of John Snow, deputy undersecretary of transportation during the Ford administration and one of the early proponents of deregulation. In a 1975 memo to several other high-level policymakers, Snow, a Ph.D. economist and lawyer, warned against giving Congress aggregate estimates of social savings. He said it was politically counterproductive because the larger the estimate, the greater the implied adverse impact on labor and capital.

Snow's advice was probably sound at the time. In the early 1970s, when DOT first produced estimates of what deregulation could save consumers, the political opposition was so intense that the agency spent considerable time just defending its figures. More generally, the attitude of many congressmen toward the notion of economic efficiency was almost hostile at that time, because efficiency implied a reduction of jobs.[41] That adherence to Snow's advice seemed so unthinkable five years later was an indication of just how far the political center had shifted on the issue of deregulation, and of how much the political "market" had improved—at least temporarily—for a policy reform that promised diffuse savings to the public.

Reflecting these political changes, deregulators did not play down the fact that reform would make losers out of the trucking industry (though they said little about the risk of bankruptcy to many marginal firms). Instead they portrayed the industry as something of a villain—with much talk of "monopoly profits," "price fixing," and "collusion that in any other business would be a felony."

The approach to labor was more cautious. Deregulators maintained that reform would not necessarily mean fewer jobs, because firms that had turned to private carriage as a way around regulation would return to common carriage under decontrol, bringing with them potential Teamster jobs (private trucking is largely non-Teamster)—an argument they only half believed. On the wage question, deregulators played up the potential for reform to put downward pressure on labor costs absent the price-fixing cartel. But they never went so far as to argue (as some reformers felt they should) that deregulation was the only way to "break the back of the Teamsters."

Coordination between analysts and other advocates. The substantive case for reform was sensitive to strategic factors in part because there was effective communication and coordination between the analysts and those on the political front line. Logistics aside, the two groups learned from one another. Gary Broemser, the director of DOT's Office of Regulatory Policy, attended weekly meetings of the ad hoc coalition supporting reform. Coalition members received from him the latest DOT reports and analyses on trucking and expressed to him any lobbying problems they had encountered where analysis might bear. The chairman of the coalition gave Broemser and the DOT analysts "high marks" for their efficiency and political sensitivity.[42]

This coordination of analytic and political effort produced prompt and effective counters to ATA claims. Refuting the ATA's CPI comparison with the economist's technical answer (changes in the composition of a ton-mile) would have been far less convincing than what politically attuned analysts worked out—the truckload versus less-than-truckload comparison, which cleverly turned the ATA's argument on its head.[43]

Another politically tailored statistic proved critical to the most important Senate vote on the trucking bill. The ATA maintained that the expanded agricultural exemption approved in markup would affect 21 percent of the regulated trucking industry's total tonnage. That figure was the key to the industry's lobbying campaign against the expanded exemption, which provided the major test of strength on the Senate floor. The administration's figure was quite different; it claimed that only 3.7 percent of total interstate truck traffic by revenue would be affected. It's not hard to reconcile the two figures if one reads the fine print: they measure different things. In a political vacuum, the administration would doubtless have explained the difference, but under the circumstances, fighting fire with fire was deemed appropriate.

Good internal coordination also meant that the dissemination of analysis was well timed. DOT rushed its survey of Nevada small communities to completion in order to present the findings at Cannon's field hearing in his home state. Several months later, Commerce Committee staff members saw to it that CBO's small-communities analysis was completed in time to have dramatic impact; Cannon read the favorable conclusions to a packed room on the last morning of the Senate hearings. CBO's $8 billion estimate was also obtained just in time for dissemination before the full Senate vote.

Despite close coordination of effort, systematic differences in attitude toward policy evidence separated many of the reform advocates on the front line from those carrying out the analysis. Some lobbyists, particularly those trained as lawyers, were "dubious of numbers." "I didn't use the figures on total savings," said one trade association representative. "My lawyer's background made me hesitant; I know you can prove almost anything with numbers. But it was a good point for the newspapers." In dealing with members of Congress, a majority of whom are lawyers themselves, lobbyists often preferred to rely on what seemed to them "commonsense" arguments.

Even the most dubious lobbyists found the DOT small-communities surveys useful in persuading congressmen who shared their skepticism of numbers. But, ironically, the reluctance of some professional analysts to perform nonscientific research was an obstacle to carrying out these surveys initially. "There are two kinds of economists," observed one high-level DOT official, "the one who says it will take three weeks (to gather evidence), and the one who says it will take three years. . . . There was lots of fighting over that within DOT (on the small-communities issue). Finally I went to the White House people and said—I need anecdotes. . . . That's what led to the small-community studies."

Eventually the political battle became one where economists did more than "make the bullets that lawyers fire at one another." Analysts from DOT and the ICC went on the firing line themselves, delivering speeches to groups antagonistic to deregulation. Though forbidden by law to lobby, they presented their evidence—both scientific and anecdotal—on small-community service and other reform issues. "The economists became much more political," recalled a DOT official. "One of them said it was the best experience he'd ever had."

At the same time, noneconomist reformers became much more sophisticated about substance (a phenomenon that chapter 7 will discuss further). "The economists became lawyers and politicians and vice versa," said the DOT official. "There was lots of fighting initially. But eventually, everyone became all-around advocates. It was really an interdisciplinary approach."

What—If Anything—the ATA Did Wrong

Senator Cannon opened his first hearing on trucking deregulation with a guarantee that the Commerce Committee would "decid[e] the issues based on a factual analysis and not the decibel level of the advocates on either side." That the ATA-Teamster alliance had the edge on decibels went without saying. The irony is that when it came to the presentation of "factual analysis" by both sides, the ATA was hopelessly outshouted.

For every study the ATA offered in evidence, the administration offered three or four and often more to counter it. One DOT representative liked to begin speeches on small communities by showing his audience two stacks of studies: one, a towering pile, was what the federal government had produced on the subject; the other, a lone pamphlet, was the ATA's contribution. Goldschmidt too liked to hit the ATA where it was weak:

> Where are the studies to show that there is a cross-subsidization of small town service? That the current system saves fuel? That minorities have been allowed into the truck system? That the small communities receive good service because of the existing system? The debate has raged for years and yet the opponents of reform have come forward with assertions and rhetoric and little else. On the other hand, the administration and others have submitted literally dozens of serious studies documenting the case for reform.[44]

Ultimately, the ATA was hampered greatly by the lack of empirical support for its arguments and by credibility problems with much of what evidence it had. The trade group consciously placed a low priority on empiricism—a decision for which some have criticized it. But faced with limited resources, the ATA chose to put its money on public relations.

When the Ford administration proposed to deregulate trucking in 1975, the ATA prepared a public-relations film, *The Dividing Line,* narrated by newsman Frank Blair. The title referred to the distinction between good—economic—regulation and bad—social and environmental—regulation, a favorite industry theme. The public-relations campaign intensified in 1979, when the ATA hired Hill and Knowlton to help sell Congress and the public on the benefits of continued regulation.

Hill and Knowlton's campaign may have been effective in small towns, where it was primarily aimed, but in Washington, D.C., the public-relations firm was perhaps best remembered for a laughable poll it conducted. Hill and Knowlton held simultaneous press conferences in five cities to publicize the results of a survey taken by a subsidiary, the Group Attitudes Company. The poll, cited in a number of regional newspapers and wire-service reports, showed "virtually no public support for the move in Congress to deregulate the nation's trucking industry." A closer look revealed that of 405 people asked to identify some businesses and industries that should be regulated or deregulated, only 15 people mentioned trucking at all. Of those, 12 said it should be deregulated and 3 said it should be regulated.[45] The accompanying press release neglected to mention that the poll was taken by a subsidiary of a firm campaigning against deregulation.

Hill and Knowlton was admittedly not hired for its social science capability. Besides, the ATA had its own internal analytic shop. But there were problems there as well. The man who directed the ATA's economics division up until 1977 did not have an undergraduate degree. When he left, the division was without a director for a year. Said one ATA analyst, "At the time when we should have been doing the empirical work to prepare for the political fight, we just didn't have the bodies with the brains."

ATA subsequently recruited the appropriate degrees. A Ph.D. economist who taught agricultural economics at Pennsylvania State University for many years took over the division in 1978. Under him were two department heads, both with advanced degrees. In 1980, the division employed over twenty people and occupied most of one floor of the ATA's six-story office near DuPont Circle in Washington, D.C.

During the last year of the political battle, a handful of analysts from ATA's economics division worked primarily on trucking deregulation, though the summer, 1979, gasoline crisis diverted some of that manpower. For the last six months of the fight, ATA analysts did little else but respond to the latest opposition study. They critiqued virtually every report the administration put out during that period (primarily small-communities studies). When the Senate Judiciary Committee released its draft report on Kennedy's hearings just weeks before the Senate markup, the ATA prepared a point-by-point rebuttal. That document appears as an appendix to the published committee report. The rest of the ATA's critiques were never circulated outside the building.[46]

The lack of empirical studies was damaging to the industry on almost every contested question, but nowhere more than on the issue of small communities. According to ATA analysts, a major problem was the inaccessibility of certain vital information sources—the CTS tapes, for one—which they say would have shown that there really was a geographic cross-subsidy. This seems unlikely. Cross-subsidy or not, the CTS tapes would not have revealed the true answer; they don't contain enough information about corridor costs. ICC analysts, who obtained the tapes from the Judiciary Committee, had the same idea, but decided the CTS data wouldn't be dispositive.

Lacking CTS data, the ATA put its money on a second bet—a survey of small-town shippers and their attitudes toward regulated carriage. Using Dun and Bradstreet listings, the ATA drew a national sample of 3,000 shippers and mailed them questionnaires. But the response rate was only 15 percent, which the ATA says was too low to make the results worth reporting. Here again, one can't help but react skeptically. Hill and Knowlton's poll notwithstanding, the ATA's 1976 survey of carriers, "Small Town Blues," was based on a mere 26 percent response rate, and the trade group relied on that as ammunition for four years.

Why a survey of shippers which, at best, could provide only indirect evidence that small towns would not benefit from deregulation? Was there a reluctance to ask carriers directly, for fear of what they might say? More generally, do trade association analysts feel that certain questions are better left unasked because of what the answer might be? "Absolutely not," said the head of the ATA's economics division, Wesley Kriebel. "I don't make policy. I don't want to make policy. Our job is to provide data [however unflattering] to those who do."[47]

However apolitical its analytic shop, lack of credibility is a serious problem for a trade association. Sometimes the members bring it directly on themselves. "Our carriers told us they were serving those small towns and we believed them," said one ATA analyst. "Too late the data showed they weren't. We were caught in a credibility gap." (Another ATA analyst was skeptical that anyone could be so naively believing. "That's silly," he said. "People here should have known there was not much geographic cross-subsidy occurring.")

Other times just being a trade association is enough to cast a shadow on credibility. That's no doubt one reason the ATA emphasized public relations over substance. Said one ATA analyst when asked why the trade group didn't produce hard evidence, "Would one more study with our imprimatur really have done any good?"

The ATA's credibility was damaged by its inability to line up any serious academic support. The only well-known economist to be identified with regulation advocates was Michael Evans, a supply-side advocate who testified that, on the basis of his macro model, deregulation would push trucking rates higher. What academic support the ATA did have came from a handful of business school professors—most notably D. Daryl Wyckoff of Harvard. (Wyckoff's background as a trucking company manager cast doubt on his credibility, however.)

The ATA was quick to play up Wyckoff's Harvard ties but even quicker to mock "ivory-towered economists and academicians" in general. One ATA analyst felt that approach alienated potential support. "We never should have started swinging at academics. It made for great speeches, but it was strictly a short-term gain. It's a classic error. The ERA people made it when they mocked the housewife."

But academic support for deregulation was so overwhelming that the ATA's public-relations approach can hardly be viewed as a significant contributor. The analyst's hindsight is less useful as strategic advice than as an indication of how many ATA people—even the analysts—saw the fight: as a battle of personalities and symbolic politics without real substance. In their commonly expressed perception, the Democrats needed somebody to beat up on in the name of less government intervention, and we were it. "If we could have just called it 'bananas' instead of 'regulation' we would have been okay," said an ATA analyst.

Given this attitude, it's not surprising that the ATA analysts, despite a faith in the political worth of hard evidence, bore no ill will toward Hill and Knowlton, expressed no feeling that money spent on public relations could have been better used on studies. Rather they felt that better public relations could have saved the day. Avoid swinging at academics. Call it "bananas" instead of "regulation."

One detected a hint of jealousy, though, toward the money and support lavished on the ATA lobbying operation. On the ATA organizational chart, the economic and lobbying divisions appear as equals. In practice that's far from true. The Government Relations Division has its own separate building—a modern, expansive red-brick structure just down from the House office buildings on Capitol Hill. In 1980, the seven lobbyists headquartered there (all white, male Protestants) were the ATA's golden boys, seen as rainmakers by many in the industry. "The director of this division doesn't have the power of [the ATA's lobbying director]," said one analyst. "If I was running the show, the Hill office wouldn't be the tail wagging the dog."

From the industry's standpoint, the two divisions—economics and government relations—probably ought not have equal power. The ATA is foremost a lobbying organization, after all. But it might have helped the lobbying effort had there been better coordination with the analysts. "We never . . . mapped out a strategy linked to the available data," said one ATA analyst. "We never sat down and said—Where are our strong points, our weak points? Where do we have data? What are the three key issues where we need it?"

On the one hand, it seems surprising that one of the most powerful trade groups in the country, in a battle for its survival, would never have mapped out a plan for strategic use of analysis—especially considering that economists were the heart of the opposing army. On the other hand, it's not surprising when one considers how minimally analysis figured into the ATA's overall battle plan.

In retrospect, the ATA may have devoted too little effort to empiricism, especially given the questionable effectiveness of its public-relations campaign. Even if trade association studies are skeptically received on Capitol Hill, there may be a critical mass when it comes to substantive evidence: Any more won't help a group very much, but any less and its analytic arguments are dismissed altogether as self-serving. The ATA failed to reach that critical threshold, and credibility problems undermined what little evidence the industry group did have.

But precisely because of those problems, the ATA's decision to stress public relations over substance was sound. No amount of attention to empiricism would have helped the industry's case significantly. The evidence simply wasn't there. (One ICC economist, asked what he would have done had he been on the ATA's side, said without hesitation, "I'd have bought people off. There's no way you could convince them with the numbers.") Any studies would inevitably have had credibility problems.

Moreover, stress on public relations served the ATA's internal needs. Unlike statistical studies, films and catchy advertisements are highly visible to members and serve to reassure them that the trade association is doing everything possible in their interest.

In short, the facts simply weren't on the industry's side. Eventually, members of Congress came to see that. But while deregulators merit considerable credit for that outcome, the ATA deserves little blame.

Soft Numbers

Despite the skepticism of some lawyers and others in politics toward "numbers," they imply precision and certainty, so there's a strong incentive for both sides in a policy battle to quantify even that about which they're less than sure. Outright fabrication is the exception; the process is too adversarial to permit that. But there is a tendency to engage in "creative calculating" and to make soft estimates appear much firmer than they really are.

Lana Batts, who in 1980 headed ATA's Economics and Planning Department (one of two sections in the economics division), likes to quote Batts's Laws on this subject: He who has a number is one up on him who does not. And, he whose number is bigger is more credible. (Batts's corollary to that: If you can't make your number big, add five decimal places.)[48]

The challenge is not just to make a more convincing case than your opponent, but to get the attention of Congress in the first place. Numbers have to be big to do that, as Everett Dirksen's oft-quoted line about federal dollars implies: "A billion here, a billion there; pretty soon you're talking real money."

The figures on the effect of exempting processed food from regulation are an example of creative calculations. One ATA analyst described what happened after the first vote on the exemption amendment was tabled, in part to give both sides an opportunity to quantify the impact it would have on the trucking industry: "The [ATA] lobbyists said to us, "Give us the numbers." [They didn't say] "Do you have any numbers?" We scrounged around, but we didn't have much." The measure ATA analysts produced—showing that the exemption would threaten 21 percent of the regulated carriers' total tonnage—was dramatically large. It also concealed the fact that most of that tonnage was transported by (regulated) contract carriers, who supported deregulation (though they opposed the exemption).

The administration's measure—showing that only 3.7 percent of total interstate truck traffic by revenue would be affected—was also carefully crafted. Neither figure gave any clue as to what the savings or cost to society would be; Congress didn't ask about that, only about who would lose and by how much.

This preoccupation with winners and losers can lead to use of numbers that confuse distribution with efficiency. In 1976, in response to Thomas Gale Moore's well-publicized estimate that the cost of trucking and rail regulation might approach $15 billion a year, the ICC (then a close ally of the industry) did its own cost-benefit analysis. The commission concluded that ICC regulation benefited the nation to the tune of $4.4 billion a year, almost all of that from trucking regulation.[49]

The ICC's analysis was strikingly poor. (A *Business Week* "Commentary" said its authors deserved an *F* in Economics 101.) Most notably, the analysis failed to distinguish between income transfers from one group in society to another and net social costs or benefits. It calculated as benefits the redistribution of income through cross-subsidy but neglected to consider that some pay for what others receive.[50] Most economists at the ICC today cringe at the mention of their predecessors' methodology. But these same analytic and statistical flaws were common in the industry's arguments for continued regulation.

Even a good case gets bloated. CBO's estimate that deregulation would save as much as $8 billion took on a life of its own, even though it was based not on an original CBO study—as newspaper headlines implied—but rather on CBO's review of existing studies. Moreover, there is considerable subjectivity involved in any such review—which studies to include, how much to weight individual ones, how to present the conclusions.

The issue of data presentation is particularly relevant. CBO's $8 billion bottom line represented its estimate of the potential impact of deregulation by 1985 (expressed in 1980 dollars). Presumably that date was chosen as a time by which the effects of deregulation would have had a chance to work through the economy (the bill before CBO preserved antitrust immunity until 1983). Only in the accompanying text did one learn that the bill "could result in increases in certain rates over the short term" (precisely because of the preservation of antitrust immunity). That effect, the text went on to explain, "would likely be overwhelmed" by the effects of increased competition—but only in the "longer run"—that is, by 1985. In short, the estimate distorted the magnitude of potential long-term savings by ignoring potential interim costs.[51]

Nowhere in the trucking debate were the numbers softer than in estimates of energy impact. The administration claimed that reducing empty backhauls would save 220–320 million gallons of fuel a year; the ATA said increased competition would put more trucks on the road using additional fuel. Neither side had much to back up its claims.

The first effort to quantify the energy impact of deregulation came about in 1975, when the trucking task force asked the Federal Energy Administration for its estimate. Lacking the necessary information, the FEA turned to the MIT Center for Transportation Studies for an answer. Working under a two-week deadline, Paul Roberts and James Kneafsey, associates of the center, produced an estimate that the net effects of both trucking and rail deregulation would be to increase fuel use by 15 million barrels a year (the equivalent of a day's use).[52]

The Roberts-Kneafsey estimate looked solely at the effect on energy due to expected diversion from rail to truck; it ignored altogether potential efficiency increases within the trucking industry—the raison d'etre for reform. DOT commissioned an independent assessment which concluded that, taking into account intramodal efficiency gains, deregulation would save 22 million gallons annually.[53] The FEA endorsed the Roberts-Kneafsey report and sought to present the results in congressional hearings on the Ford administration's trucking reform bill. However, the Office of Management and Budget refused permission and told the FEA to resolve its differences with DOT.[54]

The 220–320 million gallon estimate of fuel savings from deregulation cited by Carter administration spokesmen also had questionable parentage. It can be traced to a figure in a Charles River Associates study. In 1978, when the Department of Energy (successor to FEA) testified on a bill to provide for limited backhaul authority, the Charles River figure was "inflated in a very unscientific way," according to one DOE analyst. DOE later told other agencies that the figure was not well founded, but that caveat was never properly communicated to, or else was ignored by, some administration spokesmen who continued to cite the estimate.

Meanwhile, DOE had contracted for a study from Cambridge Systematics (CS), a Boston consulting firm, on the energy impact of deregulation. (DOT protested giving the contract to CS on conflict-of-interest grounds; CS had also done a study for the ATA.) Preliminary results showed that there would be a slight net fuel increase from both truck and rail decontrol. DOE was never asked to testify on the question, however, and release of the results was successfully delayed. In March, 1980, after the Senate hearings were over, DOE presented the preliminary results to the Commerce Committee staff. DOE's message to the committee was that energy consumption should not be a major consideration in deciding the fate of trucking deregulation.

When President Carter signed the motor carrier act, his Rose Garden speech highlighted the energy savings that would result. Said one DOT analyst, "We kept trying to get that out of Carter's [signing] statement, but somehow it kept getting put back in."

The estimated savings represent an insignificant amount of oil, but the size of the number is not the issue. The issue is that deregulators made it appear far more certain than it really was that reform would reduce the use of fuel. The impact of deregulation on fuel consumption depended on two big unknowns—potential diversion of traffic from rail to truck, and shippers' demand for service under decontrol (a third factor, the potential intramodal efficiency gain, is more of a known quantity). Any estimate of savings was highly speculative.

Arguments Seldom Heard

One reason it was so hard to estimate the energy impact of deregulation is that no one knew how shippers' demand for service would be affected. If their demand goes up, all else equal, that will increase fuel use. From an efficiency standpoint, that's perfectly all right. As long as shippers face the true social cost of their increased demand (which they don't insofar as oil prices are controlled), it must mean that the cost to them of additional transportation service is more than offset by other savings—for example, reduced inventory costs.

In short, fuel efficiency and economic efficiency are not always synonymous: Sometimes it's cheaper to take a taxicab. But deregulators were careful not to make that argument on Capitol Hill in view of the oil shortage. It lacked appeal to the layman. It also violated the cardinal rule of lobbying: Keep it simple. Like a trade name with an unflattering acronym, some efficiency arguments don't reduce well.

Other efficiency arguments were downplayed in the political debate because their implication was all too clear. If there are economies of scale in the trucking industry, as the ATA mentioned, from an efficiency standpoint society should be allowed to benefit from them. Senator Cannon made that point to an audience of motor carriers, but deregulation proponents refrained. On Capitol Hill, small business is akin to Mom, apple pie, and Senate bean soup.

The economist's argument that regulation can keep rates too low is another one that doesn't agree with most congressmen. Even if the trucking industry were correct in claiming that regulation had kept rates artificially low, that would imply a basic misallocation of resources, and regulators would have ill-served the nation, at least in efficiency terms. But absent dramatic evidence of scarcity due to price controls—like the gasoline lines in the late 1970s or the meat shortages a decade earlier, both of which prompted a strong congressional reaction—that argument has little political appeal.

Other efficiency arguments are unpopular because they can be made to sound inhumane. The ATA's small-communities argument was an example of the "widows and orphans" defense: "We can survive fine under deregulation," says the regulated industry. "We just won't be able to provide for the widows and orphans any more." The widows and orphans defense implies a cross-subsidy in the tradition of Robin Hood. In strict economic terms, if society desires to subsidize widows and orphans, that's best accomplished directly, through a lump-sum tax, rather than indirectly, through the price mechanism. But that theoretical notion is not very credible as a political proposition, and one isn't apt to hear savvy economists advocating it to Congress.

Proponents of trucking deregulation were fortunate. In the case of energy consumption and industry concentration, the facts were such that reformers could avoid making the unpopular efficiency argument. More important, there weren't sticky distributional problems. There really were no widows and orphans (with the possible exception of some small shippers). The big losers were truckers and Teamsters, and deregulators were able to portray at least one of those groups as a villain.

Conclusion

While the trucking-deregulation issue moved relatively quickly once it was on Congress's agenda, the economic case for reform was a decade or more in the making. As early as the 1950s, economists applied their basic theoretical model to the trucking industry and concluded that the potential efficiency gains were large, but the lack of data inhibited further scholarly research. In the early 1970s, recognizing that theory alone would not go far on Capitol Hill, government economists began building an empirical case that would answer questions and counter threats concerning decontrol. By the late 1970s, when persistent inflation and an energy shortage had created a conducive political climate, the economists, like surfers waiting for the big wave, were ready to ride it in.

Economists bore the burden of proving the substantive worth of their case to a Congress reluctant to tinker with "the finest transportation system in the world." They met that burden by demonstrating that the system was "broke," that an alternative existed, and that the transition to it would be relatively painless. Their substantive case was heavily documented, and the evidence was well tailored to the political debate, reflecting the close cooperation between economists and those on the political front line. The ATA relied largely on public relations to make its case on the merits, which was probably a sound decision given the inherent weakness of the case.

Economic evidence and analysis had a considerable impact on Congress, both directly (at least in the Senate) and indirectly through its influence on interest groups and the press. Even absent hard evidence, the lineup of groups supporting reform was enough to suggest that deregulation would produce savings (though the existence of a single numerical estimate was helpful). Fear of the unknown still remained, however. Thus, data and analysis made their greatest contribution by demonstrating that well-functioning unregulated markets existed and that conditions that would lead to transitional disruption and displacement of nonindustry groups were absent.

The considerable importance of economic arguments distinguishes the trucking (and airline) battle from most others. At least with respect to distributive issues, policy analysis generally has limited influence on congressional decisions. Economists are concerned with aggregate efficiency and net social benefits, members of Congress with how a measure will affect their district. But double-digit inflation in the late 1970s helped to create a better "market" on Capitol Hill for reforms that promised aggregate social savings. Efficiency went from being a pejorative to a rallying cry. Even client groups cloaked their arguments in the language of economists.

Because trucking was a textbook example of a competitive industry, economists were virtually unanimous in calling for deregulation. That, and the consistency of the data, also explain their greater-than-usual influence. Though economists share a theoretical approach, that theory can usually be made to support diverse policy positions. Even if only a small minority disagrees, Congress is often left with the impression that there is no professional consensus. In the case of trucking decontrol, there was but one professional view; only those with a transparent self-interest argued for continued regulation.

Economists' unanimity reflected the unambiguous nature of the theoretical and empirical case for efficiency through deregulation, but it also reflected the belief that equity would be served simultaneously, and this is another explanation for the importance of economic arguments. Economists' judgments concerning efficiency are often rejected because they don't coincide with the public's perception (right or wrong) of equity. Events only partly bore out the prediction noted earlier that reformers would succeed only if they converted deregulation "from a technical case promising improved efficiency to a moral case promising an end to monopoly profits and privilege." The case for efficiency proved surprisingly appealing in its own right, but it prevailed only because it coincided with the equity case.

Yet another explanation for the centrality of economic arguments in the trucking battle is their intuitive appeal. While the regulated industry was itself complex, and few members of Congress understood the difference between TL and LTL, the logic of the competitive market was familiar territory. Thus, it was relatively easy to explain the "illogic" of barriers to entry and collective ratemaking. Moreover, there weren't complex questions of implementation and administration to confuse the issue, beyond assuring a smooth transition. Deregulators needed "simply" to dismantle the existing regulatory system for the market to operate. Finally, "deregulation" was a relatively simple and comprehensive policy principle for purposes of political mobilization.

In all three respects, economic deregulation differed from other pet policy proposals of economists, such as the notion of a market in pollution rights. That notion is not intuitively appealing to noneconomists, it would require a complex administrative apparatus to implement, and it resists reduction to a simple and understandable principle for purposes of political mobilization. As one regulatory expert observed, "Save the Bay Efficiently" is an unlikely bumper sticker.[55]

Environmentalists, who presumably would benefit the most from a cleaner environment—at least psychically—have been slow to embrace economists' proposals for creating markets in air and water pollution rights.[56] By contrast, those groups that stood to benefit from trucking deregulation were strongly supportive of economists' arguments—a final reason these arguments carried such weight. As chapter 5 will describe, the reform coalition contained virtually every eligible interest group, and these groups were generally agreed on the need for open entry and elimination of collective ratemaking.

In sum, the issue of deregulation had inherent strengths that made it a good candidate for a case to Congress on the merits, but that case would not have gotten very far without the efforts of economists in DOT, Justice, and elsewhere over a period of many years. It attracted some of the most talented and respected economists in government and academia, and they put together a case for reform that was both substantively thorough and politically persuasive.

In making their case, economists took advantage of the public concern over inflation and energy, and the growing acceptance of efficiency and the competitive-market ideal, but they also contributed to that acceptance. Hearings served to educate members of Congress and the press, and successful decontrol of one industry contributed to the momentum for deregulating others. More than riding in on a big wave, economists unleashed a small flood, and deregulation became a powerful idea in its own right.

5

The Ad Hoc Coalition: Strange Bedfellows Make Good Politics

What cause could possibly unite Ralph Nader, Inflation Fighter Alfred Kahn, the National Association of Manufacturers and the American Conservative Union in enthusiastic support of Teddy Kennedy?
—*Time*, February 7, 1979

Policy analysis is persuasive on Capitol Hill only insofar as it's consistent with the political lineup on a proposed reform: who's for it and who's agin it. No amount of economic evidence will convince Congress that a reform will help farmers if farm groups themselves don't favor it.

More than just a proxy measure for the merits, organized group support is a guide to legislators' own self-interest. The more widespread and active the support for reform, the more likely a congressman is to feel he can oppose the powerful vested interests without suffering significant electoral damage.

To demonstrate that a policy reform is in "the public interest," then, requires a showing of diverse interest-group support. To defeat the opposing client group in Congress requires yet more—a broad coalition of interest groups actively lobbying and demonstrating popular support for the reform.[1] An ad hoc coalition provides a way for organizations to share information, coordinate strategy, and overcome the inherent limitations of any single member group—in short, a means to maximize their joint strength.[2] But if the advantages of coalescing are great, so are the obstacles.

The initial problem of *forming* such a coalition—an organization of organizations—is comparable to the familiar problem of organizing individuals to act collectively. By the "logic of collective action," rational self-interested individuals will not join large organizations in order to pursue their common interests: Each individual will see his own stake as small and his potential contribution as irrelevant. Moreover, since the benefits sought are collective—that is, nonexclusive—in nature, the nonmember will receive them equally with the member. Thus, if there is any charge for joining, an individual will find it rational to be a free-rider except under certain conditions: if the organization can coerce him into joining (e.g., through closed-shop laws, which restrict employment to union members); if his stake and hence his contribution is significant (the smaller the group and the more powerful the individual, the more likely this is); or if he is offered some selective inducement to join (e.g., information unavailable elsewhere, low-cost insurance, or discount airline fares).[3] Applying the same logic to interest groups as potential members of a coalition aimed at securing a collective good, each group will have an incentive to free-ride on the efforts of the others unless the group perceives that its contribution would be significant or unless there is some selective inducement to join (coercion seems improbable).*[4]

Even if one overcomes the major problem of mobilizing latent support, there are serious obstacles to trying to coordinate this support effectively. Organizations may endorse the same legislation for antithetical reasons, which can lead to conflict within a coalition. They may even disagree about what the policy aim itself should be, based on differing ideologies or practical objectives. At best, internal conflict distracts a coalition from its collective interest. At worst, it results in one member taking independent action which is damaging to the coalition as a whole.[5]

---

*The free-rider problem is what distinguishes a coalition of interest groups organized to influence public policy from the kind of coalitions that game theorists and political scientists have traditionally studied—e.g., governing coalitions of political parties in multiparty countries.

Whereas a *policymaking* coalition seeks a collective good, a *simple* coalition seeks a fixed reward that is divisible only among members—e.g. control of the government. Since membership is a requirement for payoff, not only is there no incentive for potential members to free-ride, but there is a tendency for simple coalitions to exclude those who are not essential to victory, so that there are fewer parties among whom to divide the payoff. Stating this as a general principle of strategic behavior in *n*-person, zero-sum games, William Riker has theorized that the equilibrium size of a winning coalition is always minimal. Riker, *The Theory of Political Coalitions* (New Haven: Yale University Press, 1962).

In this respect, political coalitions are like economic cartels, which face the constant danger that one member firm will shade its price (or raise quality) so as to increase its market share. Independent action by a cartel member is ultimately self-defeating: Other firms promptly counter, leaving the initiator with the same-sized share of a smaller profit. But the danger, particularly within diffuse cartels, is ever present nonetheless.

In sum, two fundamental problems confront any effort to organize a broad coalition of organizations so as to achieve a collective good: the incentive for individual organizations to do nothing and hitchhike on the good efforts of others (the free-rider problem); and the tendency for member organizations to take independent action harmful to the coalition as a whole (the cartel problem). An additional problem, which is not organizational in nature, may also confront a coalition. Where groups do not accurately represent their members, or where more than one voice represents a particular interest—such as farmers or business—the problem of who speaks for whom may arise.

These problems are not unique to ad hoc reform coalitions. An opposing client group faces the free-rider problem so long as the benefits to members of the industry or profession are nonexclusive—industry-wide price supports or tariff protection, for example. Moreover, within an organization formed to secure special-interest benefits, conflict over the distribution of those benefits is inevitable.[6] When multiple client groups coalesce to preserve a shared set of special-interest benefits, other distributional conflicts threaten internal compatibility.

This chapter looks at the problem of forming and maintaining coalitions in the setting of the trucking deregulation battle. The basis for the chapter is (1) the belief that reformers' victory was in good part due to the creation and effective coordination of a broad coalition of organizations supporting decontrol, and (2) the prediction that a comparable coalition is a necessary (though not sufficient) condition for terminating any major client policy. The first section of the chapter describes how the ad hoc coalition for trucking reform arose and operated against formidable opposition from the ATA and Teamsters Union. Section two looks at the three problems described above as they applied to the ad hoc group. Section three briefly examines the ATA as a coalition itself. Finally, the chapter looks at the question of whether political organizations accurately represent the interests of their members.

In this chapter, "ad hoc coalition" generally refers to the alliance of interest groups and private companies that actively supported trucking reform. The administration can be thought of as a member of the coalition as well, and with respect to the cartel problem, it was unquestionably the most important member. Thus, this chapter looks in a limited way at the strategic behavior of the Carter White House, but a more thorough discussion of that topic is reserved for chapter 7.

Fighting Depth with Breadth—The Ad Hoc Coalition

> *Any movement that lines up such diverse organizations as the Consumer Federation of America, National Association of Manufacturers, National Federation of Independent Business, American Farm Bureau Federation and Common Cause on one side [with] the American Trucking Associations and the Teamsters union on the other, must be in hot pursuit of sound public policy.*
> —*Barron's*, March 5, 1979

For good reason, the Carter administration opted not to tackle trucking reform until it had won the fight for airline deregulation. The trucking battle, warned political veterans, would make its airline counterpart look like a friendly spat.

Trucking deregulation was a more ambitious goal than airline decontrol in three respects. First, the opposition was much stronger. Individually, the trucking industry and the Teamsters Union had reputations as awesome powers on Capitol Hill; in tandem, they were considered unbeatable by many. Second, the trucking industry was not likely to divide internally as the airline industry had done. Whereas individual airlines had broken ranks to support reform, thus rendering the industry trade group ineffective, the trucking industry was generally unified in its opposition to deregulation. And third, the savings would be less visible than were those from airline deregulation; hence consumer support would be harder to mobilize.

The heart of the opposition—the American Trucking Associations— had for years been viewed as one of the three or four most politically powerful industry lobbies in Congress (along with the medical, insurance, and oil lobbies). With over 16,000 firms, the regulated industry was a presence in every congressional district in the country—and one that made itself felt. Trucking companies are major employers in many of these districts; hence letters, calls, and visits from trucking executives—which pour in by the thousands at the ATA's command—are taken seriously by their representatives in Washington.

For sheer grass-roots power, the Teamsters' reputation was even more renowned. The union represented about 300,000 truck drivers in 1980 (down from 500,000 several years earlier), but its legendary clout derived from a membership of nearly 2.5 million. The Teamsters' Washington, D.C., headquarters is a huge marble edifice at the foot of Capitol Hill. The boardroom, lined with portraits of past union leaders, has a large picture window facing the Capitol. According to one visitor, the window frames the scene in such a way that the domed Capitol on the hill looks like "the Teamsters' little toy."

Powerful lobbies don't flex their muscles on every issue that affects them. But trucking deregulators had every reason to feel that their cause would elicit the opposition's full horsepower. For the ATA, it was "the issue"—a threat to the economic well-being of many members and to the organizational survival of the trade group itself. The industry's massive offensive in 1976 had stopped the Ford administration bill cold. The Teamsters also feared for their bread and butter. For years, the union had benefited from its shared monopoly with the regulated trucking industry. Open entry into that industry threatened loss of jobs to new, nonunion carriers and an end to the fat wage hikes that monopoly pricing had made possible. "[Deregulation is] the one issue that the man standing on the loading dock understands," commented a Teamster lobbyist during the summer of 1978, adding his confident prediction that the administration wouldn't "meet with much success if [it chose] the legislative route."[7]

To take on this kind of opposition, deregulators needed a sizable coalition supporting reform. The coalition had to be broad—representing the basic interests that opponents claimed would be hurt by deregulation: business and agriculture (shippers), as well as consumers. And it had to be active, to counter somewhat the pressure the trucking industry and the Teamsters would exert on members of Congress (an even show of force was considered out of the question). Specifically, the coalition would have to serve three functions: one, testify at upcoming hearings on motor carrier deregulation so as to establish the legitimacy of the issue; two, lobby congressional offices directly; and three, mobilize grass-roots support of two kinds—mass letter writing and one-on-one contact by influential constituents in key members' districts.

The basis for a trucking coalition existed long before the battle took place. Trucking reform had been a recognized consumer issue at least since 1970, when Ralph Nader published his attack on the ICC, the *Interstate Commerce Omission*.[8] Farm groups had long been active supporters of deregulation; their lobbying had kept unprocessed food exempt from regulation in the 1935 act, and they had jealously protected that exemption from industry encroachment over the years.

Corporate shippers, the third group essential to any reform alliance, were actually the first to organize in support of deregulation, though on a very limited basis, a full decade before the reform bill was eventually passed. In 1970, representatives of the Council of Economic Advisers, wanting to assure President Nixon that there was business support for trucking and railroad deregulation, contacted a number of reform-minded companies. In response, General Mills, Quaker, DuPont, Sears Roebuck, and eleven others formed a group called COMET (Committee for Efficient Transportation). COMET worked largely for railroad deregulation, the focus of Nixon's decontrol campaign. When President Ford resumed the effort to deregulate trucking in 1975, COMET regrouped and changed its name to CURRENT (Committee Urging Regulatory Reform for Efficient National Transportation).

Despite this potential, there was no certainty that deregulators could mobilize the latent support for trucking reform. The concern about consumers was noted earlier: Would they and the groups that represented them rally for a cause that promised a one-cent price reduction on a can of peaches? Moreover, many corporate shippers were reluctant to risk antagonizing their carriers by speaking out for reform when the prospect of congressional action seemed so remote.

The airline deregulation effort accomplished much of the groundwork of building a trucking coalition. Many of the groups that later coalesced in the name of trucking reform first allied themselves around the airline bill. (At least one shipper supported airline reform in good part because of the perceived spillover from that to the company's main concern—trucking deregulation.) What's more, airline deregulation marked the first major issue ever to unite such ideological odd couples as Ralph Nader and the National Association of Manufacturers. As a formally organized group with elected officers and a full-time, paid executive director, the airline coalition played a major role in enacting the 1978 decontrol bill.

The momentum of the airline victory carried over to the trucking issue. Members of the airline coalition formed a "reporting group" that began meeting in late 1978 to monitor developments in motor carrier reform. This informal assemblage included representatives of the four major constituencies for airline deregulation: consumers, business, conservatives, and state and local government groups, as well as a fifth—agriculture—that had been only marginally involved in the airline fight.

The group first surfaced publicly in early 1979, when Senator Kennedy, newly designated chairman of the Judiciary Committee, staged a press conference to announce legislation to eliminate the trucking industry's antitrust immunity. The Massachusetts senator made that announcement—which ignited his fight with Commerce Committee chairman Howard Cannon for jurisdiction over trucking reform—flanked by an assortment of supporters whose diversity was guaranteed to catch the media's eye: Ralph Nader, Alfred Kahn, representatives from the National Association of Manufacturers, the American Conservative Union, the National Federation of Independent Business, the Independent Truckers' Association, the Contract Carrier Conference of the ATA, Mattel, Inc., and others.

Most members of the reporting group backed Kennedy in the jurisdictional fight, believing that Cannon was friendly to trucking and Teamster interests. Cannon's victory demonstrated the strength of both the Nevada senator and the ATA lobby, which pulled out all stops to get the bill referred to his committee. "They blitzed the Hill," a Kennedy aide told the *Wall Street Journal*. "We were totally outclassed."[9]

The reporting group continued to meet irregularly throughout the winter and spring of 1979. Several member groups developed trucking reform bills of their own. Some of them, like the Farm Bureau's bill, were quite limited in scope. The most comprehensive was the American Conservative Union's proposal, which called for a six-year phaseout of all trucking regulation, tempered by compensation for displaced Teamsters. (The bill was never introduced.) The ACU also asked interested groups to sign a letter of support for trucking reform addressed to all members of Congress, with the list of signatories to serve as the basis for setting up a more formal coalition.

That spring also marked the beginning of hearings by the Senate Commerce Committee at which reporting group members, among others, testified. In May, the Transportation Consumer Action Project (TCAP), a Nader group set up specifically to promote trucking reform, held a symposium on "Trucking Regulation and Consumer Prices." Senator Kennedy was the featured speaker, appearing alongside representatives of the administration and groups on both sides of the deregulation issue.

The existence of interest-group support for trucking deregulation during this time served to keep the issue warm as White House interest appeared to wane. That appearance was in part strategic. Teamster-industry negotiations over a three-year master freight contract, which began in late March, represented a critical test of President Carter's newly established wage-and-price guidelines. The administration put deregulation on the back burner in anticipation of those negotiations and strongly hinted that a settlement which conformed to the president's inflation guidelines might cause the White House to reconsider its support of a strong control bill.

Equally important to keeping reform on the public agenda during this time was Ted Kennedy, Carter's chief rival for the Democratic presidential nomination in 1980, whose continued efforts toward drafting his own comprehensive bill served (quite intentionally) to goad both the White House and the Senate Commerce Committee. Kennedy's staff counsel, Jay Steptoe, represented the focal point of trucking reform for members of the reporting group for many months.

The long-awaited appearance of an administration bill gave the reporting group something concrete to coalesce around at last. Member groups were called in for comments on the draft proposal, and when Carter and Kennedy announced their joint legislation at a White House ceremony on the first day of summer, the other erstwhile opponents supporting the bill, such as the ACU and Common Cause, were prominently displayed. Lobbyists remained skeptical that the White House would push for a strong trucking bill, however, particularly as the 1980 election drew near. Thus the reporting group remained just that throughout the summer and early fall of 1979. There was no set schedule or location for meetings. The convener changed from one meeting to the next. Even the membership was fluid.

The summer saw continued debate among group members over whether to organize officially, as the airline coalition had done. While some lobbyists wanted a tighter organizational structure, corporate shippers, skittish about taking a visible stand on the trucking issue, preferred to keep the low profile of a loose alliance. Reflecting the uneasiness of their members, National Association of Manufacturers (NAM) representatives were also reluctant to make the coalition more formal.

The reporting group decided to remain informal, but key members agreed on the need for additional leadership. (What central direction the group had received up until then came largely from two individuals, both long active in the trucking reform movement, who carried on a friendly rivalry for leadership.) An informal nominating committee selected Frank Swain, a young attorney and lobbyist for the National Federation of Independent Business (NFIB). Swain had not been particularly active in the group up until then; his major appeal was that he represented small business—an ideological middle ground acceptable to both the conservative and consumer members of the group. His charge as chairman was to give the group cohesiveness, develop a coherent lobbying strategy, and get group members to respond and follow that strategy if something should occur to cause the trucking issue, then seemingly stalled in committee, to move forward.

That "something" occurred almost immediately, when Howard Cannon, responding to recent and dramatic reforms announced by the ICC, delivered his "we're-mad-as-hell" speech to the commission. Cannon's promise to have a bill on the president's desk by June 1, even coming from one still thought to be friendly to the industry, was a green light to deregulation supporters because it meant that Congress would have to take action of some kind.

With Swain as chairman, the reporting group took on a new name—the Coordinating Committee for Truck Regulatory Reform—signifying its transition to an action group. At Swain's urging, the more active members of the coalition began systematically lobbying, and there was talk of holding a symposium on the Hill to publicize the broad support for reform and to educate staffers, most of whom knew next to nothing about trucking regulation. However the group was still preoccupied with internal disagreements. Ann McBride, a lobbyist for Common Cause and vice-chairman of the coalition, put together a "statement of principles" that provoked much debate.

By late fall, coalition members' recognition of the difficult lobbying task that lay ahead, together with Swain's conciliatory influence, produced a working balance within the group. White House aides applauded the group's internal accomplishment and urged the coalition now to step up its outside effort. Specifically, the aides wanted the coalition to hire an individual to coordinate the group's lobbying effort. (Coalition leaders were told that the presence of a coordinator, as evidence that the group was serious in its commitment to reform, would in turn help the aides get a strong commitment from the White House. However, the real motivation behind the pressure to hire a coordinator was the Carter aides' belief that having such an individual would make the coalition a more effective lobbying group.)

There was considerable reluctance to hire a coordinator on the part of Swain and other members of an informal, self-designated "steering committee." Hiring a law firm—a common practice for such purposes—would cost more than the group wanted to spend. More important, there was concern that an outside person would become the tail wagging the dog—another common phenomenon with ad hoc groups. However, the committee eventually found someone satisfactory to all—Cornish (Con) Hitchcock, a young Nader attorney with a strong technical background in transportation regulation (he directed Nader's Aviation Consumer Action Project, an important player in the airline-deregulation battle), a low-key personal manner, and an affordable, Nader-rate price tag.

To pay for Hitchcock's time and other expenses, the steering committee set up an "information service." For $250, a subscriber received a monthly newsletter and copies of bills, committee reports, and the like. Except for the newsletter, the material disseminated this way was almost all available to the public at no cost. But $250 seemed to the committee a modest fee to charge for what private companies would spend much more to track down on their own.

The coalition had all of this organizational structure in place by January 1980, before the Commerce and Public Works committees had released their bills, on which the political debate would focus. That same month the group held its long-planned symposium on Capitol Hill. It was a watershed for the coalition. The day-long event attracted a large audience, primarily shippers and congressional staffers, and the press took note of the turnout. Two weeks later the group got another boost when Cannon introduced a bill far stronger than was anticipated.

By the time the Senate markup neared, a month later, the coalition machinery was in place and functioning relatively smoothly. The group was meeting regularly. The members were lobbying in teams—each representing the four major interests backing reform: consumers, small business, big business, and agriculture—systematically visiting key senators and their staffs. Information provided by coalition members at the end of each lobbying day was incorporated into a centralized head count.

The coalition met formally on Wednesday mornings in a boardroom at NAM's headquarters, just a block from the White House. Attendance averaged about thirty, picking up noticeably after the Senate markup, when the prospects of victory increased dramatically. There was enough turnover from week to week that Swain began each meeting with self-introductions. A typical coalition meeting found representatives from the following organizations sitting around the table: the administration (the ICC, DOT, the Council on Wage and Price Stability, and the Domestic Policy Staff), the Senate Judiciary Committee, Nader's Congress Watch and TCAP, Common Cause, Consumers Union, the Consumer Federation of America, the Farm Bureau, NAM, NFIB, the National Council of Farmer Cooperatives, CURRENT, the National Retail Merchants Association, the National Industrial Traffic League, the Food Marketing Institute, the National Audio-Visual Association, DuPont, Lever Brothers, Procter and Gamble, Kimberly Clark, General Mills, 3M, Sears Roebuck, Union Carbide, International Paper, Flying Tiger Line, Federal Express, United Parcel Service, the Private Trucking Council, and two dissident ATA conferences representing the contract carriers and private carriers.

Coalition meetings were informal and fast paced. The forum was designed to update members on recent legislative developments, coordinate lobbying and drafting of amendments, and provide an opportunity for exhorting members to do more lobbying. There was almost no visible dissension or acrimony, much joking, and exhortations were strictly soft sell. While disagreements between members arose, they were generally handled outside of the weekly sessions.

Coalition meetings preceding key events—committee meetings and floor votes—served to alert members to what to watch for and to last-minute lobbying they could do:

<blockquote>
Rick Neustadt (White House representative): *The guts of this [upcoming Senate markup] will be reflected in the vote on the ATA's amendment on the National Transportation Policy statement. That vote will come right at the beginning and will be the test vote. If that amendment prevails, then we've essentially lost the vote.*
</blockquote>

DuPont rep.:   *Who will offer the debilitating amendments?*
Neustadt: *The rumor is [Sen. Ernest] Hollings.*
DuPont rep.:   *Is there any way to cool his ardor?*
Others: *Unlikely.*
DuPont rep.:   *We are the single largest employer in South Carolina*
                (Hollings's home state).
Neustadt: *If you can do anything, please do.*
Sears rep.:   *The test vote on the National Transportation Policy*
                statement will show if Cannon has control. If the
                amendment prevails, showing he doesn't have control,
                then you'll see [debilitating] amendments coming in
                like pigeons at the end of the day in Farragut Square.
Neustadt: *Without meaning to be a guru about this, I'll offer a*
                suggestion and list of key senators to contact. Getting
                substantive matters to staff is no longer of any use;
                only thing at this point is telegrams and calls from
                home states. . . . When you're interrupting corporate ex-
                ecutives today to ask them to make phone calls to
                [senators] on the Hill, you might tell them that the Pres-
                ident interrupted his work on foreign policy today to
                make some phone calls on this bill.
Swain: *Where you have plant managers and CEOs (corporate*
                executive officers) from key states, have them call. No
                one [on the committee] is pinned down; if the first vote
                goes against us, we've got problems.
DOT rep.:   *I saw Sen. [James] Exon this morning; he got 50 Mail-*
                grams today from opponents of deregulation.
Swain: *Phone calls to senators should say not just to support*
                S. 2245, because that will be reported out by a 16 to 2
                vote in any regard. They should say to hang tough on
                entry [and other key provisions]. Say to support the
                leadership and don't weaken the bill. Full court press.
                Now is not the time to concentrate on substance; now
                is the time to concentrate on firepower.

Several meetings were devoted largely to reviewing the list of House and
Senate committee members so as to get a rough "head count" and help
coalition members know where to focus their lobbying efforts:

> He doesn't understand how the different groups stand on this, but his staffers
> are figuring it out. He's especially interested in consumer issues.

He will follow [Public Works subcommittee chairman] Howard.

Forget him; he's still hollering about airlines.

He's good, though he won't take a leadership position; he finds the subject boring.

He should be okay; he thinks Ronnie Reagan is too liberal.

He's tied up the next few weeks with [another] committee. His [administrative assistant] is leaving at the end of the next month, unfortunately. Beware of the conflict between him and [another congressman].

He will follow [Congressman Allen] Ertel [a strong advocate]; but he needs to be visited. We're not counting on him as a for-sure bet.

He's very adroit at saying nothing at all. Originally we thought we could swing him around, but he's really on the wrong side on this. He could really poison the well for us; any contacts you have. . . .

He's better than the pope; seems to want total deregulation.

He said he has 200 trucking companies headquartered in his district. He'll probably go with the chairman (of the subcommittee).

He's getting hit hard; won't commit.

He's not the most cerebral congressman; needs lots of work.

He's looking for money. See him personally; his staffer is bad on the issue.

Supposedly good all the way, but could still use visiting.

He made awful statements at hearings. While he was talking his staff member was in the back of the room shaking down the ATA for money.

He has a very cordial administrative assistant. But he's in a tough reelection campaign; I don't think he can afford to be a statesman.

Most important, the meetings provided an ongoing opportunity for Swain and others to inspire the team and plea for more calls, letters, visits—in short, "full court press."

Trade association rep.:	*Next Tuesday, there's a big ATA breakfast here in Washington, and then the truckers will hit the Hill. After they're done, it will look like the locusts have been there.*
DOT rep.:	*The Teamsters have generated an unbelievable amount of mail on this. Out of 400 pieces of mail that a Hill office gets, maybe six pieces will be pro reform. Many staffers have talked to 20 people from the other side, some to twice that many. Staffers have begged us to get some groups up there so the senators will have something to hang their hats on.*
Swain:	*Just to agree. . . . Lots of staffers have begged us for mail. They say, "We're inclined to support you but when our senator goes to vote and asks for the mail count, [what can we say?]" If we lose [the Stevenson amendment exempting food], it will create a herd attitude. The result may be a horrible rollback on what the ICC has done.*

The coalition ultimately fulfilled each of the three functions envisioned for it—providing testimony at congressional hearings, direct lobbying, and display of grass-roots support. NFIB members sent more than 100,000 pieces of mail to their senators and representatives. Common Cause and the Farm Bureau also made a strong grass-roots showing. NAM provided quality, if not quantity, in the form of contacts from corporate executives and plant managers in key districts. Congress Watch and Consumers Union representatives did extensive direct lobbying, as did lobbyists from NFIB, NAM, Common Cause, and the Farm Bureau.

In addition to those six groups, which were the most visible members of the coalition, a number of others lobbied actively—the ACU, Food Marketing Institute, and Consumer Federation of America, to name just three. A minicoalition of farm groups organized around the Farm Bureau, representing everything from farm cooperatives to poultry producers. A handful of private companies—Sears, Lever Brothers, and International Paper among them—lobbied extensively, often reaching senators and representatives whom no one else could in districts where they had plants.

In terms of sheer firepower, the coalition was hopelessly outgunned by ATA-Teamster lobbying. The Teamsters produced a dense "snow-down" of mail—hundreds of thousands of letters opposing deregulation. The ATA orchestrated a massive lobbying campaign. In the weeks preceding the Senate floor vote, legislative assistants in many offices spent four to five hours a day on the telephone with ATA members. The ATA block-booked

500 hotel rooms for trucking executives who flew in from around the country for the Senate vote. (The Senate leadership moved the vote up a day partly to spare members from the barrage of last-minute lobbying.) ATA lobbying on the House side was, if anything, even heavier. Many Hill staffers said that the ATA-Teamsters effort represented the heaviest lobbying campaign on any issue in years.

Vote counts reflected the massive lobbying against deregulation. In districts where trucking companies were a significant presence, congressmen tended to vote in line with the industry position. For example, Preston Trucking Company, a Maryland-based firm with employees in 125 congressional districts, lobbied heavily against the bill. On a crucial amendment on the House floor, 70 percent of the representatives with ten or more Preston employees in their districts voted the "right way."[10] In the Senate, several problematic amendments originated with members who generally favored deregulation but who had a strong constituency to appease.

Where the regulated trucking industry was not a major threat—either because industry pressure was minimal or because reelection was not an immediate concern—senators and representatives were relatively free to vote on the basis of the merits. Most of them eventually supported regulatory reform. For this, the coalition deserves considerable credit.

Breadth and diversity were what made the coalition so effective. "In my twenty years in Congress, I've never seen such exotic alliances," said one retiring representative. Team lobbying was probably the most visible (to Congress) embodiment of that diversity. Congressmen and their staffs were struck by the rare experience of having a team representing consumers, business, farmers, and conservatives come calling to make a united appeal. The reaction was often the same—anything Nader, big business, and the ACU can agree on must have merit.

Packwood maintained that the coalition was the key to victory on the Senate floor. His statements during the floor debate suggest just how that victory was achieved: On issue after issue, Packwood pointed to interest-group support as proof that deregulation would not have the undesirable effects that opponents claimed it would.[11] On small-community service:

> We will hear lots of rhetoric about small towns [losing] service. ... The National Federation of Independent Business, perhaps the best cross-section of small business in this country, its membership is disproportionately in small towns ... supports this bill with a vengeance.

On the amendment to preserve the regulation of processed food which its sponsor, Ernest Hollings, claimed would help consumers and small towns:

Do we think those groups* would [oppose] a Hollings amendment if they thought it would injure [consumers]? They are opposed to the Hollings amendment.

Think it will hurt small towns? The National Association of Counties, the principal lobbying organization for the counties of this country, not cities, but counties, principally the rural areas, is opposed to the Hollings amendment.

On the argument that deregulation would raise the cost of transportation:

If indeed the transportation of food is so cheap, why do the American Retail Grocers Association and the Wholesale Grocers Association support the bill . . . ?

On trucking deregulation in general:

[The ATA and the Teamsters Union] are the two organizations that principally oppose this bill and, understandably, from their individual standpoint. On the other side, you have almost every other conceivable combination. [See table 5.1 for list of deregulators.]

Why do all these groups support this? They think they will get a better deal out of this bill than they have out of the present system. The ATA and the Teamsters think they will get a worse deal. . . .

In short, the breadth and diversity of the coalition were the ultimate evidence—far more politically persuasive than numbers alone—that trucking deregulation was in the public interest. Had any one of the major groups affected by deregulation—consumers, farmers, or corporate shippers—not favored it, or even been significantly divided in its support, that probably would have assured defeat. But as it was, the line of supporters stretched all the way from Common Cause to the ACU, with very few gaps in between.

For congressmen worried about their own political well-being, the broad support represented by the coalition did not necessarily offer safety in numbers. A vote against the ATA and Teamsters was potentially far more politically damaging to most legislators than a vote against an ad hoc coalition with little means of retaliation. (The Teamsters Union carried through with its threat against Carter; the labor group endorsed Ronald

*Common Cause, National Consumers League, Consumer Federation of America, Community Nutrition Institute, Public Citizens (Nader), Consumer Alert, Consumers Union, Congress Watch, American Association of Retired Persons, Friends of the Earth.

Table 5.1
Trucking Deregulation Supporters

Air Florida
Alta Freight Systems
American Association of Retired Persons
American Conservative Union
American Enterprise Institute
American Farm Bureau Federation
American Institute for Shippers Association
American Paper Institute
American Retail Federation
Anchor-Hocking Corporation
Association of General Merchandise
Beatrice Foods Company
Boise Cascade
Frank Borman, President, Eastern Airlines
Burger King Company
Center for Auto Safety
Champion International
Chemical Manufacturers Association
City Products
Civil Aeronautics Board
Clorox
Common Cause
Community Nutrition Institute
Congress Watch
Consumer Alert
Consumer Federation of America
Consumers Union
Continental Airlines
Cooperative Food Distribution of America
Cooperative League of the U.S.A.
Council for a Competitive Economy
Crown Zellerbach
DuPont
Federated Department Stores
Federal Trade Commission
Food Marketing Institute
Food Ways National
Friends of the Earth
General Mills
Georgia Pacific
Charles Horn, Mayor, Kettering, Ohio
The Hubinger Company, Keokuk, Iowa
International Management Consultants
International Paper
Kraft, Inc.
Lever Brothers

Frank Lorenzo, President, Texas
    International Airlines
Mattel Toys
Mead Corporation
Minority Trucking Transportation
    Development Corporation
Delmar Mitchell, President, Buffalo City
    Council
Ernest Morial, Mayor, New Orleans
National Agricultural Transportation
    Association
National Association of Counties
National Association of Furniture
    Manufacturers
National Association of Manufacturers
National Association of Retail Stores
National Association of Wholesale Grocers
National Cattlemen's Association
National Consumers League
National Council of Farm Cooperatives
National Farmers Organization
National Federation of Independent
    Business
National Grain and Feed Association
National Grange
National Home Furnishings Association
National Independent Meat Packers
    Association
National Industrial Traffic League (except
    for antitrust immunity)
National Meat Association (except for food
    exemption)
National Restaurant Association
National Retail Merchants Association
Ore-Ida Foods, Inc.
Orlon Industries
Owens Illinois
Pacific Southwest Airlines
Peninsula Transportation District
    Commission, Hampton, Virginia
Pittsburgh Plate Glass
Private Truck Council of America
Public Citizen
The Ripon Society
St. Regis Paper Company
Scott Paper

(continues on next page)

Table 5.1 *(cont.)*

Sears Roebuck & Company	Union Carbide
Spiegel	United Parcel
Starkist Food	Western Airlines
Super Valu Stores	Weyerhaeuser
Tiger International	Whirlpool
Truck Renting and Leasing Association	Coleman Young, Mayor, City of Detroit

Source: Adapted from *Congressional Record*, 96th Cong., 2d sess., vol. 126, no. 57, p. S3591.

Reagan in the presidential election, citing Carter's support for deregulation as a major reason.)

This political reality was reflected in the Senate floor vote on the all-important Hollings amendment: Of the twenty-eight senators up for reelection in 1980, nineteen supported the Hollings-ATA position; eleven out of those facing reelection in 1982 voted with Hollings; and only ten senators not due to campaign until 1984 supported the amendment (see table 5.2).[12]

Trucking deregulation presented congressmen with a no-win issue. That was nowhere more apparent than in the House Public Works Committee, a body that thrives on a diet of "pork." Trucking legislation offered no money, jobs, or pet projects to lavish on the home district. Rather, it offered a choice of two unappetizing alternatives—vote against "the public interest" and be spared the ire of the ATA and Teamsters; or incur their wrath but with little thanks in return from consumer constituents, who would see no readily visible benefit from deregulation. Committee members asked the same question repeatedly of the leadership: Why are we being faced with this issue in an election year?

The existence of the coalition served to make the second alternative at least somewhat more palatable. For the congressman facing a tough reelection campaign who "couldn't afford to be a statesman," no ad hoc coalition could have made the difference. But for those who could afford such luxury, the coalition provided as unambiguous a proxy measure for where the public interest lay as Congress ever sees.

Proof of the merits notwithstanding, coalition lobbying persuaded certain members of Congress that a vote for deregulation was in their political self-interest. Corporate members of the coalition were especially important in this respect. By bringing their corporate executive officers and plant managers in to Washington for selective lobbying, those firms could exercise political clout in districts where they had plants comparable to that of regulated trucking companies. Lobbyists for business associations, particularly NAM, also sought to exert their influence by arranging targeted contacts from member companies in key districts. "Congressmen support business not because they like business," said one trade association lobbyist, "but because of the importance of jobs to their district."

Obstacles to Building a Coalition:
The Free-Rider Problem

Dairy farmers are the most selfish lot. If they can't hear the milk hitting the bottom of the can, they don't want to get involved. That's the only music they hear.
—Consumer Lobbyist

Dairy farm groups never joined the ad hoc coalition, and the quote, from a lobbyist who worked on trucking reform, suggests the reason: Why would any organization devote its resources to an effort that promises collective benefits—benefits that can be enjoyed whether or not one contributes to their production? A look at several members of the trucking coalition and how they came to participate tells something about the incentives and disincentives to being a free-rider in the lobbying arena.

Consumers Union

The Consumers Union began lobbying late in life. Founded in 1936 as a product-testing organization, up until recently CU exerted political pressure only indirectly, through its respected magazine, *Consumer Reports*. Several articles favorable to airline deregulation represented CU's involvement in that issue.

In early 1978, CU hired its first lobbyist and legislative staff person— Sharon Nelson, a young attorney and recent occupant of the "Warren

Table 5.2
Senators Supporting ATA, by Year of Reelection Campaign

	Vote on ATA-Supported Amendment	
When Facing Reelection	For	Against
1980	19	9
1982	11	16
1984	10	19

Magnuson chair" on the Senate Commerce Committee staff—a one-year spot that was unofficially reserved for a top graduate of the University of Washington law school, alma mater of Senator Magnuson, when he served as chairman of that committee. Nelson outlined what CU's legislative priorities should be and included among them trucking deregulation—an issue she was familiar with from her tenure on the Hill. Coincidentally, a writer on the editorial board of *Consumer Reports* was very interested in the trucking controversy, and her proreform article appeared in the issue of June, 1979—the same month that Carter and Kennedy introduced their joint bill. That made CU a player.

CU's top management staff in Mt. Vernon, New York, approved Nelson's overall plan to lobby on trucking deregulation. The executive director of the four-person Washington, D.C., office (the Mt. Vernon headquarters has 300 employees) signed off on specific positions that CU subsequently took.

Congress Watch

Given Ralph Nader's long-standing interest in reforming the ICC, there was never any question that the Nader-based Congress Watch would get involved in the trucking debate. That the group gave the issue such a high priority was due largely to a personal interest in trucking reform on the part of Nancy Drabble, a staff attorney, and to Congress Watch's preference for playing a dominant role in any issue that it tackles. Personal interest aside, Drabble felt that trucking deregulation was a good candidate for Congress Watch support because it had the earmarks of a winner: Regulatory reform was a timely issue; it had diverse (if unorganized) backing; and the White House was committed to the issue. In addition, trucking reform was a regulatory issue on which Congress Watch could urge a vote for less government control—a desirable step given the increasing liability of the group's proregulation image.

National Federation of Independent Business

NFIB adopts policy positions on the basis of "Mandate," a periodic poll of its 600,000 members. In 1976, the members voted overwhelmingly to support regulatory reform of the trucking industry, a result which guaranteed that NFIB would, at the least, strongly endorse reform. But it was in good part because Frank Swain chaired the coalition that NFIB produced over 100,000 letters supporting reform and otherwise made it a high priority. NFIB's extensive involvement came about gradually. When Swain took on the chairmanship, he did so with the understanding that his time commitment could be reduced at any point if other, more important issues arose. None did; no other issue that would have required a major NFIB commitment—a tax or minimum-wage bill, for example—reached a critical lobbying stage during the trucking fight. Moreover, Swain's boss was agreeable to letting the group's involvement in the trucking issue increase over time.

Lever Brothers

In the late 1970s, Lever Brothers conducted an internal study of its transportation costs and concluded that it could save $7.5 million a year if the trucking industry were more competitive. At first, the company was reluctant to make its findings public; eventually it decided to speak out, and the company lobbied extensively for the deregulation bill on the basis of its estimated savings—a figure that congressmen found highly persuasive.

The Incentives at Work

Beehives

Lever Brothers' reluctance to support trucking deregulation publicly was typical of private companies. Many companies weren't willing to get involved in the coalition until a number of other corporate shippers did so. Others agreed to attend meetings because the coalition was informal and they didn't have to attach their name to an official organization. Of those that lobbied, at least one refused to visit Capitol Hill offices as part of a team of coalition members, preferring instead to lobby independently and selectively.

Such reluctance is understandable. In addition to the fact that a private company has little to gain from speaking out—the benefits of deregulation will go to silent as well as vocal supporters—there are real costs to taking a political stand. Political advocacy appears unbusinesslike: private firms want to be thought of as manufacturers of good products, not as parties to political deals. Moreover, by taking a position on a controversial public issue, a company inevitably alienates some group—customers, suppliers, workers. "Why kick a beehive," said one business lobbyist, "so long as someone else is getting honey from it [for you]."

Various beehives surrounded the trucking issue. Teamster threats were one: Some nonunion companies were warned not to support deregulation lest they find union organizers visiting their plants. Much more common were "threats" by regulated carriers who said they would have to raise rates or even discontinue service if the deregulation bill passed. Even shippers who doubted the sincerity of the warnings were reluctant to jeopardize often long-standing relations with their carriers by speaking out for decontrol.

Why then did some companies join the coalition? Economic interest was clearly the primary motivation. The companies that endorsed, and even more so those that actively lobbied for, deregulation were those that stood to profit the most—manufacturers of consumer and retail products, predominantly, for whom transportation costs are a significant fraction of total expenses.

Most private firms in the coalition had large plants in several locations; as major employers in those districts, they felt they could exercise some leverage with individual senators and congressmen. (As a matter of policy, most companies lobbied only congressional representatives from districts where they had plants.) Thus their political involvement was perfectly rational from an economic standpoint: even though they would profit from deregulation whether or not they spoke out, the stakes were high enough that the potential value of their marginal contribution outweighed the risks of kicking beehives and the cost of lobbying itself. In short, like dairy farm groups that lobby for issues close to home, these firms could "hear the milk hitting the bottom of the can."

Not all shippers recognized their economic interest in deregulation, much less lobbied for it. Companies with sophisticated transportation operations were more likely to appreciate the potential savings from, and thus speak out for, regulatory reform. Firms that still had "traffic departments" were less likely to appreciate this and, indeed, where the green-eyeshaded traffic clerk spoke for the shipper, as he often did, the message was typically one of partial opposition to deregulation. These traffic managers had a personal stake in preserving the regulated system, a phenomenon discussed later in the chapter.

One coalition member with a highly sophisticated transportation system was Sears Roebuck. Sears had become interested in transportation regulatory reform many years before, when it replaced traffic managers with distribution managers—sophisticated professionals who "thought big and wanted change," according to Stanton Sender, Sears's transportation counsel. As a result, Sender helped organize the early shipper alliances for deregulation—COMET and CURRENT. Sears was also active in airline deregulation, for which it received considerable criticism from opponents of decontrol who accused the company of, among other things, wanting to start its own airline.

Sears's involvement in trucking reform was motivated by economic interest, but the extent of involvement was due considerably to Sender's personal interest in the issue. His enthusiasm was contagious as well.

Sender was an officer in a major shippers' association, and through that network he recruited many of the large companies that actively participated in the coalition.

This personal element was extremely important in determining the makeup of the coalition. Whether companies got involved at all and, if so, how much, was in good part due to the personal interest of company representatives in Washington and those at "home." They didn't always agree. Several Washington lobbyists whom coalition leaders knew were "chomping at the bit" to lobby the trucking bill were overruled by the home office—either because participation seemed like an unnecessary headache or because the company had higher political priorities.

In part because of the headaches involved in direct lobbying, companies join trade associations. Umbrella business groups give private firms the means to exert political leverage without having to speak out individually. But even trade group lobbyists sometimes avoid taking a political stand for fear of beehives.

Internal dissent is the beehive most feared by voluntary organizations, for whom survival is paramount. NAM's board of directors voted unambiguously to support trucking deregulation, but some member companies opposed reform, and NAM was reluctant to take an active role until deregulation was a politically feasible proposal and not just a gleam in economists' eyes.

NFIB kicked the beehive and suffered the consequences. The trade group represented more than half a million small-business men and women, some of whom owned regulated trucking companies and staunchly opposed deregulation. NFIB alienated members because of its visible role in the trucking battle. One field representative complained to the Washington office that he had lost more members over trucking reform than over any issue in ten years.

Two major business groups—the Chamber of Commerce and the Business Roundtable—stayed silent altogether on the trucking issue because their members disagreed internally. The chamber excused its silence by saying that it never takes a stand on legislation specific to an industry. But in fact, the chamber came out against the "superfund"—a proposal to have chemical companies pay jointly for damages from a large-scale chemical accident—and in support of hospital-cost containment, both of which are industry-specific policies. A better explanation is that there were several trucking-company executives on the chamber's policy board, which made it impossible for the group to reach a consensus on reform. (Carter administration representatives enjoyed pointing out in their speeches that on the biggest regulatory reform issue of the year, the GOP-oriented Chamber of Commerce chose to remain silent.) The head of the Business Roundtable

was Thomas Murphy, president of General Motors, a company that supported continued antitrust immunity for rate bureaus.[13]

Trade associations weren't the only interest groups that faced internal
pressure to keep quiet on the trucking issue. Shortly after Kennedy's press
conference on trucking reform, the ACU received letters from several
members severing their ties with the conservative group. Said one letter
from a trucking company executive, "I like to have had a relapse when I
noted that the ACU attended a press conference orchestrated by Sen. Teddy
Kennedy's aides and that [the ACU] issued a stirring statement, along with
Ralph Nader. . . ." The ACU's appearance alongside Nader and Kennedy also
prompted a letter from a conservative southern senator outlining his decidedly unenthusiastic attitude toward trucking deregulation. At the top of
the letter appears an ACU staffer's handwritten editorial comment, "File
under Bullshit."

ACU staffers met with far greater resistance as the battle wore on
because of some unique ties to the trucking industry. The ACU's chairman at
the time was Rep. Robert Bauman; Bauman's congressional district, the
Eastern Shore of Maryland, was the home of Preston Trucking Company,
one of the largest and most profitable regulated carriers. The executive
director of the ACU, Ross Whealton, was formerly Bauman's administrative
assistant. Prior to joining Bauman's congressional staff, Whealton had
worked for Preston for many years.

The ACU lobbied for trucking deregulation with little direct interference from Whealton or Bauman up until the end. Jeffrey Hollingsworth, a
pipe-smoking young ACU staffer, attended coalition meetings regularly,
lobbied the Hill, kept ACU members updated on the progress of the
trucking bill, and issued a position paper to members of the Senate shortly
before the floor vote. Just before the House vote, Hollingsworth prepared a
similar position paper to go to all representatives. Much to his dismay,
Bauman stopped the letter from going out altogether.

The Competition for Groups and Issues

The ACU went as far as it did in lobbying for reform because trucking
deregulation was a quintessential conservative issue and political visibility is
good for business—ACU business, that is. The ACU is an organization of
ideologues. Members join in order to express strongly held beliefs about
the role of government in society. ACU activity expressive of those beliefs
enhances the organization in the eyes of existing and prospective members.

Consumer groups were similarly motivated. Members join organizations such as Common Cause and Congress Watch largely to contribute to
the attainment of worthwhile political causes rather than for any individual,

tangible benefits.[14] To appeal to these individuals, consumer organizations must be able to demonstrate their commitment to and efficacy in furthering such causes.

Broadly based business associations such as NAM and NFIB also thrive on political visibility and a reputation for legislative effectiveness. Such groups attract members largely on the basis of appeals to ideology and a sense of duty to support broad political goals.[15] These goals generally have some economic impact on the members, and certain members may have considerable financial stake in particular issues. But the major appeal of these groups is their ability to further broad political and economic goals rather than to provide immediate, tangible rewards.

Not all, or even most, political organizations can survive largely by carrying out political activity. Plagued by the free-rider problem, most survive by offering individual, material incentives to prospective members, such as information or low-cost insurance. But even these materially induced organizations—such as farm groups and industry trade associations—benefit from being able to show existing and prospective members evidence of the leaders' ability to secure economically beneficial legislation.

In sum, organized interest groups need issues. For some groups, evidence of their political activity and efficacy is the primary incentive offered to members. For other groups, individual, material benefits are primary, but political visibility nevertheless enhances their appeal. In either case, quite the opposite of private businesses, interest groups thrive on exposure and display their political bearskins proudly on the wall. That fundamental need for issues from which to derive visibility and opportunities to take credit is the single most important counter to the free-rider incentive in coalition politics.

More than just needing issues to lobby, groups seek to dominate them. Because ACU staffers saw trucking deregulation as a "tailor-made issue for the conservative movement," they had early hopes of leading the reform effort. Internal ACU memos written during the winter and spring of 1979 reflect the sense of ideological competition for dominance:

> ACU has laid the foundation for a coalition similar to the [airline coalition], of which ACU was a charter member. We could take the lead in the reform movement if we choose. [A] consumer organization has gotten up front and is hosting a seminar . . . on the effects of trucking regulation on consumer costs, etc. ACU . . . will attend the conference to further our own interests.

Another memo recommended that the conservative group make certain compromises in order to broaden its base of influence:

My goal [is] to have sponsors of ACU's bill play [the] leading role in drafting and steering of any final legislation. This will involve compromising, but without [that] the ACU [deregulation bill] will not receive significant recognition. However, if the Carter Administration decided to push legislation . . . , conservative support . . . will be essential to the leadership. They will be forced to play ball with us. . . .

Groups at the other end of the ideological spectrum display this same preference for playing a dominant role. At Congress Watch, it's stated policy, according to staff attorney Nancy Drabble:

We like to be the lead group on any issue in which we get involved. There are exceptions—cases where we just sign on to a letter. But generally, we like to make a real organizational commitment, jump in feet first. That way, we feel we have some control over what happens.

While all interest groups need issues, the availability varies among groups. For some groups, particularly smaller ones, starvation is a constant threat. A representative from the National Audio-Visual Association regularly attended the trucking coalition meetings out of an interest in the implications of deregulation for damaged freight. That's a fairly peripheral concern—an indication that the audio-visual group is one that's chronically hungry for issues.

For other, generally larger, groups the plate is always too full. NFIB falls in that category. Congress shows great deference to small business, so everyone wants small business on its side. NFIB's problem is to pick and choose from a surplus of issues. NAM is in the same position. "Issues seem to find us," said a NAM lobbyist. They come from several sources, including NAM's standing committees and congressmen with pet projects, as well as staff members themselves.

Because many groups have a surplus of issues, ad hoc coalitions face the problem of persuading potential members to join initially and then to lobby actively. In addition to the groups that decline to get involved at all, coalition leaders confront two kinds of free-riders—those who send a representative to meetings to take notes but no more, and those who get involved only when it becomes clear there's going to be a successful bill. Coalitions are also plagued by unreliable paying riders who can't be counted on for the lobbying support they promise. In some cases, members-as-free-riders are desired by a coalition—for example, because they provide ideological ballast. But in general, a group is of little value unless it's active.

The trucking-reform coalition had its share of free-riders. Getting groups to "join" the coalition was not the problem. Except for the two organizations that were internally divided—the Chamber of Commerce and the Business Roundtable—virtually every group that should have been represented in the coalition was; the "big six" groups formed a well-rounded lobbying team, and those six brought others in. The problem was getting organizations (corporations especially) to commit resources. Swain's "greatest frustration" was in failing to get certain groups moving, and succeeding with others only through "constant hortatory." As the coordinator for the coalition, Con Hitchcock continually faced the problem of lobbyists failing to appear for scheduled team visits on Capitol Hill. He put pressure on them "by appealing to their better sense: 'We're really counting on you.' or 'Congressman so-and-so really listens to you.' . . . Pleading, flattery, cajolery." But in the end, a handful of coalition members was responsible for the bulk of activity, which came as no surprise to them. "No matter how many groups and people are involved," observed one active consumer lobbyist, "it inevitably comes down to around four who do most of the work."

In short, free-riding doesn't end with a group's decision to join a coalition. For coalition leaders, the key question is how high a priority the issue is for the individual lobbyist and the group he or she represents. Is a consumer organization prepared to turn out 100,000 pieces of mail? Is a trade association willing to get member companies to send their CEOs to Washington? How much capital is the organization willing to spend?

How Political Organizations Decide

In the competition for groups and issues, how do political organizations decide what to lobby and how much in the way of resources to invest? Without trying to answer that question exhaustively, one can point to several factors illustrated by the case of trucking reform. A fundamental consideration, certainly, is *the expressed will of the membership*. Business groups in particular had concrete evidence that trucking deregulation was something their members supported—a strong "Mandate" from NFIB members, a unanimous vote of approval from NAM's board of directors.

A less concrete indication of members' will is an *organization's broad statement of purpose*. The board of directors vote was a specific affirmation of NAM's overall policy directive to reduce unwarranted federal intrusion. Trucking deregulation was thoroughly consistent with the ACU's "Statement of Principles," which maintains that "capitalism is the only economic system of our time that is compatible with political liberty."

Organization memberships are rarely homogeneous, however. Since internal strife is a threat to survival, potentially divisive issues are almost always avoided. Even if only a few members have interests inconsistent with the majority's, that's often sufficient to inhibit action by the organization, as evidenced by the absence of the Chamber of Commerce and the Business Roundtable from the trucking coalition.

The membership's consensual will—as expressed through issue-specific communications or through more abstract principles—provides the broad framework for selecting issues. But within that framework, certain constraints limit the choice. *Timing*—what else is on the legislative agenda—is one. The ACU was much less active in the trucking battle than it had initially planned to be (and less so than it was in airline reform) in part because two other issues—SALT and the Panama Canal treaty—took higher priority. Environmental groups, some of which expressed early support of trucking deregulation because of its implications for energy conservation, never really joined the fray. The coalition made no particular attempt to recruit them, knowing that an environmental battle with a capital *E*—the Alaska Lands bill—was being waged at the same time. Like NFIB, however, most groups found themselves relatively free of demands to lobby other *major* issues during the critical months of the trucking battle. (Nevertheless, the ever present problem was that trucking deregulation was the only issue for opponents, while it was one of many issues for coalition members.)

In addition to timing, *who else is involved* in different issues may limit the agenda. Armed with limited resources, groups prefer to lobby where their potential contribution is the greatest. Coalition leaders feared that one particular consumer group would drop out of the alliance, saying, in effect, What can we add? Moreover, groups are reluctant to share credit, particularly with rival (as distinct from opponent) organizations, with whom they compete for members.[16] Thus for organizations that represent the same broad constituency—such as consumers or small business—it often makes sense to avoid overlap.

Cooperative lobbying also raises "concern for the company one keeps."[17] The ACU member who "like to have had a relapse" over the conservative group's appearance next to Nader and Kennedy illustrates the problem strongly ideological groups confront when they ally themselves with their erstwhile enemies. Even friends can pose a threat to a group's reputation. The Consumers Union does not like to join coalitions as a matter of policy: management feels that working with other consumer groups jeopardizes CU's image as being more cautious and conservative than the rest. (The trucking coalition posed an additional, conflict-of-interest problem since CU-rated products were manufactured by some of the corporate members of the group.)

Most consumer groups actively prefer to work with coalitions. But that represents a dramatic change from the early days of the consumer movement, when alliances were a threat to the separate and emerging identities of the movement's nascent groups.[18] Competition with rivals aside, groups trying to make a name for themselves must often take extreme positions and antagonize legislative opponents—actions inconsistent with the requirements of a coalition.[19] Even for established groups, cooperative lobbying poses a threat to their cherished autonomy. "The Farm Bureau speaks for the Farm Bureau," that organization's leaders like to say, expressing an attitude that is typical of interest groups.

CU's lobbyist worked with the ad hoc trucking group despite management's policy because she felt that "in Washington, you can't get anything done without joining [a coalition]." NAM lobbyists prefer to work in alliances for that same reason: "Association work is nothing more than coalition building," said one. While coalitions require a sacrifice of independence, they also increase the likelihood of success. Under certain conditions—when a group is trying to make a name for itself, for example—position taking may be more important than winning. But overall, *the probability of success* is a key consideration in selecting issues. Being associated with a losing cause damages the reputation of interest groups and the legislators who "carry water" for them. Even more costly is the opportunity foregone—the lost chance to use the group's resources and political capital for some other, more promising issue. Among other things, a reputation for success makes a group more attractive to potential members.

If a bill looks like a potential winner, another consideration to prospective coalition members is the *precedential or symbolic value of victory*. Some groups lobbied the airline bill particularly hard because success there would increase the chances for trucking reform. Ideological business groups like NFIB and NAM saw the trucking issue as symbolizing the still larger fight against unnecessary government interference.

For consumer lobbyists more than any others, trucking deregulation was the right issue at the right time. This reflects another factor important in selecting issues—how the choice will contribute to *the group's internal agenda*. After a decade as a growing political movement, consumerism lost favor in the late 1970s when its goals became linked in the public's eye with increased government spending and inflation. Business groups attacked the movement anew for being out of touch with reality and for favoring the same solution to every problem—more regulation. Despite President Carter's proconsumer stance, the movement's legislative agenda suffered major defeat in the Ninety-fifth Congress (dubbed "the corporate Congress" by Nader's Congress Watch).

Consumer leaders responded to this defeat pragmatically—with plans to "move away from that pure view of 'consumerism' as a group of isolated issues standing apart from other areas of concern" and begin to portray it as an integral part of the war on inflation and big government. As an item which consumer groups felt would "strike the anti-inflation chord," trucking deregulation, while not a new consumer issue by any means, took on new importance to the movement.[20]

While trucking deregulation was a good issue for groups to lobby for all of these reasons, it was not necessarily an automatic choice, given competing opportunities and the potential for beehives. Thus, for many groups, the decision to join the coalition reflected considerable *discretion on the part of staff members*. Some groups would not have gotten involved at all had individual lobbyists not found the issue important or interesting. Other groups would have participated in any event, but the level of participation was largely a matter of staff discretion.

In general, those organizations where lobbyists and other staff members had the most discretion in picking issues were the consumer groups. Such groups tend to be supported by foundations and direct-mail grants from contributors who do not seek to put much of a stamp on day-to-day activities. If the contributors don't like what the group is doing, eventually they vote with their checkbooks and stop contributing. Thus decision making is highly centralized. Even democratically organized Common Cause, which takes frequent polls of its members, had ample discretion under its broad mandate to pursue regulatory reform. (Consumers Union is an exception to this pattern of centralization. Because it is primarily a product-testing rather than an advocacy group, with virtually all of its funds coming from sales of its magazine, CU is more bureaucratic than most consumer groups.)

Groups with a strong ideological orientation were also characterized by considerable staff discretion in choosing issues—the ACU, NFIB, and, to a lesser extent, NAM. Highly centralized leadership is the rule among such groups. This accurately describes NFIB—whose periodic polls of members are permissive rather than directive—as well as the ACU. NAM is the exception to the rule in that it is controlled by a board of directors.

Most constrained were staff members in the Chamber of Commerce and the Business Roundtable—groups with a decision-making structure designed to ensure substantial member involvement and avoidance of issues that might cause internal conflict based on intrabusiness differences between members. Also constrained in the choice of issues were the representatives of groups that rely largely on individual benefits to attract members, since these groups are generally limited to issues in which their members have high stakes.[21]

(Staff discretion at the outset, in selecting issues to lobby, is not the same as staff discretion later on during the debate. A lobbyist may have a broad mandate to "get involved" with an issue, but later in the debate, he may have less freedom to take specific positions without consulting influential members of the group. The following section on the cartel problem discusses this further.)

Even more subject to staff discretion than the actual choice of issue is the amount of its resources—staff time, political chits, grass-roots capability—a group devotes to an issue. The lobbyist's interest in the issue is key here. "Some [lobbyists] were really turned on by the trucking issue," said one coalition leader to explain the varying levels of commitment. "Others viewed it as just another bill to lobby. Some work out of a bushel basket— agreeing to take on everything, but then picking out just what suits them when the time comes."

Coalition builders, who take the phenomenon of staff discretion for granted, use it strategically. The Common Cause representative, Ann McBride, was selected as the trucking coalition's vice-chairman ostensibly for ideological balance (the chairman represented business). But there was a hidden agenda—to increase McBride's personal commitment to the trucking issue and, in turn, the resource commitment of Common Cause. (Whatever the reason, McBride eventually became one of the most active members of the coalition.) Ironically, that was not a rationale for selecting Swain as chairman, but not surprisingly it had the same effect. Swain's prominent role in the coalition "raised the consciousness" of other NFIB staff members to the trucking issue, and the result was a massive lobbying effort by the business group.

Curb Service

A final incentive to join coalitions is the opportunity for groups to get individualized benefits from legislation that would not otherwise be available. Like the need for visibility and opportunities to take credit, this incentive serves to counter the free-rider problem because groups that desire such benefits don't have the luxury of hitchhiking. More accurately, they can get the same free ride as everyone else, but if they want individual stops along the way—curb service—they have to contribute.[22]

Curb service was a particularly strong incentive in the trucking battle, given the complexity of the bill and the diversity of the economic interests affected by truck transportation. International Paper Company lobbied actively for the deregulation bill in general, but particularly for a two-word addition to the provision exempting certain products from regulation— "wood chips." Flying Tiger airline, an all-cargo carrier, joined the ad hoc group as a way to secure two very narrow provisions of interest to virtually no one else in the coalition. A half dozen other air and motor carriers and carrier groups participated in the coalition as a way of getting specialized benefits.

Food and agricultural products were the focus of a number of groups that joined the coalition largely to seek specialized benefits. While the Farm Bureau's goal of exempting processed food from regulation was so generally important that consumer and business groups also made it a priority, other proposed agricultural provisions—for example, those affecting farm cooperatives—distributed benefits more narrowly. Food-manufacturing and food-distributing groups each used the trucking bill as a vehicle for seeking their own, conflicting provision with respect to zone-delivered pricing of groceries—an issue that was only indirectly related to trucking deregulation.[23]

Obstacles to Internal Compatibility: The Cartel Problem

Some groups have a reputation for getting 98 percent of what they want and then pulling out at the last minute to try and get the other 2 percent for themselves.
    —White House Representative

A cartel faces the constant danger that one member firm will take independent action—shading its prices to increase market share—which is contrary to the interest of the group as a whole. Political coalitions face a comparable problem. It goes by various names—single-shooting, breaking ranks, cutting one's own deal, selling out, caving in, or splintering—depending on who does it and why, but it's essentially the cartel problem.

For individual coalition members, the counterpart to increased market share is legislation favorable to the group's particular needs. Sometimes one coalition member supports a provision that another opposes. More often coalition members disagree as to how strong certain provisions should be and what weight to assign them.

The lowest common denominator for the trucking coalition was open entry. Virtually everyone in the alliance favored, or at least did not oppose, getting the most liberal entry provision possible. On the issue of rate bureaus, there was slightly less agreement: some groups sought complete elimination of antitrust immunity, others only elimination of immunity for single-line ratemaking. (One "shippers'" group had a peculiar reason, to be discussed later, for opposing any change in the rate bureaus' immune status, though it did favor other rate-bureau reforms.) The third key issue was rates: Coalition members disagreed over the amount of freedom carriers should have to raise and lower rates without being subject to ICC approval, and over proposals to tie this zone of rate freedom to some sort of price index. Finally, there were reforms that virtually everyone in the group agreed were desirable. Some of them (restriction removal and agricultural exemption) were important to nearly everyone; others (provisions dealing with private carriage, contract carriers, air cargo, and food cooperatives, for example) were critical to some coalition members and inconsequential to the rest.

In addition to disagreements about individual reforms, there were conflicts over their relative importance. Most groups regarded open entry as the single most important reform objective. A few coalition members placed elimination of collective ratemaking ahead of open entry. And others gave top priority to narrow provisions that affected them selectively.

Differences of Degree

The biggest inhibitor of disagreement over how strong to make certain provisions and what weight to assign them was the low level of information on Capitol Hill regarding trucking reform. When Frank Swain began chairing the coalition, the members were spending much of their time quibbling over minor organizational matters—what to call the group, whether to get a letterhead—and debating the intricacies of the rate, entry, and other provisions. His major task initially was to convince coalition members that if the group didn't get up to Capitol Hill and begin lobbying on the big issues, they would never have the luxury of worrying about the finer points of reform.

Once coalition members began visiting Hill offices, the point became clear. Few legislative staffers understood what open entry involved, much less the difference between single-line and joint-line immunity from anti-trust laws. For coalition members, it was a little like having argued over whether to have their chateaubriand-for-two cooked medium or rare only to find that the menu offered nothing but hamburgers.

Outside of the Senate Commerce and House Public Works committee staff offices, the level of information about trucking deregulation remained low, even as the legislative battle progressed. In their allotted ten- or fifteen-minute appointments with members of Congress or their aides, lobbyists could generally get across simpler points—on entry, and backhaul and commodity restrictions. But trying to explain the more technical issues of rate bureaus and pricing zones was, as one coalition member put it, like watching water roll off a duck's back.

The low level of information on specific issues is a fact of life on Capitol Hill. It reflects the excessive demands placed on the time and resources of staffers and members of Congress. A single representative is confronted with a great many issues, only a few of which are of real importance to his constituents; he can't possibly have more than a rudimentary understanding of most of them. The cardinal rule of lobbying is "K.I.S.S."—Keep It Simple, Stupid. The keep-it-simple rule applies to lobbyists' wish lists as well. "You have to limit what you ask of congressmen," commented one coalition member. "If you ask for more than A, B, and C, you're overloading the circuits."

Both out of a need to keep it simple and a recognition of their differences, coalition members lobbied for essentially two things: open entry and elimination of antitrust immunity for (single-line) ratemaking. With respect to those two issues, which most members agreed were the highest priorities, reform lobbyists spoke the same tongue.

A more ambitious agenda might have split the group. For example, when Representative Howard disingenuously proposed the possibility of total deregulation, coalition members were sharply divided over whether they could support a sunsetting of the ICC. (Alternatively, had they been forced to choose between open entry and elimination of antitrust immunity, members would have split somewhat.) But recognizing the need for simplicity, coalition members lobbied successfully for their lowest common denominator.

Single-Shooting

The need to keep it simple meant that the coalition could avoid public disagreements about relatively important concerns. But it also discouraged "single-shooting." Confronted with the low level of information on the trucking issue, coalition members with only very narrow interests in reform had little choice but to lobby the whole bill.

The Private Trucking Council is a case in point. The council is a trade association of companies that have gone into private carriage. (Some PTC members also belong to the Private Carrier Conference of the ATA, one of two ATA conferences that joined the reform coalition.) PTC members' interest in regulatory reform can be summed up in two words—*intercorporate hauling*. The 1935 Motor Carrier Act prohibited private carriers from transporting goods for other members of their corporate family—even wholly-owned subsidiaries. Private carriers had always viewed that prohibition as a nuisance and an obstacle to filling many empty backhauls, but not until oil prices soared did it become a priority corporate problem. Unsuccessful in getting relief from the ICC, the Private Truck Council decided legislation was the only answer.

Initially, the council hoped to get its reforms included in some noncontroversial piece of legislation, such as an energy consumption bill.

Richard Henderson, the council's director of operations, told his bosses the bad news: The only (legislative) way to remove the ban on intercorporate hauling was to amend the 1935 act. They concurred but warned him that he'd get caught up in the whole deregulation fray.

Henderson did his best not to. He attended coalition meetings but tried to lobby his narrow issue and no others, to the dismay of fellow coalition members, particularly Kennedy's aide, Jay Steptoe, who admonished Henderson for single-shooting. In addition to feeling peer pressure, Henderson met with a lot of blank stares on the Hill when he tried to explain how intercorporate hauling tied in with deregulation. So he became part of the team, lobbying the big issues—entry, rates, and rate bureaus—and only secondarily promoting his own concern.

The head of the Contract Carrier Conference of the ATA faced an even more difficult problem in joining the coalition. His members favored a few narrow and specific provisions in the bill, but they opposed others (primarily the expanded agricultural exemption). He walked a fine line with his members, eventually bringing them around to support a position of broader-based reform that he felt was necessary to be credible.[24]

Single-shooting is not a major threat to a coalition unless the marksman happens to be one of the strongmen in the group. There the danger is that the lone member will lead legislators to believe that other provisions are unimportant or will undermine a compromise that ignores his needs.

When the administration cut its deal with the Public Works Committee, the compromise did not include the hard-fought (in the Senate) exemption of processed food. The Farm Bureau accepted the deal reluctantly, but when Public Works announced that it could not fulfill another term of the compromise critical to farmers, the Farm Bureau felt it was free to seek to amend the compromise bill on the floor of the House. Other coalition members joined in the subsequent effort to add the food exemption to the House bill. The White House favored the exemption on the merits, but feared that if the amendment passed (it did not), the entire compromise would unravel.

Caving In

The last-ditch effort by the Farm Bureau to exempt food from regulation was less an example of single-shooting than an illustration of a bigger problem the trucking coalition faced—one that had to do with bottom lines and bearskins. The problem occurs even when coalition members can agree completely on what issues are important and what weights to assign them, but where they disagree as to what is (1) maximally attainable, and (2) minimally acceptable. The coalition's interest may suffer if one or more heavyweight members accepts too little or demands too much.

Representatives of the president—any president—are often viewed as "cavemen"—political agents who cave in too quickly in a tough legislative fight. That view reflects differences in motivation. A president's motives are electoral; to a greater extent than those of other participants, he wants the bearskin on the wall—the appearance of legislative victory as evidence that he is an effective leader. Demanding too much from one's opponents can jeopardize agreement on legislation. Interest-group representatives also need legislation in order to claim credit, but compared to voters, interest-group members are more apt to know a good bill from a bad one. So interest-group lobbyists are more likely than the president's agents to reject a proposed legislative compromise as worse than no bill at all.

Since the trucking bill came up in an election year, pushed by an unpopular president with few legislative victories he could point to, coalition members were particularly wary that the administration would sell short. Veterans of the 1979 railroad deregulation fight were the wariest of all, feeling that they had been burned once by the Carter White House in that experience.

The administration's senior point man on the trucking bill was Ronald Lewis, an articulate, soft-spoken attorney and deputy to Alfred Kahn, Carter's chief inflation fighter. Lewis began work on the trucking issue in the winter of 1979 and had as thorough an understanding of the substance of the issue as anyone in the administration. He was sensitive to the coalition's fear of cavemen, and at the group's weekly meetings, Lewis made it a point to stress the president's commitment to a strong bill. Sharing command with Lewis was Richard (Rick) Neustadt, a young lawyer and former political writer for CBS television. Neustadt was a member of the Domestic Policy Staff and reported directly to Stuart Eizenstat, Carter's chief domestic policy adviser.

A handful of administration representatives took part in the final negotiations on the trucking bill. But it was Lewis and Neustadt who ultimately said, "It's a deal." Whether they settled too soon—that is, whether they could have negotiated a more favorable compromise or, alternatively, done better by accepting a weak House bill and then fighting it out in the conference committee—will be long debated by those who fought in and followed the trucking battle (and further discussed in chapter 7). Some coalition members say not. Others feel the White House did compromise prematurely (at a celebration following the bill-signing ceremony, the coalition awarded Lewis a "moveable bottom line"), though their major objection was to the fact that the White House cut the final deal without consulting coalition members and presented it to them as a fait accompli.

Comments at the coalition meeting following the Public Works Committee approval of the compromise indicate the divided mood of the group:

> Swain: *Many of us were involved in the discussions with Public Works. At some point, it got away from us. We're not sure why. The White House people decided the votes just weren't there [in committee]. Rather than going ahead with the fight, getting a bad bill out of committee and trying to win in conference, the decision was made to negotiate the bill through ahead of time. It was a political decision. We've all spent lots of time trying to determine whether it was the right one. . . . Some of us [in the coalition] think it's a pretty good bill. Others of us think it's pretty bad. Still others—NFIB included here—don't know, but feel it's lukewarm at best.*
>
> DOT rep.: *Just remember what those vote counts [in Public Works] looked like two weeks ago. Keep that firmly in mind.*

Once the deal was made, the administration was very eager to have it ratified, first in committee markup and then by the full House. The longer it took to schedule the House vote, the more likely it was that certain coalition members would decide that specific provisions of the compromise were unacceptable. "The grapes were bitter anyway," said one coalition leader. The floor vote was delayed long enough for the Farm Bureau to organize its effort to reinstate the agricultural exemption, but there were no other serious challenges to the compromise itself. There, as elsewhere in the trucking battle, the extraordinary speed with which the issue moved served to inhibit dissension and splintering.

Walking Out

Bottom lines can slice two ways. If a coalition member demands too much of opponents, it can also undermine the group interest. Making strong demands isn't itself a problem. The damage comes when a coalition member whose price isn't met pulls out and abandons the bill or endeavors to defeat it.

The coalition member with the most demanding bottom line was the National Association of Manufacturers. The most dramatic illustration of that came less than a week before the Senate floor vote, when NAM's two representatives on the coalition announced to the assembled group that they were going to advise NAM to oppose the Cannon bill. The two spokesmen—James Carty, a veteran of the airline-deregulation fight, and Robert

Ragland, a third-year law student—said they felt their organization had made too many concessions in accepting the bill that came out of the Senate markup. While most reform advocates felt the markup was a major victory, one amendment—which indexed carriers' pricing freedom so as to take account of inflation—was particularly bothersome to NAM members and other shippers. The final straw for the manufacturing group was the just-released Commerce Committee report, which contained some surprise language that NAM found unacceptable. Carty and Ragland said that Cannon had tipped his hand with the language in the report and could no longer be trusted. They maintained that their organization would be better off having no bill and letting the ICC continue to deregulate on its own.

On the surface, the dramatic announcement stemmed from factual disagreements. ICC and DOT representatives at the meeting maintained that the objectionable amendment and report language would have a benign effect given the ICC's power to control anticompetitive rates. Carty and Ragland disagreed on the basis of calculations supplied by member companies on NAM's task force on trucking deregulation—companies from whom the two NAM representatives were no doubt feeling pressure to correct the situation.

Behind the appearance of factual disagreements, ideological differences were at work. NAM, more than almost any other member of the coalition, attached symbolic importance to having free entry and competitively set rates in the trucking industry. Said Ragland to the coalition:

> The bottom line for the manufacturing community is that we have an obligation to assure competitive prices. If they're 100 percent higher, okay, so long as they're set competitively. The [amendment added in markup] took away from that. The [language in the committee report] took away from that. God knows what else will take away from it. We're not going to be betrayed.

As a group for whom ideological appeals are the primary draw, NAM had to take a strong position in order to satisfy its membership.

Had NAM been cooperating with a Republican administration, betrayal wouldn't have been a major fear. But the GOP-oriented group was deeply suspicious—far more than most other groups in the coalition—that it would be sold out by the Carter White House. That ideological distrust contributed to what was perhaps the major explanation of NAM's threat to walk out: bruised organizational egos—a feeling that the White House and the coalition had not paid enough attention to the powerful manufacturing association. "When you represent 75 percent of the manufacturing community," observed one coalition leader about NAM, "there are some fragile egos. Occasionally you need to see everyone running around fawning over you."

Insofar as Carty and Ragland were sincere in their intention to withdraw NAM's support for the Cannon bill, it was a self-defeating strategy from an economic standpoint. They were willing to rely on the ICC to deregulate without legislation—and this was now their preferred alternative—yet they were unwilling to trust the ICC to resolve the particular problem created by the amendment and report language, seemingly a far simpler task. Moreover, by withdrawing its support, NAM would not be increasing the chance of getting *no* legislation, since the ATA wanted *some* bill as much as the deregulators. Rather, the more likely outcome would be a bill favorable to the industry, which would undo much of what the ICC had already accomplished.

Economics aside, NAM's behavior made sense from an organizational point of view. "Nothing looks better to a group like the NAM task force than to see the executive branch quaking with fear [over your threat to walk out]," said the coalition leader. "You really feel like you're getting your dues worth then."

In an effort to nurse NAM's bruised ego, coalition leaders were sympathetic, and offers were quickly made to have the ICC chairman and high-level administration officials contact NAM and discuss the problem. Most important to resolving the conflict, the White House promised to try to "fix" the indexing problem in the House bill. Ragland still advised NAM's trucking task force to oppose the bill, but members overruled him in deference to the White House. (The administration was not able to fix the indexing problem in the compromise with Public Works. NAM again threatened to oppose the bill, though it conceded that its opposition would have little effect at that late stage. Ultimately, Carty and Ragland came up with a noncontroversial amendment that they maintained made the indexing provision at least tolerable.)

Under other circumstances, NAM's threat to walk out would have been much more serious. Had the coalition been a formally organized group, as it was in the case of airline deregulation, splintering of any kind would have been extremely damaging. It was a conscious decision by the trucking group to remain informal, and it unquestionably proved to be the right one.

The advantage of organizing formally is that a coalition can speak with a single voice. That's significant, because it establishes the group as a special player and guarantees that it will be listened to. The disadvantage is that because it speaks with a single voice, an official coalition must be highly unified. Disagreements that an informal alliance can agree to live with are sufficient to lead groups to secede—or avoid joining in the first place—when the alliance is formal.

The risk of schism in a formal coalition is compounded by outsiders' expectations. A formally organized alliance is expected to be monolithic. The focus of interest—particularly in the trade press—shifts from substantive issues to internal politics: Can the group hold itself together? When a headline reads, "NAM Breaks from Coalition over Rate Issue," the alliance must spend undue effort bringing the group back on board, largely for the sake of appearances.

By remaining a "free-floating coffee klatch," as one coalition leader described it, the ad hoc group faced less external scrutiny. The general perception in Washington was that coalition members all signed off on the compromise with Public Works. In fact, some did not, including the Farm Bureau, several consumer groups, and owner-operators. But that lack of unanimity escaped notice because of the informal nature of the coalition.

Sideline Conflicts of Interest

Had the coalition been formally organized, the appearance of unity would also have been threatened by two direct conflicts that were actually tangential to the deregulation debate. One of the conflicts pitted two food giants—the Grocery Manufacturers Association and the Food Marketing Institute—against one another over a proposal to allow food stores to pick up their own groceries so as to receive a discount off the zone-delivered price. The administration sided with FMI (in favor of the proposal), in part because of a political judgment that FMI's active support of trucking deregulation, the unstated quid pro quo for administration backing, would be more valuable than GMA support.

The other issue that split the coalition was "lumping"—referring to the problem owner-operators in particular have had with being coerced into paying "lumpers" to load and unload their trucks. This issue put the Farm Bureau and owner-operators at odds with FMI and others.

Both conflicts were major battles in their own right. The food industry skirmish brought out a vast amount of power and pelf, including Sen. Russell Long as a champion for the distributors (FMI) and former DOT secretary Brock Adams as a lobbyist for the manufacturers. The lumping controversy required nearly as many hours of closeted negotiations as did all other provisions of the trucking bill put together. But neither issue was central to the rest of the bill (opponents of the "Long amendment" on food tried to delete it as nongermane), and neither sideline skirmish threatened the basic unity of the coalition.

Ideological Balance

"I hear you've got a new symbol," joked the farm lobbyist to the ACU representative, "an eagle with no left wing!" In jest, ACU staffers referred to Common Cause as "Communist Cause." Ideological differences are good for a laugh in political circles, but they're also serious business when the aim is to unify groups as ideologically diverse as those in the trucking coalition.

Conservatives can be knee-jerk skeptics about any cause that has liberal backing, even one as promarket as trucking deregulation. The ACU could not get any of its traditional spokesmen to introduce the group's deregulation bill in 1979, so closely linked was the issue then with Ted Kennedy. Similarly, many conservative congressmen voted against the amendment to deregulate processed food, even though it had strong ACU endorsement. Because the provision was sponsored by New Jersey congresswoman Millicent Fenwick, some House conservatives suspected it was "another liberal scheme."

The ideological clashes so common in Congress did not have their counterpart in the trucking coalition. Aside from NAM's threatened walkout, there was almost no ideology-based friction within the group. Neither the ACU nor the Congress Watch lobbyist, representing the two ideological poles, felt the balance was at all fragile.

In part, the issue lent itself to compatibility among supporters. The most common basis for liberal-conservative conflict is the question of what the federal government's role in a policy area should be. Everyone in the trucking coalition agreed that the answer to that question was "less" rather than "more." Finer discriminations that might have split the coalition never had to be made.

Other things that could have caused friction didn't. Money is one. An early ACU memo discussed the potential for generous business-group support of the (still unformed) coalition but warned that funding should be "handled carefully [because] it would be a sensitive point with several potential liberal members. . . ." That turned out not to be a problem, and consumer groups enjoyed the luxury of access to good Xeroxing facilities and other physical resources provided readily by corporate members of the coalition.

Coalition leadership was another potential problem that never materialized. Frank Swain was interviewed for the chairman's position by an informal nominating committee of coalition members representing Common Cause, Congress Watch, and the ACU. The ACU lobbyist, anticipating that "the liberals" would be reluctant to support a representative of business—even small business—was prepared to "hold solid for Frank." But Swain impressed the group personally so much that his affiliation wasn't an issue.

When the coalition hired Con Hitchcock as its coordinator, Swain wrote a memo to the members at large announcing the action. Swain omitted any mention of Hitchcock's Nader affiliation so as not to give the business and conservative members reason for doubt. They soon learned of his ties to Nader, but by then they appreciated his value to the coalition.

No single group tried to take control of the coalition, which did away with another potential source of friction. The power was shared fairly equally among NFIB, NAM, the Farm Bureau, Common Cause, Congress Watch, and Consumers Union.

Ideological inflexibility was another thing absent from the coalition. The member lobbyists were professionals—politically pragmatic despite strongly held personal beliefs. At one meeting, as coalition members were discussing how to approach various committee members, the name of a particularly conservative congressman was mentioned. A Nader lobbyist who had already been to see the congressman said with a smile, "Just say [to him], 'Less government regulation.' I almost gagged [on the words]!"

Finally, there was a remarkable absence of personal conflict among coalition members—over ideology, or anything else for that matter. One member contrasted it with other ad hoc groups she'd participated in: "With the trucking coalition, there was some good mix there that worked; there was genuine affection. That was an intangible glue." The shared sense (accurate or not) of being underdogs created a bond, strengthened by what one coalition member termed the ATA's "stand in the schoolhouse door" approach to regulatory reform. That, the brute lobbying force displayed by the industry and the Teamsters, the sympathy-evoking image of owner-operators getting the crumbs left by the regulated carriers, the stacks of economic studies supporting deregulation—all of this combined to make the trucking fight seem like an old-fashioned battle between good and evil, white hats and black hats. Every coalition needs a villain.

It's probably true that two Washington lobbyists—one from Congress Watch, the other from the ACU—have more in common than the ACU lobbyist does with a card-carrying member of his group who sits on the Chamber of Commerce in Akron, Ohio. In that sense, perhaps it's not surprising that there would be such personal compatibility between coalition lobbyists, many of whom were lawyers, under age forty, with previous experience working on Capitol Hill. Still, that compatibility came as a surprise to many of the lobbyists themselves (even more so in the airline-reform coalition, since it was a novelty there), who were used to thinking of one another as permanent foes. "The whole adversarial nature of lobbying is such," said one coalition member, "that when you can work with your usual enemy, it's especially satisfying and memorable."

In part because of the novelty of working with people against whom they previously had fought hammer and tong, coalition members enjoyed the trucking battle more than most fights. "A lot of people really had fun lobbying the trucking bill," noted one coalition member who recalled how nostalgia set in as soon as a bill was imminent: "As someone said, the final coalition meeting was like the last day of high school!"

Who Speaks for Whom?

The "green-eyeshade" era is over.
—Roland Ouellette, General Motors

There is a working assumption on Capitol Hill that groups speak accurately for the people they purport to represent. There is a tendency, moreover, for Congress to view broad interests—business, labor, agriculture—as being more internally homogeneous than they actually are. These are simplifying devices, necessary for coping with the mountain of complex issues and bills that confronts Congress each session. But they can make life for a coalition more complicated.

The National Industrial Traffic League claims to be the oldest and largest nationwide association of shippers and receivers. So when the NIT League spoke out against any elimination of antitrust immunity for rate bureaus, many people assumed that shippers favored the status quo. (The league did favor open entry and procedural rate-bureau reforms.)

To understand why the NIT League's position was so far apart from that of other shipper groups, one must examine it through a green eye-shade. Transportation issues rarely reach the corporate boardroom. So the league's voice was not the voice of the corporate executive: it was primarily the voice of the traffic manager—the green-eyeshaded clerk responsible for the day-to-day logistics of transportation pickup and delivery.

Traffic managers faced altogether different incentives than corporate executives. First, they had spent years mastering the regulated system—no small task given that there were over a trillion rates on file at the ICC. They feared precisely the scenario envisioned by the director of transportation affairs at General Motors when asked about the impact of deregulation: "The most important result will be a small margin of error for transportation managers, who will have to be highly skilled and professional. The 'green-eyeshade' era is over. Exit the rate clerk—enter the transportation professional."[25]

Second, traffic managers were less interested in cutting absolute shipping costs than they were in assuring that their counterpart at a competing firm didn't get a comparatively better price. The regulated system was ideal, then, because it assured them rates that were predictable, stable, and "nondiscriminatory." Under regulation, traffic managers were price takers. Deregulation would force them to become price seekers, a much tougher job.

Third, traffic personnel had been the target of massive lobbying by the regulated transportation industries. Kennedy's hearings on rate bureaus included testimony drawn from ICC audits showing that millions of dollars a year in gratuities went to traffic managers of shipping companies (as well as to ICC and DOT officials).

The "traffic-manager phenomenon" created much confusion and misunderstanding on Capitol Hill, especially early in the trucking fight, when many shippers who favored deregulation declined to speak out and risk antagonizing their regulated carriers. It would have taken but a few minutes to explain away that confusion. But when a lobbyist had just that much time to brief a busy member of Congress on the entire deregulation issue, "the green-eyeshade story" rarely got told. As one Commerce Committee staffer said, "We just told [senators] that some shippers favor reform and some oppose it, and we left it at that."

The traffic manager–ATA connection was largely responsible for another shipper voice speaking out for collective ratemaking. In early 1980, General Motors, Firestone, and five other companies formed the Committee of Truck Shippers (COTS). COTS presented itself as the voice of large shippers who were heavily dependent on regulated common carriage, and testified in favor of continued antitrust immunity for collective ratemaking. A *Wall Street Journal* article drew considerable attention to the group, prompting NAM representatives as well as individual corporate shippers to reiterate their commitment to deregulation in a Washington, D.C., press conference.

The coalition referred to COTS as the Committee of Truck *Suppliers* and tried to discredit its position on that basis. GM is a major truck manufacturer, and five of the other six COTS members were GM suppliers. Deregulation should lead to more efficient use of existing truck capacity, and hence less demand for additional trucks.[26] Thus, a supplier qua supplier might well oppose deregulation.

The ATA sought to use its influence as an important customer to get GM to oppose deregulation. But contrary to what most people felt, that pressure was applied not to GM's sales division (GM the truck supplier) but rather to GM's traffic and logistics division (GM the shipper).[27] GM in turn pressured its suppliers to do the same. Most did because, as a representative of Pittsburgh Plate Glass put it, "When GM sneezes, we get a cold."

A company like General Motors was understandably wary of big changes in the transportation system it had grown up with. (GM spent nearly a billion dollars a year on common-carrier trucking and railroad services in 1980. According to a NAM lobbyist, that transportation demand is so time-sensitive that a strike by a railroad in one state led to GM layoffs in another state that same day.) But GM's action represented the traffic-manager problem writ large—the problem of policy decisions getting made by individuals whose incentive was to reduce risk rather than maximize profit.

COTS disappeared from the scene almost as quickly as it had appeared. The publicity the group received scared away several potential members. And GM backed off of its pro-rate bureau stance, seemingly in response to pressure from the administration. Sen. Donald Riegel of Michigan voted the "right way" in the Commerce Committee markup; deregulators, who felt his vote could tip the balance, had feared that he would heed the adage, "What's bad for GM. . . ." All in all, little damage was done.

In addition to the shipper, the other coalition member who heard another voice claiming to speak for him in opposition to reform was the owner-operator. Actually, many voices claimed to speak for owner-operators—one reason that those members of this group who favored deregulation fared no better than they did.*

Owner-operators fell into two camps on the question of deregulation. Favoring reform were the exempt haulers—owner-operators who primarily carried unregulated agricultural commodities. They sought two key provisions—a broadened agricultural exemption and authority to carry regulated goods on the return leg (backhaul) of an exempt haul. The name most often associated with this group was Mike Parkhurst, the colorful Los Angeles–based editor of *Overdrive* magazine who dramatized the plight of the independent trucker—an individual "forced to sit in the back of the financial bus" and settle for "crumbs from the table set for the regulated carriers," while rate bureaus operate as "price-fixing pimps" for the large carriers.

---

*At one congressional hearing, the last speaker on a panel of owner-operators was Karl Murphey, a plain-speaking man who represented the Washington State independent truckers. Senator Cannon asked Murphey what he could add to what had been said by the other owner-operators who preceded him. According to several lobbyists who were there, Sen. John Warner of Virginia had left the room just minutes before Murphey, apparently unaware of Warner's notoriety-by-marriage, responded roughly as follows: "Senator Cannon, I feel a little like Elizabeth Taylor's fifth husband. I know what I'm supposed to do, but I don't know how to make it very interesting."

Opposing deregulation were the independents who operated on a permanent lease basis to ICC-certified carriers—primarily to haul (processed food and other) regulated agricultural goods. They particularly opposed any deregulation of food, since that would cut into their lease market. (They did support a limited backhaul provision.)

Many advocates of deregulation shook their heads in exasperation at this second group of independent truckers, feeling that they were misguided in supporting a system that kept them in bondage. This underestimated them. Leased owner-operators behaved essentially like Teamsters. Their approach was to seek a share of the industry's monopoly profits in the form of higher wages. Lacking organization, they had been less successful than the Teamsters, but they were not misguided.

Lack of organization is the owner-operator's critical problem. He is, by definition, independent. No one could have reconciled the two disparate positions these truckers took on deregulation; advocates of each were acting in their own best interest. The fact that they all called themselves owner-operators only served to confuse. But organization was absent even among those owner-operators who supported reform. They were effectively absent from the coalition, and thus largely ineffective.

The ATA as a Coalition

[If] we don't all hang together on this deregulation threat we will surely hang separately.
—ATA Board Chairman, 1976

Soon after Congress passed the airline deregulation bill, a Delta Airlines vice-chairman spoke to the annual meeting of the ATA and offered some hard-earned advice:

> I would urge you as strongly as I can . . . to agree on common principles with respect to [deregulation] within your industry. We were splintered. Our trade association was absolutely unable to be effective on Capitol Hill. . . . And as a result, we went down to a resounding legislative defeat.[28]

For the truckers, the danger was not so much that major carriers would break ranks as did United Airlines, the largest air carrier, when it came out in support of deregulation. United had been held back by regulation precisely because it was so large; the CAB awarded new routes using a handicapping system which favored smaller, less profitable airlines. By contrast, in the regulated trucking industry, the large carriers had been well served by ICC controls.

Roadway Express, with annual revenues of a billion dollars the largest general freight carrier in 1980, testified that it could survive in a deregulated world. And after the Senate vote, when the situation looked most bleak for the industry, some of the giant carriers—Roadway, Consolidated Freightway, Yellow Freight—made sounds about preferring total deregulation to some middle ground between that and regulation. But when push came to shove, and they had the opportunity to support sunsetting of the ICC, they voted thumbs down.[29]

For the ATA, avoiding splintering—and the resulting fate of the airline industry—meant maintaining unity among the national conferences that comprise the industry group. In 1980 there were thirteen of them, each organized around a specific branch of the trucking industry. Every conference has its own officers and staff and is financed exclusively by its own members.

The Regular (Route) Common Carrier Conference (RCCC) is the heavyweight of the group. RCCC members—the predominantly less-than-truckload general-freight carriers like Roadway and Yellow Freight—contribute the lion's share of ATA dues and dominate ATA policymaking bodies. A distant second in terms of influence in 1980 was the Irregular Route Common Carrier Conference, representing the typically smaller firms that hauled specialized goods—primarily regulated food—in truckload lots (the IRCCC has since merged with the Contract Carrier Conference). Other ATA conferences represent carriers specializing in shipments ranging from munitions to household goods to motion picture film.

The "bastard child" of the ATA is the Private Carrier Conference, representing nontransportation firms that do their own (private) hauling. Historically, a shipper resorted to private carriage only when it was dissatisfied with the regulated service available; hence there was a basic incompatibility between private and regulated carriers, and the PCC was (and is) more a shipper group than a trucker group. Despite this, private carriers were brought into the ATA many years ago so that the trade group could say it spoke for the entire industry.

When the Ford administration's trucking bill came out with a provision authorizing intercorporate hauling for hire, a reform long sought by the PCC, transportation trade journals began writing of the imminent crack in the ATA's theretofore solid front. ATA officials made emotional pleas to resist the divide-and-conquer strategies of deregulation advocates: "This bill was dangerously constructed ... purposely done ... to divide the industry and defuse our opposition. We need to reject all of it. We need to stand together in total opposition. There are 16,000 motor carriers under ICC regulation. If we present a united front, our position cannot go ignored."[30]

The ATA's then-chairman of the board went still further—suggesting that deregulation was just a ploy to accomplish something even more sinister: "We cannot help but wonder if nationalization is not the only goal of those in favor of deregulation. Is this what the bureaucrats in DOT are really after? To the bureaucratic mind nationalization of transportation has a definite appeal."[31]

Appealing to private carriers on the grounds that their threatened defection in pursuit of self-interest would weaken the ATA's united front against deregulation seems a remarkably brash approach. Continued regulation was certainly not to their benefit; private carriers were engaged in transportation, after all, only because the regulated system served them poorly. Yet it was an approach that had considerable success. The PCC's longtime director was extremely loyal to the ATA; many of the conference members also felt a strong bond to the industry group. Don't-rock-the-boat sentiment ran strong.

Two years later, the ATA worked out a compromise with the PCC. The agreement allowed for compensated intercorporate hauling for wholly owned subsidiaries—a "100 percent rule." That failed to satisfy the independent Private Truck Council, and it continued to seek from the ICC and Congress a 50 percent rule. But the 100 percent rule, which was later codified in the 1980 act, actually solved much of the private carriers' problem, since two-thirds of all opportunities for intercorporate hauling involve wholly owned subsidiaries.

A second issue came along to divide the private and regulated carriers anew. Historically, the ICC barred private carriers from serving other shippers for hire on their otherwise empty backhauls. In 1978, the ICC reversed that policy in its landmark decision, *Toto Purchasing and Supply Company, Inc.* The ATA and Teamsters joined in a major effort to overturn *Toto* both in the federal courts and through legislation.

Partly in hopes of codifying the *Toto* decision, the PCC joined the reform coalition. The private carrier group also sought to codify the 1978 ATA-PCC compromise on intercorporate hauling, which the ICC had yet to act on, in part because of contradictory ATA statements in legal proceedings. The PCC was represented on the coalition by a gracious but aggressive outside attorney, William Borghesani.[32] But Borghesani kept a low profile in the ad hoc group, in keeping with the PCC's still strong bond to the ATA. As one ATA conference director said, "The private carriers never really left the reservation."

The ATA group that did up and leave the reservation was the Contract Carrier Conference. It was inevitable. Contract carriers, truckers who "dedicate" their operation to particular shippers, compete directly with common carriers. Like private carriage, contract carriage offers an alternative for shippers whose needs aren't met by common carriers. Furniture manufacturers, for example, rely heavily on contract service. Furniture is bulky but light; it "cubes out before it weighs out," making it undesirable as common-carrier freight.

ICC regulation served to keep contract carriers from their market in several ways. Most significant, it limited the number of shippers they could serve—through the "Rule of Eight"—and barred them from serving certain types of shippers. Operating authority was difficult to get, and contract carriers were forced to file repeated applications with the ICC to get broad enough commodity and geographic authority to service their shipper-customers fully.

Contract carriers first toyed with the idea of supporting regulatory reform in 1975. The Ford administration bill, introduced that year, contained provisions attractive to contract carriers, but the CCC made no overt move toward the side of reform. That would change upon the arrival of a new managing director, Thomas Callaghan, in late 1976. Callaghan, a young attorney with a Boston accent and a strong Irish wit, began raising eyebrows as soon as he hung a Manet nude on the wall of the conference office.

Callaghan felt that the CCC needed an easy-to-understand issue with which to rally its members and justify its existence. Regulatory reform "was exactly what the conference and its members needed," said Callaghan. "We could argue that it was unfair to limit the number of customers contract carriers could serve and thereby punish them for their success. The issue was appealing to the membership and an easy story to tell to the outside world."[33]

There was some effort toward compromise. At the suggestion of the ATA's policy committee on regulatory reform, the CCC began presenting its case to the other twelve conferences in hopes of gaining inside support. Midway through that process, ATA president Bennett Whitlock put the issue of redefining contract carriage to a vote before the ATA's executive committee where it was summarily rejected. "Bennett Whitlock short-circuited the process," said Callaghan. "He didn't like the idea of another personality taking a high profile within the family."

Whatever Whitlock's motivation, CCC members felt that they were clearly on their own. They in turn became more aggressive, and Callaghan felt the time was right to establish "the Kennedy connection"—an offer of some regulated industry support for Kennedy's still early campaign for trucking deregulation. "Our members are conservative businessmen," said Callaghan. "Normally they never would have established a political connection with Teddy Kennedy, but they were peeved and feeling feisty."

Callaghan wrote a long letter to Kennedy, who was then holding hearings on antitrust immunity for rate bureaus, suggesting that ICC regulation of contract carriers had antitrust implications. Kennedy's people welcomed the CCC with open arms. Callaghan testified at the rate-bureau hearings and later appeared at the much publicized press conference at which Kennedy announced his intent to introduce a bill repealing antitrust immunity for the motor carrier industry.[34] (That appearance prompted Whitlock and others to try, unsuccessfully, to oust Callaghan.)

When the ATA drafted its own bill, the common-carrier interests partially accommodated the CCC by including language that would eliminate the "Rule of Eight." That, by itself, was not sufficient to bring the CCC back into the fold, however, and contract carriers teamed up with the ad hoc coalition.

Other rifts within the ATA were successfully healed internally. In 1976, the Local and Short Haul Carriers Conference threatened to break with the ATA and support deregulation, when the conference's effort to get ATA backing in a fight with the ICC was blocked by the common carriers. Whitlock interceded and got the ATA's board of directors to vote its support of the conference. The conference was appreciative but cocky. "I am pleased that we have ATA's support. . . ," said a spokesman. "If ATA is to win their battle, they will need short-haul carriers."[35]

From the standpoint of sheer firepower, the ATA probably didn't much need the short-haul carriers or any other of its small conferences so long as it had common-carrier support. Moving the contract carriers and private carriers from one side of the chessboard to the other had an insignificant effect on the balance of power. But the ATA had always prided itself in speaking for the industry with a unified voice. It was an irritant to the giant association to testify as *the* voice of the regulated trucking industry, only to be followed on the program by the pipsqueak contract-carrier conference singing a different tune. And it prompted Congress to revise slightly its image of the ATA as a monolithic power opposing reform.[36]

With respect to its major conferences, the ATA remained relatively monolithic to the end, but not without sacrifice. The various conferences had little direct conflict of interest, but they had priorities so different as to create almost the same dilemma.

What separated the conferences was the importance of preserving entry controls versus antitrust immunity. The less-than-truckload common carriers, represented by the powerful RCCC, set most of their rates collectively; thus antitrust immunity was of great importance. Entry controls were less important, because LTL transport requires large terminal facilities where small shipments can be consolidated and distributed; the cost of these facilities creates a natural barrier to entry. For other carriers, the priorities were reversed. Some didn't even belong to rate bureaus, but they were extremely vulnerable to the effect of a liberal ICC policy on entry.

The ATA gave up early in the fight on preserving strict entry controls and made collective ratemaking its top priority. In part, that choice reflected the political power of the large common carriers within the ATA. In addition to these carriers, who were dependent on collective ratemaking, the rate bureaus were themselves a potent force within the industry group. There are a great many rate-bureau employees in the trucking industry; like traffic managers, they feared that deregulation would make their specialized skills obsolete. These employees were a strong voice within the ATA when it came to setting the industry's lobbying priorities; there was no comparable constituency concerned about the issue of entry.

Internal politics aside, the industry's lobbying priorities reflected the ATA's assessment of what was realistic. ICC reforms had already removed the major controls on entry. The industry trade group felt it couldn't turn back the clock.

Whatever the rationale for deemphasizing the preservation of entry controls, the choice caused considerable conflict within the ATA. The conferences representing tank truckers and local and short-haul carriers were upset from the start. When the ATA drafted its own bill in an effort to appease critics, industry insiders privately conceded that the reforms called for were purely cosmetic. But the tank-trucker conference said the bill was a sellout and threatened to bolt. A year later the director of that conference teased deregulators, saying he'd break with the ATA if the reform side could come up with a way "to keep the riff-raff out."[37]

The irregular-route common carriers became upset by later events. The irregular-route carriers were concerned about entry regulation insofar as it limited competition for their mainstay—the hauling of regulated agricultural products. When the Senate voted to exempt processed food from regulation, that provision hit the irregular-route conference so directly and so hard that it severely threatened the ATA's united front. The conference threatened to break away, and it did go so far as to hire its own lobbyist—a former congressman—to help delete the provision on the House side. Ultimately, the ATA had to give up on trying to preserve collective ratemaking in order to reinstate the agriculture exemption and keep the irregular-route conference from breaking ranks. That important tradeoff (described in more detail in chapter 7) was the heart of the final compromise between deregulators and the ATA. Unity was maintained within the ATA, but at considerable cost to general-freight carriers.

The ATA-Teamster alliance suffered from the same conflict over the importance of entry versus collective ratemaking. To Teamsters, entry regulation was the highest priority. Open entry directly threatened jobs and indirectly threatened an end to above-market wage rates. The Teamsters faulted the ATA for not recognizing the importance of preserving entry controls to its own self-interest.[38]

The ATA and the Teamsters operated less as a coalition than as a de facto alliance. Their differences—historical animosity, conflicting priorities with respect to deregulation—were too great. In addition, the ATA risked jeopardizing its image by closely associating with the Teamsters, who were poorly regarded by many in Congress. As it was, many people viewed the unlikely pair of lobby groups as an unholy alliance. For the Teamsters, however, the lack of a cooperative agreement was damaging. When the ATA cut its deal with deregulators, the union was left out in the cold.

Do Groups Represent the Interests of Their Members?

If I wanted to know what the position of [an interest group] was I would be inclined to listen to the people who speak for them, and if they do not speak for them . . . they will not hold those positions very long.
—Sen. Robert Packwood, April 15, 1980

The traditional, pluralist view of interest groups was that members joined and quit on the basis of their agreement with an organization's political goals and activities. Therefore, the group's goals and behavior were presumed to reflect the members' preferences.

Mancur Olson implicitly disputed that long-standing view with his important work on "the logic of collective action." If, as Olson posited, "the membership and power of large pressure-group organizations does not derive from their lobbying achievements, but is rather a by-product of their other activities"—chiefly the provision of individual material benefits— then one cannot assume that the group's political activities will reflect the preferences of the members.

As other students of interest groups have shown (and as earlier pages of this chapter suggest), Olson's by-product theory does not explain the power of established ideological groups like NAM and NFIB nor of the relatively new wave of public-interest groups. Selective material inducements are not unimportant, but the primary incentive these organizations provide has to do with the group's involvement in attaining broad political goals that are consistent with members' private interest or their private conception of the public interest.[39]

Even among groups that offer primarily political incentives, however, lobbying activities do not necessarily reflect the preferences of the members on every issue. The centralized decision-making structure that characterizes ideological and public-interest groups allows for considerable staff discretion.

The type and extent of discretion that an organization's leadership and staff members have depends on the structure and purpose of the group.

James Q. Wilson has observed that executives of ideological groups, with their centralized policymaking structure, have both more and less freedom of political action than executives of more participatory organizations: ". . . more in the sense that policies need not be compromised to fit a wide range of diverse interests, less in that the ideologically motivated inner circle will not often countenance any softening of language to make policies more palatable to those in government or elsewhere whose actions and approval are being solicited."[40]

Expanding on Wilson's analysis, one can divide political organizations into four rough categories to indicate a high or low degree of staff discretion in (1) picking issues to lobby and (2) taking specific positions and agreeing to compromises in the course of lobbying the issue (see fig. 5.1).

Type A organizations are best illustrated by consumer and other public-interest groups: Their centralized control allows for discretion in selecting issues. And the absence of a strongly ideological inner circle in such groups means that staff members have more freedom than in purposive organizations like ACU or NAM—type B groups—to agree to a softening of legislation language and other politically expedient changes. Type C groups tend to be ones that exist primarily to provide individual material benefits to their members. These organizations, such as the Farm Bureau, are limited by scarce resources to supporting issues that have a reasonably direct bearing on their members, but the members exercise little control over how the staff executes that support. Type D groups are those whose primary incentive is the promise of shared economic benefits from political action—typically trade groups in industries small enough that the free-rider problem isn't an obstacle to organizing members. Staff members in these groups follow a lobbying agenda limited primarily to securing and preserv-

Discretion in Choosing Issues to Lobby

		High	**Low**
	High	A	C
Discretion in Taking Specific Issue Positions	**Low**	B	D

Figure 5.1.   Staff discretion in lobbying

ing the benefits around which members are organized; moreover, staff members' freedom of action to take specific positions or agree to compromises is limited by the fact that group members have a strong economic interest in the outcome.

Because staff discretion is known to characterize many political groups, lobbyists employ certain techniques in part to avoid being challenged as unrepresentative of their members. NFIB feels that the use of internal polls gives it an edge on groups without evidence as to their members' preferences. Lobbyists commonly take local-group members with them when they visit Capitol Hill offices.

No amount of evidence as to member preferences will prevent certain challenges to a group's credibility. On the Senate floor, Ernest Hollings tried to discredit the NFIB poll of its members by implying that the questionnaire was loaded. (NFIB's poll offered pro and con arguments for trucking deregulation. Hollings read only the "pro" statements and failed to mention that they were so labeled and accompanied by "con" statements.) However, as Packwood's response to Hollings's ploy illustrates, the assumption that groups know what's best for their members dies hard:

> The last refuge . . . of the argument of [Senator Hollings] is that the National Federation of Independent Business does not know what it is talking about. . . .
>
> I am not going to look behind how the National Federation of Independent Business came to its conclusion. It has over 600,000 members. It has a permanent full-time paid, and I find qualified, staff here. . . .
>
> If [Senator Hollings] wants to say they do not know what they are talking about, they do not understand their members, it was a stacked questionnaire and their members are too dumb to understand it, that is his business.
>
> All I am saying is that if I wanted to know what the position of the National Federation of Independent Business was I would be inclined to listen to the people who speak for them, and if they do not speak for them . . . they will not hold those positions very long.[41]

Do groups in fact speak for the interests of their members? Chapter 6 considers this question again with respect to the ATA and Teamsters Union. The present chapter, with its focus on the groups that supported reform, suggests a qualified yes.

Some would point to the NIT League as an obvious counterexample. The league purported to represent corporate shippers who are presumably interested in efficiency and profitability, yet it spoke through and for traffic managers, the green-eyeshaded clerks who preferred certainty and stability to efficiency and profitability.

The NIT League is an interesting example, to be sure, but not of a group that misrepresents its members. The league's "members" are traffic managers by and large; it is they who attend the meetings and who vote (at large) on policy positions. Staff members merely carry out those positions. The league is an example, rather, of a group that misrepresents the membership for which it speaks.

The Private Carrier Conference of the ATA comes closer to exemplifying a group that didn't represent its members in the trucking battle. The PCC chairman is a longtime ATA employee. One could argue that his loyalty to the industrywide trade group prevented him from advocating certain reforms (namely intercorporate hauling at the 50 percent level and deregulation of processed food) that were clearly in his members' interest.

Two extenuating circumstances should be noted, however. First, there was considerable reluctance to break ranks on the part of the members of the PCC themselves. This raises one immediate question: Do members know what's in their own best interest? If the answer to that is no, then the next question is more philosophical: Is an interest group remiss in choosing to lead by following?

Second, presumably the PCC receives certain benefits from being a member conference of the ATA—for example, legislative representation on issues where the interests of private and regulated carriers conform. Thus the PCC has to weigh the benefits to it from breaking ranks against the cost that involves—primarily the weakening of the ATA as a permanent lobbying power.

One could argue that NFIB didn't represent its members insofar as the association's level of involvement exceeded its membership's interest in the issue. But NFIB staffers viewed trucking deregulation as (among other things) a test issue that would set a precedent for other policy reforms of interest to small-business owners. Members are less well situated than the staff to recognize the spillover benefits (and costs) of lobbying particular issues.

In short, the question of whether groups represent their members has no easy answer. It raises empirical questions—Do members know their own interest? Questions of judgment—Do the spillover benefits and costs to other policy issues justify action (or inaction) by an organization? And philosophical questions about the role of leadership.

Trucking deregulation provides few examples of interest groups that sinned by omission or commission. To say that staff members exercised considerable discretion is not to say that they did whatever they pleased. Their decisions were largely consistent with broader organization goals and ideology. Examples of groups that, by their absence from the battle, ill served their members are limited to the ones paralyzed by internal conflict.

The trucking-reform coalition included every other group with a significant stake in deregulation.[42]

Conclusion

Deregulators were able to defeat a single-interest lobby in part because they put together a broad-based coalition that actively supported reform. The lobbying effort of the ad hoc group was no match for the ATA-Teamsters offensive as measured by sheer volume of letters, calls, and visits to Capitol Hill. But it was sufficient to give congressmen who were favorably inclined toward deregulation "something to hang their hats on." More important, for members of Congress who were free to support the merits, the sheer breadth and diversity of the coalition was convincing evidence, fully consistent with the economic analysis, that trucking deregulation was in the public interest.

The basis for a trucking coalition had existed for many years; potential gainers knew who they were. But they had always viewed deregulation as a political impossibility because of the strong, organized opposition to it. That any coalition came together when it did is a result of many forces, most immediately the political agendas of Kennedy and Carter. That it ultimately attracted nearly every eligible group and elicited such a strong commitment from them is due to other factors as well.

The most general explanation one can offer is this: Groups need issues, and trucking deregulation was an issue that served the needs of many groups. It was a good free-enterprise issue for conservatives. It was an ideal anti-inflation issue with which consumer groups could counter their pro-regulation image. It was a pocketbook issue for consumer, business, and farm groups. It symbolized two causes with popular appeal—reducing burdensome government regulation *and* diminishing the power of special interests. In short, it offered something for everyone.

No matter how ideal the issue, the perception that victory is at least possible is a necessary condition for groups to sign on to a coalition. The passage of airline deregulation accomplished that much for the trucking-reform effort. To get groups to begin active lobbying takes more. Cannon's "We're mad as hell" speech—promising a bill on the president's desk by June 1—probably best marked that watershed for the trucking group. Sheer momentum and external events—the introduction of Cannon's bill, the Senate markup, subsequent votes—kept the coalition's lobbying effort going and expanding. In addition, many lobbyists had a strong interest in the trucking issue and the discretion to pursue it actively.

Blessed with an issue that lent itself to compatibility among ideologically diverse supporters, the trucking coalition spent far less energy than many such groups maintaining its own internal unity. Also responsible for such harmony was the low level of information on Capitol Hill, which allowed for a lowest-common-denominator approach to lobbying, and the behavior of individual coalition members, who had the inclination and the discretionary authority to be politically pragmatic.

What internal strife there was reflected a classic problem of some members wanting to hold out longer, or compromise sooner, than others. Predictably, the coalition player whose motives were largely electoral settled for less than what those driven more by political gain thought was attainable. That strife also reflected the problem of organizational egos: Powerful groups need to feel that the rest of the team is listening to them. Because the coalition chose to remain informal in structure, internal dissent was inconspicuous to outsiders and hence less troubling to the group itself.

For the ATA, a permanent coalition of industry groups, independent action by individual members was a somewhat more serious organizational problem. The ATA's strength derived from its representation of the entire industry. Segments of that industry were never well served by regulation; other segments became ill-served over time. So it was inevitable that the issue of deregulation would cause splintering. Moreover, even among the great majority of ATA member carriers who benefited from regulation, there was enough heterogeneity that agreement on political priorities— entry, rate bureaus, food exemption—was impossible. Nevertheless, the ATA successfully maintained the appearance—and the reality—of general industry unity.

Industry coalitions like the ATA are nothing new, but ad hoc coalitions have only recently become a way of life in Washington, D.C. Such coalitions almost never become permanent—that would jeopardize individual groups' cherished autonomy—although certain combinations (consumer groups and labor, for example) appear repeatedly. Carter administration spokesmen strongly urged trucking coalition members "to keep the heart of the group together" for future battles, and NAM hosted a reception several months after the trucking battle ended in an effort to keep the alliance going. NAM's agenda called for a reduction of health and safety regulation, however, and the consumer members of the group—who had helped push that regulation through Congress initially—were not sympathetic. Airline and trucking deregulation had provided a fairly rare combination that appealed to liberals and conservatives—lower prices *and* less government.

Moreover, the timing was right. Ten years earlier, consumer and public-interest groups were only bit-part players on the political stage. By the late 1970s, the consumer movement had achieved stardom and begun to fade; still a box office draw, the movement was looking for a new image to fit the changing times. At the same time, business groups were in ascension.

The consumer movement had shaken groups like the Chamber of Commerce out of their lethargy, and they were finding support in the same concerns over inflation and excessive government regulation that were sapping the strength of consumer groups. Like two shoppers who pass on opposite escalators and exchange a momentary greeting, business and consumer groups paused briefly to join in support of deregulation.

In sum, much as we saw in chapter 4, larger political and economic forces set the stage for the deregulation drama, and qualities inherent in the issue contributed to the unusual degree of consensus—and even passion— among supporters. Still, political skill and strategy are evident at every turn. As both cause and consequence of the issue's prominence, it attracted a high caliber group of lobbyists (much as it had attracted high-caliber economists in and out of government) with the resources and flexibility to mount an effective campaign for reform.

6

Picking Up Where Brute Sanity Leaves Off: Transition Strategies for Reducing Opposition to Change

Reformers have the idea that change can be achieved by brute sanity.
—George Bernard Shaw

M uch opposition to change represents resistance, not to the change itself, but to problems associated with the transition. Stated differently, people's fear of what will happen in going from Here to There, rather than any principled objection to There, is often the real obstacle to change. Economic arguments on the merits, and the confirming evidence of interest-group support, can at best allay only some of that opposition to problems of the transition.

One common transition problem arises when people resist change out of uncertainty and fear of the unknown. Following the devastating 1980 earthquake in Italy, the Italian government tried to move the homeless to unoccupied resort hotels along the coast—far from the threat of postquake epidemics and harsh weather. Most victims refused to go, however, wary of the unknown no matter how dismal the future.

People prefer certainty to uncertainty, even under adverse circumstances. For years, the airline industry suffered poor financial health under CAB regulation; in 1977, the major trunk lines earned only about 11 percent on their equity. Yet the carriers fought to preserve regulation because it was a known quantity. They might not prosper under it but at least they would survive. Bauer, Pool, and Dexter observed the same behavior in their classic study of (unregulated) businesses engaged in foreign trade. They concluded that "fear of loss is a more powerful stimulus than prospect of gain."[1]

Another transitional obstacle to change involves a different choice of the lesser evil. It arises when people recognize that change is itself desirable but fear that getting from Here to There would be so destructive that, on balance, they would be worse off. A baseball coach may see that his pitcher is tiring but do nothing for fear that the "start-up costs" of substituting a new player would be too great. Or an incompatible couple may stay married, believing that separation and divorce would be even harder on the children than their continued fighting. Similarly, some congressmen readily conceded that the airline industry was inherently competitive, but they feared that, after forty years in a regulatory hothouse, the industry would wither in the transition to a free market.

Perhaps the most stubborn obstacle to change is the problem of transitional losses. It arises when people perceive (accurately or not) that they will lose something valuable in the course of moving from Here to There. The object of value may be job security. Postal workers resist automation because it will render their skills obsolete. Lawyers are no less opposed to no-fault systems of insurance and divorce—the bar's equivalent of automation.

Alternatively, the transitional loss may involve an asset that dwindles in value as change comes about. Racial prejudice aside, southern slaveholders fought emancipation because it would deprive them of valuable property. For the same reason, stockbrokers resisted decontrol of their rates by the Securities and Exchange Commission. That 1975 reform reduced the value of a chair on the New York Stock Exchange from $500,000 to $30,000—less than the $50,000 price of a (regulated) taxicab medallion in New York City.[2]

Still another kind of transitional loss involves market share. Some airlines opposed deregulation even though they accepted economists' predictions that, absent regulation, the industry's revenue from increased passenger demand would more than offset the loss from the drop in fares. Their concern was that they would suffer relative to other carriers in the process of moving to a deregulated system. Likewise, savings and loan associations worried that the transition to decontrolled interest rates would give banks, their main rival, a competitive edge.

Transitional problems are not absolutely unyielding, however. Abraham Lincoln could do little in his lifetime to lessen racial prejudice and avert a civil war that way. But insofar as slaveholders opposed emancipation because they would suffer economic loss, this country might have been better off had it purchased the freedom of the slaves outright.

That approach—compensating potential losers to neutralize their opposition—represents one broad transition strategy. Other transition strategies look to solutions that reduce the (perception of) uncertainty and turmoil associated with change—a directive from the pope to victims of a tragedy; a joint custody arrangement that allows children to see their divorced parents equally; a pitcher's bullpen in Shea stadium or, the political equivalent, a transition-team headquarters in Washington, D.C., where an incoming presidential administration can warm up.

Transition strategies share one thing—a recognition that the only practical way to bring about change is to minimize the social disruption in moving from Here to There. Economic regulation ws imposed initially with the help of such strategies: grandfather rights, for example, allowed those already in business to continue. Likewise, removing a long-standing system of regulation requires sensitivity to the problems of transitional uncertainty, chaos, and loss.

In sum, the issue of transition is important to reformers for two reasons—first, because transitional obstacles are the root cause of much opposition to change; and second, because where change is desirable, these obstacles are far more yielding than the principled objection to change itself. The solution may require an act of Congress, a court decree, or a charismatic leader. But the fact that a solution is possible offers hope.

Compensating Losers

The public deserves to be freed of this Depression-inspired legislation, even if it means buying back our freedom.
—*New York Times* editorial, November 13, 1977

Truckers and Teamsters had fire in their belly for good reason: deregulation posed a serious economic threat. Most of the multibillion-dollar annual cost to consumers of ICC regulation represented monopoly rents to capital and labor. A competitive system would make monopoly pricing impossible.

For regulated trucking firms, decontrol threatened loss of valuable operating certificates. If profits were normal, no one would pay for the right to enter the trucking industry; and ICC certificates—valued at billions of dollars in total—would be worthless. For trucking firm employees, deregulation threatened downward pressure on wages. Absent barriers to entry by new (nonunion) firms and without the rate-bureau mechanism for passing along industrywide cost increases, Teamsters' above-market wages would have to become competitive with those in other industries—a loss to union members of well over a billion dollars a year.[3] Many Teamster jobs might disappear altogether as nonunion firms attracted a larger share of the market.

The prospect of suffering such enormous losses fired the opposition to a point that it seemed unbeatable. At the same time, the enormity of the continuing cost to consumers made reform urgent. If the politics of the issue were discouraging, the economics offered a possible solution in that trucking regulation presented a classic opportunity for what economists describe as a "mutually advantageous exchange between gainers and losers."

To elaborate, economic theory tells us that where resources are inefficiently allocated, there's always room for a deal. That's so because the gains to those benefiting from the misallocation are never as great as the loss to others; a little bit is lost in the process—what's called the deadweight loss. By moving from an inefficient to an efficient allocation, then, in theory it is always possible to compensate the "losers" fully, such that they are indifferent, and still be better off by an amount equal to the deadweight loss.*

Economists like Charles Schultze have argued that compensation offers a general solution to the problem described in chapter 1: the ability of narrow groups to block policy changes that would benefit the general public.[4] Because transportation deregulation offered such a striking example of that problem, it was the subject of numerous specific proposals for compensation, such as the following, which appeared in a 1978 article in *Regulation* by Gordon Tullock:

> Policy makers, and especially reformers, should realize that it is a good deal easier to get a program through the political process if they do not try to impose severe losses on anyone. Hence, if deregulation is the goal, we would probably be wiser to forgive the "monopolists," forget their past monopoly profits, and buy them off, rather than engage in a political struggle to take their money away from them.[5]

A sign of the appeal of the economists' message was its echo in a *New York Times* editorial entitled, "Let's Buy Back Capitalism on the Road." "If truckers were deregulated and compensated in cash for their loss of monopoly privileges and then left to compete freely," wrote the *Times,* "the gains to society in lower freight costs would far outweigh the loss to society in payment of tribute."[6]

While political expediency was the major argument for compensation, it was not the only one. Trucking deregulation represented a change in long-standing "rules of the game"—rules around which people had built

---

*In this way, the compensation principle provides a theoretical test for efficiency. If gainers can compensate losers fully and still have something left, then the total value of output must be greater and the change an efficient one. Conversely, if there are insufficient gains to compensate losers, the change must not be efficient.

their businesses and lives. Thus there was at least a case for compensation on the grounds of equity—particularly for truckers who had purchased their operating rights. Unlike the recipients of grandfather rights—for whom regulation produced a windfall—those who bought certificates earned no more than a competitive rate of return, taking into account the cost of the certificate.[7] Moreover, the equity of compensation would seem to coincide with efficiency in that regard, because if policy changes continually confounded the business expectations of firms and investors, it would become difficult to raise capital privately. In short, compensation for losses due to deregulation stood to further several policy goals simultaneously, making it a course of action that, in the words of one economist, "St. Francis of Assisi, Boss Tweed and a board composed of the last three winners of the Nobel Prize in economics would all advise. . . ."[8]

The idea of compensating for the sake of political expedience wasn't new to policy reformers. The Trade Adjustment Assistance Act of 1962 provided for severance pay to workers hurt by lowered trade barriers. In the mid-1970s, railroad employees who stood to lose from the formation of Amtrak and Conrail were appeased with a generous compensation package. Legislation passed in 1978 to expand the Redwood National Park called for severance pay plus weekly unemployment benefits to loggers displaced by the change.

In these instances, however, compensation was a last resort—the final step in a strategic plan that called for making concessions only to the extent that power politics failed to move opponents. The economists' proposal for compensation turned traditional strategy on its head by proposing that reformers make concessions in the form of compensation initially and avoid politics altogether. The virtue of that approach is that it would achieve reform quickly and neatly, without the prolonged battle that yields, at best, a compromise preserving much of the existing inefficiency and, at worst, no compromise at all.

Compensation schemes may well produce their own inefficiencies, as later pages of this chapter will discuss. But the general notion is a powerful one: Given the potential for compensation, no one need be harmed by—and thus oppose on that basis—an economically efficient (loss-imposing) change. Trucking deregulation presented a seemingly good opportunity to apply that notion.

Operating Rights

The proposal to silence the truckers with payment for their valuable operating rights was never seriously considered beyond the pages of policy journals and the *New York Times*. Several deregulators at one time or another intimated to the ATA that a deal could be made. But the trucking group never so much as hinted to the administration (or anyone else) that compensation might be a bargaining item. It simply wasn't an issue—at least until the bill was signed into law.

While the administration was open to a request from the truckers for (partial) compensation—in the form of tax relief most likely—it never initiated any offer. Partly that was strategic: The White House hoped to beat the truckers even without compensating them. Strategy aside, there was a logistical problem. Because of its budgetary impact, any compensation scheme would require action by the Senate Finance and House Ways and Means committees. That detour would make it virtually impossible to get a bill on President Carter's desk by June 1—a deadline both the administration and the trucking industry were eager to meet.

The jurisdiction problem was a consideration to the ATA as well. But there were more important reasons it stayed silent on an issue seemingly so important to the industry—the possibility of compensation. One reason is that the ATA felt it should play down the enormous value of operating rights in the political debate, since that was testimony to the industry's monopoly power. Publicly, the trucking group maintained that the value of the certificates represented "goodwill," but privately, ATA members recognized just how unpersuasive that argument was.

The ATA saw what political damage could come from publicity about operating rights in 1976, when Associated Transport went bankrupt and its rights were auctioned off for over $20 million. The story aired on national evening news. Members of Congress decried the fact that pieces of paper given away free by the federal government were now worth millions of dollars. Others took advantage of the opportunity to denounce costly regulation. All in all, the event served to draw the link in many congressmen's eyes between operating rights and monopoly profits.

Even more important, the ATA never proposed a compensation scheme because it viewed that as a defensive tactic—strictly a second-stage strategy. Asking for compensation would have conceded defeat. One could hardly ask to be reimbursed for the lost value of operating rights while at the same time demanding tight entry controls so as to keep the rights valuable. One ATA lobbyist, talking privately while the battle raged, described the group's strategy toward compensation this way:

> Our efforts have been devoted to the offensive, to protecting what we have, on the assumption that we still hold the cards in our hands. Asking for compensation is a defensive strategy based on trying to cut your losses. Once you adopt that strategy, you lose momentum, and you concede that what the other side is trying to do is a *fait accompli.*[9]

ATA members accepted the wisdom of this strategy almost without question. Occasionally a carrier would raise the issue with one of the ATA lobbyists, but he was quickly appeased by the response, Let's just stay on the offensive for as long as possible. When the ATA's regulatory-policy committee met before the Senate markup to discuss strategy, in six hours of talks, the subject of compensation for operating rights never came up.

Several factors help explain the willingness of ATA members to go along with the industry group's strategy on compensation. For one thing, the ATA lobbying operation was highly regarded by industry members; many carriers viewed ATA lobbyists as something of rainmakers. Moreover, many carriers independently shared the ATA's sense of strategy. If we'd thrown a request for compensation on the table, said one trucking executive after the battle, "we would have lost the whole bill."[10]

Lobbying strategy aside, some carriers were less concerned with compensation than one might expect because operating rights were no longer an important asset. For carriers who had no intention of ever selling their rights, their main value historically had been as collateral for loans. But in recent years, the uncertainty about deregulation had made large financiers look to other things—such as route structure and contracts—as criteria for extending loans.

This uncertainty had also caused operating rights to lose value, which was of concern to the average ATA member, who did view his operating right as an important asset. But members implicitly understood that if the value dropped substantially as a result of legislation, the "rainmakers" would *then* seek a tax offset to ease that problem. And that's precisely what happened.

The ATA pursued its offensive strategy—carefully avoiding any mention of compensation—until the compromise with the administration was secure. Then the industry group promptly went to work to secure favorable tax treatment. Congressman Bud Shuster, the second-ranking Republican on the Public Works Committee, laid the groundwork. At the committee markup, Shuster said if it became apparent that the effect of the legislation was to erode the value of operating rights, then appropriate relief for the industry should be considered as soon as possible—preferably by the Committee on Ways and Means. Shuster's language was incorporated into the committee report on the trucking bill. A month after President Carter signed the Motor Carrier Act, the ATA went before the Senate Finance and House Ways and Means committees to request a tax deduction worth $350 million.

The ATA's tax-relief request appealed for equity. The group said that the 1980 act had "'change[d] the rules of the game'," thus "making the value of operating rights virtually worthless compared to their previous value."

The ATA's testimony was careful to note that the previous worth of rights reflected "economic reality and . . . not . . . goodwill"—precisely the opposite of what the industry had maintained throughout the legislative debate. The testimony also contradicted statements the ATA was making to its members at that very time—claims that the bill represented a victory for the industry. The testimony all but admitted defeat:

> The 1980 Act, while not totally "deregulating" motor carrier operations, makes substantial changes in the way the industry will operate. These changes are designed to substantially increase competition within the motor carrier industry. Among the many changes is easier entry into the industry. . . . [U]nder the new legislation, the previous significant regulatory restrictions on entry and expansion are almost removed. . . . [T]he new legislation renders operating rights. . . virtually worthless compared to their previous value.

The omnibus tax bill that the ATA sought to use as the vehicle for its narrow provision died in committee. But the industry group tried again in the following congress, and that time it succeeded.

Labor Protection

Like compensation for operating rights, the issue of labor protection—that is, compensation for lost jobs—played almost no part in the trucking debate. While several advocates of reform held labor protection out as a carrot for Teamsters, the union expressed no interest until the legislative fight was nearly over. By then, the giant labor group was too late.

The most explicit example of carrot dangling was the American Conservative Union's bill, with its formal guarantee of monetary compensation and training assistance for displaced trucking-industry employees. Informally, Senator Kennedy always held labor protection out to the Teamsters as an enticement. The White House made no overt offer of compensation, but it would have been open to a provision in the final compromise giving Teamsters laid off due to deregulation the "right of first hire" by other firms.

Other players in the deregulation fight objected to virtually any guarantee of labor protection. The ATA said it would oppose any bill containing a right-of-first-hire provision. On the reform side, Howard Cannon took the position that labor protection was appropriate only if the trucking bill called for total deregulation. (Will Ris, Cannon's committee counsel, felt that it "reeked of elitism" to compensate displaced Teamsters but not others similarly situated—employees of a military base shut down by the government, for example.) Cannon had reluctantly gone along with a labor-protection provision in the airline act. But that bill, unlike the trucking legislation, provided for complete decontrol. More important, Cannon was convinced that regulatory reform would lead to more, not fewer, jobs in the airline industry, making it costless to include a guarantee of unemployment compensation for displaced workers.

Despite the potential for conflict over the issue of labor protection, it was never even a minor obstacle to getting a reform bill. The Teamsters expressed no interest in labor protection until the last minute. When the union suddenly spoke up, its demand was so unreasonable that no one took it seriously. The union threatened to kill the bill if it didn't get an acceptable provision, but it could marshal so little congressional support that its proposed amendment was offered on the floor of the House by a freshman Democrat who reportedly agreed to sponsor it only if there was no roll call vote. The amendment was defeated (by voice vote) overwhelmingly.

The Teamsters' handling of the labor-protection issue contributed to a widespread feeling that the giant labor group was ineffective at lobbying— unexpectedly so. Most reform advocates, surprised that the Teamsters waited so late in the game to ask for labor protection, attributed the omission to ineptitude. A few deregulators gave the union more credit, theorizing that the Teamster lobbyists were powerless to deal with opponents on the labor-protection issue because accepting a compromise would have been viewed by union members as selling out. But that theory assumed that the members were in a position to judge independently the tactical maneuvers of the union lobbyists. In reality, the man on the loading dock had to rely on the Teamster organization to interpret the events of the legislative battle. Thus the lobbyists did not likely feel constrained by the threat of members' ire.

A better explanation for why the Teamsters organization delayed in asking for labor protection (though not necessarily an explanation for why it waited as long as it did) posits precisely the opposite: The labor group felt that a guarantee of compensation for displaced workers would undermine members' opposition to the bill. Granted, the man on the dock would prefer work to no-work-with-compensation, but the guarantee of compensation could be enough to extinguish the fire in his belly.

In short, the Teamsters Union, like the ATA, felt that asking for compensation was a defensive strategy, to be used only when the group had no choice but to compromise. "It's a cut-your-losses strategy; hell with it," said one Teamster lobbyist privately, just before the Senate floor vote. "I keep preaching that from the steeples [to others in the union]. Our people are mobilized; they've got to deal with us."[11]

If the desire to keep union members mobilized wasn't sufficient grounds to avoid a compensation strategy, the labor organization had still another reason—fear that the promise of labor protection would ultimately prove hollow. This fear stemmed largely from early experience with the Trade Adjustment Assistance Act of 1962. The agency charged with carrying out the labor-protection provision took a very stringent, case-by-case approach to its task, and for nearly a decade almost no payments were approved. More generally, the union felt that a labor-protection provision would leave workers at the mercy of whatever federal agency was responsible for implementing it, and of Congress, which would have to appropriate the necessary funds periodically.

Interest Groups and Compensation

The "nonstory" of compensation in the trucking dispute reveals two fundamental and related forces which impede the general strategy of buying off organized opposition. The most apparent force at work is the *logic of strategic action*. So long as a bargaining offer represents less than what opponents perceive they can get from (continued) fighting, they have incentive to stay on the offensive—to hold out for more. This is true whether the offer is one of compensation or substantive concessions.

Seemingly the way around this problem is to make a better offer. Economists' buy-off schemes envision "fully" compensating losers such that they are indifferent. Several problems—one more serious than the others— arise in trying to do this, however.

One problem is that an offer of compensation may be discounted in value by skeptical opponents. Any bargaining offer is subject to discounting, but the political visibility and reversibility of typical compensation arrangements aggravate the problem. Thus arrangements that provide for a one-time payoff are preferable to those that require periodic appropriations. Tax benefits are perhaps the most preferred form of compensation; since they never appear on the budget directly, they are nearly invisible.

Another practical problem arises if opponents perceive that they can raise the compensation issue independently should they suffer losses in the political fight. Several factors determine the likelihood, and the likely extent, of independent compensation—committee jurisdiction, the strength of an equity case for compensation, the availability of a low-visibility means for compensation. Insofar as a client group believes these factors will allow it to get subsequent compensation for any losses it suffers, there is reduced incentive to be bought off initially.

The tactical decisions opponents make in response to offers of compensation—how much to discount the offer, whether to wait and ask for compensation separately—are made by professionals who lead and lobby for the membership. While they are far better positioned than the members to set strategy, interest-group leaders face different incentives from their members in situations where the organization's survival is at stake. And in two important respects, *the organization's needs work against a strategy of compensation.*

For members, political battle is a necessary means to gaining or preserving economic benefits. For the interest group, however, fighting is an end in itself. Like a declining country that breathes new life from the feelings of nationalism and patriotic pride released by war, political organizations thrive on the emotions that a good fight generates—fear of attack, dependency on the leadership, a sense of common purpose. From the organization's standpoint, compromise is anathema. Nothing lets the air out of the balloon faster than making deals with the opposition.

Any compromise is deflating, but one trading off government privilege for monetary compensation can be fatal. A special-interest group like the ATA exists largely to perpetuate political and economic arrangements that benefit its members at public expense. Terminating these arrangements in return for compensation automatically eliminates the group's major reason for being. Thus, even if group members are indifferent between the two, the group itself will favor continued inefficiency over efficiency-with-compensation.

If special-interest groups represent the major obstacle to buying off potential losers, perhaps the solution is to buy off the leaders themselves. Leaders, like members, resist change because they will suffer a transitional loss. Their specialized knowledge and talent (human capital) will be far less valuable in the new economic environment. In theory, sufficient compensation should offset that loss.

One can point to examples of the equivalent solution in other settings. In private companies, the interests of management diverge from those of the stockholders in certain situations. Thus it's sometimes necessary to buy off the managers before a company merger can take place. Similarly, before the government shuts down a military base, it must find jobs elsewhere for the colonels. At the local level, financially pressed cities often continue funding elites so as to take away money underneath without so much opposition.

However logical, direct compensation of interest-group leaders would strike most people—including the leaders themselves—as highly inappropriate. Lobbyists, like government bureaucrats and private attorneys, are not objects of sympathy in the public's eye when they are harmed by a policy change. Nor would the leaders themselves respond favorably to an offer of compensation—out of both a fear of appearing hypocritical and a sincere belief in what they promote. Thus any compensation would have to be highly indirect—for example, in the form of harmless legislative provisions that created work for the interest group.

An alternative to paying off the interest group is to make an end run around it and offer compensation to members directly. Airline deregulators did this with some success, resulting in generous payments to several airline companies that agreed to support reform. But the airline industry's trade group was weak; the stronger the group, the more likely it is to intercept any outside offers and dictate what the response will be. If union officials insist that opponents' offer of labor protection is hollow, it may be difficult to persuade the rank and file otherwise.

Airline Deregulation

Airline deregulators used promises of compensation to appease two other sources of opposition—small communities and labor. Examined briefly, these examples indicate more about the conditions under which compensation will successfully reduce political resistance.

The fear that small-town America would lose air service was the major political impediment to decontrolling that industry. Deregulators eventually overcame the obstacle by promising contingent compensation. The final bill guaranteed that any community threatened with loss of "essential air service" following deregulation would have its service federally subsidized. Many decontrol advocates felt there would never be any call for the guarantee provision. Even when loss of service did occur—requiring a $70 million subsidy during the first year—they viewed that as a bargain price to pay for legislation estimated to save consumers more than $2 billion annually.

The small-town-service subsidy illustrates where a compensation strategy can work and work well. The key is that there was no special-interest agent to feel threatened by the prospect of deregulation itself. Those lobby groups that did speak for small towns—the National Association of Counties, for one—had no vested interest in preserving regulation as such. Nor did they have any organizational incentive to fight reformers for the sake of fighting. Thus reformers' initial offer of subsidy served to appease opponents.

The second example of (contingent) compensation in the airline bill is the labor-protection provision. Reformers argued that deregulation would actually increase jobs, since the drop in air fares would cause business to expand. Unions nevertheless feared massive layoffs and one—the International Association of Machinists (IAM), the major spokesman for labor in the airline fight—pressed for protection similar to that contained in two railroad reform bills passed in the mid-1970s. In response, the airline act guaranteed that if layoffs occurred that the CAB determined were due to deregulation, displaced workers with four or more years of experience would be eligible for up to three years of federal payments.

Not all labor representatives endorsed the IAM's call for protection. The Teamsters, a relatively minor player in the airline fight, denounced that approach based on the same reasoning it followed in the trucking battle: Securing a promise of labor protection would only dilute union members' opposition to deregulation, and with no assurance that displaced workers would ever see a nickel of compensation. In the view of one Teamster lobbyist, the IAM was "bamboozled" by the administration; the machinist union's familiarity with the railroad program, which had indeed paid generous benefits to laid-off workers, led it to accept a deal. Teamster lobbyists warned against that course of action—stressing the contrary experience of workers covered under the Trade Adjustment Assistance Act—but to no avail.

Reformers' Objections to Compensation

Several years after the Teamsters' warning, the Trade Act came under attack from the reform side for overly generous and unfair compensation. In 1980, due largely to auto-industry layoffs, the cost of the program exploded from $250 million (its average cost since 1974) to $1.5 billion. A *Washington Post* editorial denounced the compensation program—not only for the sheer cost, but for its inherent inequity:

> Except for securing labor support for trade negotiations, there is no reason to provide more generous assistance to those laidoff workers who can claim some direct connection with imports than to others who are equally needy but are affected only secondarily or not at all by trade. . . . The unfairness of the current program has been starkly demonstrated in the current recession, where workers in auto-parts plants that are part of an auto-manufacturing company are receiving trade benefits while workers in an identical but independent plant down the road are not because they are only "secondarily affected."[12]

The controversy over the trade compensation program illustrated many of the problems identified by economists and others who have debated this question: Should we buy our way out of harmful regulation? Those who answer the question negatively stress the practical problems of designing and implementing compensation schemes without undermining the equity and efficiency rationales for compensating losers.[13]

The first requirement for designing an appropriate compensation scheme is to identify accurately the gainers and the losers, as well as the magnitude of the loss for which compensation should be made. With trucking deregulation, it's a fair assumption that the general public gains;

thus, it would be appropriate to finance a compensation scheme from general funds. But with other efficient policy changes—airline deregulation, for example—gainers compose a much smaller, harder-to-identify group. If, in the interests of administrative simplicity, the compensation scheme is financed not by gainers but by the public at large (as the airline deregulation act provides for), that introduces an element of distortion and inefficiency into the scheme.

Identifying losers raises additional practical problems. If one relies on compensation only for political expediency, then it would be quite simple to identify the groups necessary to buy off. But if compensation is a means of providing equity for hapless victims of a policy change, one must decide, conceptually, how far removed the injury must be before it need not be compensated. Should General Motors workers receive special compensation if they are laid off as the indirect result of deregulation that lowers the demand for GM trucks?

Identifying the magnitude of losses due to deregulation is a third knotty problem. What is the worth of a grandfather right given away free by the ICC in 1935 and carried on a trucker's books at zero value ever since? How can one determine what fraction of the decline in GM jobs is due to deregulation and what fraction to the nation's troubled economy?

The actual allocation of benefits to losers from a policy change potentially creates serious problems. Labor compensation, insofar as it is made contingent on unemployment, tends to prolong the duration of that unemployment. Paying damages to firms injured by deregulation may become even more counterproductive—by thwarting some of the very goals of deregulation. Compensation is most likely to go to the weaker, more poorly managed firms—the very firms a competitive system is designed to eliminate. Paying compensation will also tend to keep firms and workers from relocating, thus preserving the inefficiencies of the regulated system with respect to locational patterns.

The litany of practical problems with compensation goes on. One of the most serious is the potential for creating a domino effect; providing benefits to one group generates pressure to do the same for others. Groups will find it in their interest to point out how much more quickly the process will proceed if they are given compensation. Moreover, they will have incentive to seek regulation—so as again to receive compensation.

Finally, one must question whether compensation in practice actually promotes equity. One statement of the equity rationale for compensation is this: It may be necessary to compensate victims of changes in rules or institutions so as to preserve belief in the system's essential fairness. But whose belief and confidence in the system are we most interested in preserving? If the general public views compensation as a bribe that allows politically powerful monopolists to keep their ill-gotten gains, or as a ripoff unemployment scheme that pays able-bodied workers to sit idle, then it undermines rather than preserves belief in the system. Public perceptions of fairness notwithstanding, does equity require compensation of individuals injured by a change in the rules such as deregulation, given that these individuals actively fought to preserve and strengthen the original, inefficient rules for many years?

Conclusion

The threat of economic loss is the single greatest source of opposition to efficient policy reform. But in theory, no one need lose. Since the gains from an efficient change outweigh the losses, gainers can compensate losers fully and still be better off. Thus compensation strategies have the potential to make even the most ambitious policy reforms politically feasible.

In practice, compensation strategies collide head on with the organizational needs of special-interest group leaders, who dictate tactical decisions. Special-interest groups thrive on political conflict for its own sake. Thus any reform offer that aims to buy off opponents and preempt the fight altogether is anathema. This is true whether the offer is one of compensation or concessions on policy.

Even coming late in the battle, an offer of compensation will be less attractive to group leaders than substantive concessions of comparable worth to members, since the latter assure an ongoing need for the organization, whereas compensation eliminates that very need. Thus, if a compromise involving compensation comes about at all, it will come only after a prolonged battle. But compromise is more likely to take the form of concessions on policy.

Recognizing that special-interest groups will opt for substantive concessions over equivalent compensation, it follows that if you can buy off a client group, you may well not have to. Client group leaders generally won't consider the option of compensation until they are on the defensive and eager to cut their losses. But by then, they may well lack the political power to block the reform or do other damage. If that's the case, compensation would merely serve to solidify the compromise.

Compensation may not be the most desirable way to do that, however. In light of the problems of designing and implementing fair and efficient compensation schemes, it may be less costly and no less equitable to assure the compromise in some other way (where one potential cost of compensation is the loss of support for the compromise from those who object to paying tribute to monopolists). One strategy is to agree to phase in or delay reform, a transition strategy discussed later in the chapter.

These objections aside, the prospect of using compensation to bring about an efficient policy change is not hopeless in all cases. The most promising situations involve potential losers who have benefited only secondarily from an inefficient policy, since their political agents generally have no vested interest in continuing the policy. Even where special-interest groups do mediate the bargain, compensation is sometimes feasible, especially in the form of guaranteed labor protection. Since workers, unlike owners of capital, have no property rights by virtue of their monopoly position, they are more likely to seek contingent compensation as part of the political compromise rather than in subsequent legislation.

When payment is contingent on some event that reformers predict will not occur—layoffs or loss of service resulting from deregulation, for example—the result is an insurance policy more than a compensation scheme. This points up an important variation on the traditional compensation notion, which is aimed at the problem of transitional losses. Contingent compensation, by contrast, is directed more at the transitional problem of uncertainty and fear of the unknown, as discussed later in the chapter. In light of the practical problems of compensating for actual losses, a strategy of using compensation-as-insurance, particularly where the policyholder is a good risk, may be a better solution, albeit to a somewhat different problem.

Insurance

Uncertainty and the threat of unknown consequences played a major role in killing the bill.
    —Charles Schultze, on the fate of President Kennedy's proposal
    to deregulate the railroads

Uncertainty is the mother of intervention. In a competitive market, businesses are constantly at risk. Changes in technology and consumer preferences cause continual dislocation and loss; the more efficient the market, the sharper these effects. The institution of regulation responds to the fear of this risk and dislocation. Regulation blunts the sharp changes and protects human and financial interests from the ruthless blows of the free marketplace.[14]

That protection costs consumers a lot, but it persists in part because it's a known quantity. Most of us prefer the devil we know to the devil we don't know, and our fear of the unknown is an imposing barrier to change.

Deregulation: Rx for Risk

While ICC protection served to tranquilize, deregulation was a prescription for double-dosage risk. The first dose was competition itself—

inherently risky to industry; desirably so. Dose two was the transition to competition, with its undesirable uncertainty about how such a major policy change would affect a host of public concerns—highway safety, service to small communities, rates, industry concentration. The ATA's slogan—"If it ain't broke, don't fix it"—appealed directly to a fear of the unknown, and deregulators had the burden of proving that reform would not be harmful to the public.

Since there is no laboratory or wind tunnel in which to test the consequences of new public policies, that burden is difficult to bear. The interaction of economic, organizational, and technical factors makes prediction with certainty impossible. But deregulators' equivalent of laboratory results—the case on the merits described in chapter 4—was highly persuasive. And in addition, reformers used various transition strategies to reduce uncertainty and fear of the unknown.

The first strategy was *to go slowly.* Senator Cannon set 1983 as the date for ending single-line collective ratemaking to allow time to adjust. "The three-year delay provides us with an escape valve in case the reforms that are implemented do not work as well as we had hoped," Cannon said.[15] In addition, the gradually expanding "zone of reasonableness" provided a means to phase in pricing freedom over a period of years. One economist called that a way to test the water "by putting your foot in without jumping in with all your clothes on."

A go-slow approach made possible trial-and-error learning, but it was also necessary to allow for *monitoring of the change*—a second way to reduce fear of the unknown. Rate-bureau proponents felt better knowing that a study commission would be monitoring the impact of the legislation with an eye toward the future of collective ratemaking. Likewise, the prospect of annual congressional oversight reassured the ATA that adverse effects of decontrol would get prompt attention and that the "hellbent for deregulation" ICC would be held in check. "While we are not pleased with all of the sections of the legislation," said ATA president Bennett Whitlock, "I am gratified with the oversight provisions and the statements of the committee leadership that they will monitor very carefully the impact of the legislation."[16]

Both of these strategies—going slowly and monitoring—had the effect of increasing uncertainty about what the ground rules governing change would be. That consequence was undesirable from the standpoint of efficiency: the trucking industry would adjust to change more quickly if the rules were explicit and unvarying. But in order to reduce opponents' fear of unknown consequences, reformers felt it was expedient to leave the rules somewhat ambiguous.

A third strategy to reduce fear of the unknown—notable for its absence in the motor carrier bill—is to provide *insurance*—a guarantee of restitution in the event something goes awry. This is a common marketing technique in the private sector—the offer of a money-back guarantee of satisfaction, for example—to overcome initial resistance to an unknown product or service. Whether it's deregulation or antifreeze, if a new product is all it's cracked up to be, promoters should be able to put their money where their mouths are and guarantee against failure at little cost.

Robert Biller has proposed the use of explicit insurance policies for public programs—partly as a means of spreading the risks of innovation.[17] He envisions a risk-management pool for government, funded by a percentage of departments' overhead rates or with explicitly negotiated transfer payments between government jurisdictions. If a new policy such as deregulation should fail, the insurance payments would be used to restore the prior state of affairs.

Airline deregulators reduced political opposition from two sources by providing insurance—action that many reformers viewed as "hand-holding." When union interests demanded labor protection against the danger of massive layoffs, Senator Cannon reluctantly agreed to the demand "because I don't think you are going to find much use of it."[18] The guarantee of "essential air service" to small communities was a riskier offer in two regards: First, there was a greater chance that it would be triggered by the effects of deregulation (which it was). Second, such an offer might confirm rather than ease suspicions that small towns would lose air service under deregulation. Recognizing that problem, some reformers argued that a guarantee would do more harm than good, but after much debate, the risk was deemed justified.

Trucking deregulators never seriously considered including a comparable guarantee to small communities in the motor carrier act. They viewed it as an administrative nightmare: Whereas fewer than 1,000 communities were potential candidates for the airline subsidy, the comparable figure for trucking was close to 40,000. Moreover, from a tactical standpoint deregulators felt a subsidy provision would lend credibility to the ATA's forecast of "small-town blues." They preferred to treat the small-communities issue as the red herring they believed it was.[19]

Conclusion

Fear of the unknown is a powerful obstacle to change. While transition strategies can do nothing to reduce the riskiness of the marketplace itself, they can ease the uncertainty associated with moving to a competitive system.

Insurance strategies are potentially effective. In an adversary system, opponents exaggerate the risks of change; the policy equivalent of a money-back guarantee can reduce unfounded fear at virtually no cost. In some situations, no other strategy will succeed.

There are drawbacks to providing insurance, however. The guarantee may actually lend credibility to opponents' prophecies of disaster—a Catch 22 for policy reformers. Congressmen, like others, tend to accept the most straightforward explanation for things about which they know little. Thus the provision of a backup system makes it appear that a crisis is anticipated.

In the course of giving the other side ammunition, an insurance scheme complicates the political debate—another serious drawback to that as a strategy. Substantive provisions aren't added quickly and easily in the legislative process; each one requires considerable political capital. The keep-it-simple rule of lobbying reflects the scarce nature of that capital. And finally, since insurance policies amount to contingent compensation, they will encounter some of the same resistance as buy-off schemes from special-interest groups worried about organizational survival.

In sum, as with compensation schemes, the transaction costs of using an insurance strategy are high. Alternative approaches to reducing fear of the unknown—adopting change gradually, and monitoring its effects so as to adjust the rules if necessary—have more general, if less dramatic, application. Granted, these strategies may increase uncertainty about what the ground rules will ultimately be. But that may be unavoidable.

Going Slowly

The existing system [of collective ratemaking] has operated for over 30 years and both carriers and shippers must be given time to readjust. . . .
—Senate Commerce Committee Report on S. 2245

I find it difficult to conceive what benefits are to be achieved by a three-year delay . . . [P]rice-fixing is price-fixing whether it occurs in the building trades, in the sale of electrical generators, or in motor transportation.
—John Shenefield, assistant U.S. attorney general

Virtually every economic industry faced with unwanted deregulation has predicted disaster—a return to the preregulation conditions of chaos, cutthroat competition, and disregard for human and financial safety. Even if the predictions don't comport with economic theory, which describes the long-term behavior of profit-seeking firms, there is reason to fear that the transition to a competitive environment will be damaging to an industry that has never known anything but regulation.

The problem was a serious one for airline deregulators. One who confronted it was Stephen Breyer. As special counsel to the Senate Judiciary Committee while on leave from the Harvard law faculty, Breyer listened to the fears of chaos expressed by industry opponents and responded with some sympathy:

> The airline people came in and said, "We are afraid of chaos"—you know, where "chaos" is interpreted as people making mistakes. . . . I might be a little skeptical [but] I have no facts. What is there besides an inherent skepticism? I have seen the people at United and Eastern. . . . If you ask me are they prepared to start engaging in price competition and will they do it as rationally as people who have been engaged in it, I would answer that question no, because I know that they haven't had any experience.[20]

Breyer feared, among other things, that industry mistakes in the transition would lead to pressure to reregulate:

> If suddenly you tell [the airlines], "Tomorrow you are all free—do what you want," will they make a lot of mistakes? We all know that ["predatory pricing" and "chaos in the industry"] are bad economic arguments, but what might happen is that suddenly firms all over the place, because they are not certain what they are doing, misprice. They make mistakes. . . . [P]eople will see a $75 price today and tomorrow it's $60 and the next day it's $150 because [World Airways] has now driven United out. . . . If [that happens], there will be strong pressure to reregulate.[21]

The widespread fear of disruption led to general, but not unanimous, support for a policy of gradual deregulation. Some reformers, critical of that policy on economic grounds, argued that even as a political matter, "cold turkey" decontrol was the answer. "The best thing to do . . . would be to deregulate as rapidly as possible," said one, "because the benefits to consumers would appear early enough that the industry's screaming and yelling would be lost in the thunder of people heading for the airport to fly coast to coast for $50 or $75. . . ." But most reformers concluded that phased deregulation was a necessary political response to the fears of Congress and the financial community about the health of the airline industry, which had just emerged from a half decade of dismal earnings.

Alfred Kahn was a gradualist to begin with, based on substantive as well as political considerations. "I originally thought . . . we ought to move very cautiously," said Kahn, "examining the results every step of the way, in hope of minimizing the disruptions and distortions." But his experience as CAB chairman led Kahn to reject the traditional wisdom that slower is better, at least as an economically efficient approach to airline deregulation. "The way to minimize the distortions of the transition," Kahn became convinced, "is to make the transition as short as possible."[22]

One distortion Kahn feared had to do with excess capacity:

> So long as deregulation is incomplete, so long as the certificate of public convenience and necessity continues to have an exclusionary and therefore a market value, some of the airlines assure us, they will apply for more licenses than they can operate economically, and operate under them sufficiently to ensure that they are not taken away; . . . they will flood markets with more service than is economic in order to preclude competitive operations by others, in the hope of being able in the future to reap the rewards of the monopoly power they achieve and preserve in this way.[23]

Kahn argued that the only way around that problem was to demonstrate that the value of the franchises was going to be zero, and the only way to do that was to open up entry as fast as possible.

A second concern was for the unequal abilities of airline firms to compete, this largely the result of "an incredibly complicated burden of restrictions and impediments from the past" that the airline industry carries over into its present.[24] In particular, carriers' respective route structures, each the product of CAB-imposed operating authorities and restrictions, accounted for most of the differences in their costs. The CAB chairman came to believe that a rapid transition was the best solution to that problem as well:

> Moving as rapidly as possible to a system of universal free entry—and exit—is the way to deal also with the asserted inequality of competitive abilities and opportunities during a slow transition: make the transition rapid; move quickly, on as broad a front as possible, to permit all carriers to slough off the restrictions that limit their operating flexibility, to leave the markets they find it uneconomic to serve, to enter the markets they want to enter.[25]

Third, Kahn faced the problem of calibrating the liberalization of pricing and entry controls. Allowing too much entry relative to pricing freedom could lead to competition on the basis of service rather than rates. The reverse scenario—permitting too much pricing freedom for a given level of entry—would allow firms to abuse their market power by charging excessive rates.

The gradualist in Kahn worried that the CAB had created a variation on the latter problem in its haste to deregulate:

I am not certain that the increasingly permissive attitude that the Board has taken during the last year toward price reductions—to the point of almost total laissez faire—while new entry by would-be competitors continues to be embroiled in the still maddening slow certification process, has not caused us to miss the opportunity for a restructuring of the industry along more competitive lines. It is possible that by permitting incumbent carriers during the last year to introduce a vast variety of discount fares—many of them highly discriminatory and appealing to the same elastic demand travelers as the charters and Freddie Lakers—we may have enabled them to foreclose entry into the provision of uniformly low-fare scheduled service by the supplemental carriers, some of whom have been seeking this authority for years.[26]

Overall, however, Kahn concluded that the CAB had not moved too quickly and that the proper approach to synchronization was to speed up entry rather than slow down pricing decontrol. "Equalizing restrictions turns out to be like equalizing the two sides of a mustache," observed Kahn. "One can do it much more rapidly by cutting down on the longer side than by extending the shorter one!"[27]

How Fast to Deregulate Trucking

Synchronization was also a critical concern to trucking deregulators. The proposal by Public Works Committee leader James Howard to call for sudden and total deregulation was viewed as a ploy since it completely ignored the need to calibrate removal of pricing and entry controls. Even advocates of a rapid transition worried that Howard's plan would be inflationary because it would lift price ceilings before entry reforms had fully taken hold. Reformers showed less agreement about how much time was needed for the transition. At one extreme was the Department of Justice. In light of steps already taken by the ICC to liberalize entry, Justice felt that antitrust immunity (and the ICC's control over pricing that went with it) could be removed in an orderly manner within ninety days.

A delay in removing antitrust immunity would have several undesirable effects. "A lengthy transition period prolongs uncertainty, increases the difficulty of investment decisions for the industry, and causes confusion for the public," concluded the National Commission for the Review of Antitrust Laws and Procedures.[28] But more important, a lengthy transition would postpone the benefits of competition. "We simply cannot afford *not* to eliminate antitrust immunity as soon as possible in the motor carrier industry," Assistant Attorney General John Shenefield told a congressional panel.[29] Speeding the benefits of decontrol to shippers and consumers was also an important political consideration, given that there would doubtless be continuing pressure for reregulation as the increase in competition led to bankruptcies.

While the desire to reward supporters rapidly argued for a speedy transition, the more immediate need to appease critics made it imperative that trucking decontrol proceed gradually. The view was widespread on Capitol Hill, even among some deregulators, that the transition to airline decontrol was too fast. Kahn's sophisticated arguments about the distortions from a gradual approach were not central to the political debate. Instead, what congressmen heard were horror stories about towns that had lost air service during the Christmas holidays with no advance warning.

More important, gradualism was the only response to the truckers' dire predictions of chaos and destruction. A slow transition was seen as providing carriers and shippers with a chance to adjust to the new environment. It was also billed as an "escape valve"—giving Congress the opportunity to monitor the change and make adjustments to the policy if necessary. In sum, a go-slow policy showed a necessary sensitivity to the fears— legitimate or not—of deregulation critics. Senator Cannon's remarks upon introducing his bill reflected that sensitivity:

> One of the reasons why many critics of eliminating any degree of antitrust immunity foresee such grim results is because of the incredibly complicated and complex structure of motor carrier rates and tariffs. It has become abundantly clear to me from my review of this issue that there is a crying need for a simplification of tariffs and the general rate structure of the motor carrier industry. This should go hand-in-hand with a simplification of commodity descriptions and territorial limitations. Such simplifications would greatly reduce the adverse results of modifying collective ratemaking. *But such processes take time.* That is one reason why I believe it is absolutely necessary to phase-out any immunity that Congress chooses to . . . over a period substantially long enough to allow carriers to meet the demands of the new environment [emphasis added].[30]

However complex the motor carrier industry, the three years that Cannon's bill allowed for phasing out antitrust immunity was more than enough time for carriers to adjust. But a long transition was necessary simply to appease opponents. Delay permitted regulated carriers and Teamsters a last gasp of monopoly profits. In that sense, gradualism served as an alternative to explicit compensation.

Gradualism/Delay as Implicit Compensation

Throughout most of the battle, opponents of deregulation made no plea for a phase-in of reform. Like asking for compensation, that would have conceded defeat. But perhaps even more important, recognizing the existence of a transition would have belied their attitude that deregulation meant stability one day, utter chaos the next.

Once the ATA recognized that it could not preserve its cherished antitrust immunity, however, delaying the date for termination became a high bargaining priority. At that stage, the truckers' slogan might well have been, "If it ain't broke, don't fix it, or at least not for a few years." The final compromise—extending the full antitrust privilege until 1984—represented a multibillion-dollar sweetener for the truckers and Teamsters.

Delaying or phasing in policy change, which amounts to implicit compensation, has several strategic advantages over direct compensation. Interest-group leaders prefer it since, unlike explicit compensation, it implies a continued role for them. Members value delay beyond its worth as compensation because it simultaneously reduces their fear of the unknown. And others, who view compensation as a deal with the devil, look on gradualism as the responsible management of change. Strategy aside, there are good policy reasons to phase in or postpone change rather than compensate.

Implicit compensation through delay avoids virtually all the design and implementation problems of an explicit payment scheme. To recall the earlier discussion, one such problem is to identify losers—those who should receive compensation, particularly where there is a desire to be equitable rather than just politically expedient. By delaying the harm, a slow transition automatically compensates all those who would be directly or indirectly hurt by a policy change. Likewise, a strategy of postponement automatically "taxes" gainers and only gainers by delaying the benefits they receive.[31]

Compensation through delay avoids a second problem—the unemployment-inducing effects of severance pay—because no payment takes place. Moreover, it gives workers time to find other jobs before they become unemployed.[32]

Delaying the harm is more fair than explicitly compensating for it in that it automatically identifies gainers and losers, but it also *appears* more fair—a critical feature. Whereas compensation looks to some like a bribe, postponement appears to be a gesture of equity. This is particularly important when the policy is deregulation, because regulation was itself an effort to blunt the sharp changes and dislocations caused by the impersonal marketplace by introducing delay into the process. The following theory of why regulation came about initially could just as well represent an argument for the gradual transition to deregulation:

[The public feels] that the victims of economic change should not be placed at the mercy of the impersonal market, but should instead be protected by a mechanism that provides economic justice. A very primitive, minimum response to this desire is the grant of a period during which adjustment can take place and useless fixed costs be amortized. Noneconomists are great respecters of sunk costs; the transformation of useful physical and human capital into an irrelevant sunk cost by market or technological forces is a process that is easily viewed as unjust and even inhumane. In addition, substantive policy decisions are affected: people cannot be deprived of existing services at existing prices without due process.[33]

While a policy of going slowly avoids most of the problems of direct compensation, there is a lack of finality about gradual change that opponents like for good reason. Gradualism and delay can become a euphemistic cover for little or no reform. And even with the best of intentions on reformers' parts, political pressure can force continued postponement of significant change.

Conclusion

For an industry that has lived its entire life in a protectionist hothouse, the move to deregulation can be chaotic and destructive, and the fear of that chaos is a significant political obstacle. The transitional strategy of going slowly responds to that fear by giving firms time to adjust and learn gradually by trial and error. It does so, however, at the expense of economic efficiency. A lengthy transition reduces the economic benefits going to consumers. In addition, the process of phasing in policy change sometimes creates its own market distortions.

One alternative is to postpone the change altogether for a period of time and then institute it all at once.[34] That provides firms with time to adjust (though without the opportunity for gradual trial-and-error learning) while avoiding at least some of the distortions from moving piecemeal. Congress followed that approach when it deregulated brokerage rates. Stockbrokers went "cold turkey," not the day the bill was signed, but nearly a year later. When England deregulated its trucking industry, there was a two-year lag from the passage of the legislation until its implementation, which took place over a several-month period and without chaos.[35] The same strategy is used in other policy areas as well. For example, the federal government invariably gives auto manufacturers several years to prepare for stricter mileage and safety standards—standards which then take effect all at once.

Whether it's through postponement or the phasing in of change, a go-slow transition strategy gives new meaning to the expression, "time is money." Long transitions serve to compensate victims of a policy change implicitly while also avoiding many of the practical and political problems with explicit compensation. Among its advantages is that policy postponement appears more equitable than compensation.

Distortions or no distortions, major policy reforms will likely be accompanied by a long transition period. Whether the obstacle is the threat of economic loss, uncertainty, or fear of chaos, it seems there's no general strategy more well suited to reducing transitional opposition to change.

Transitional Efficiency and Political Expedience: The Delicate Tradeoff

The three transition strategies examined above—compensation, insurance, and going slowly—serve the goal of political expedience, but often at some loss of economic efficiency. The trade-off is strategically delicate. Without some sacrifice of efficiency in the transition—through a phased introduction of change, for example—it would be impossible to overcome the political opposition to reform. But if there's too much efficiency loss, supporters of reform will withdraw their backing.

Similarly, there is a trade-off to be made if one's primary goal is to have the transition from Here to There be economically efficient. There are guidelines of a sort for pursuing that goal.[36] But strict adherence to those guidelines will often create political opposition—either by aggravating perceived transitional problems or in some other way.

The trade-off between transitional efficiency and political expedience is best illustrated by the example of uncertainty or ambiguity. From the standpoint of efficiency, maximum certainty about the ground rules governing change is desirable. If truckers know for sure that they will lose their ability to collude on prices, they can take steps to reduce the injury they suffer. If they know when the change will occur, they can adjust even better. In a world of uncertainty, change is more injurious.

From the standpoint of political expedience, however, some degree of ambiguity about the ground rules is desirable. Certain transitional problems—fear of chaos, for example—are eased when opponents know the rules are flexible enough to be adjusted if necessary. Other, nontransitional problems are also reduced by allowing for some degree of uncertainty in the rules. Hence ambiguity is an important element of any bargaining compromise. The following pages examine the trade-off between transitional efficiency and political expedience—as illustrated by the example of uncertainty—in the battle for trucking deregulation.

Strategic Use of Uncertainty

Declare victory and get out [of Vietnam].
—Sen. George Aiken

The ICC's transformation from protector to antagonist left regulated carriers facing great uncertainty. For years, the commission had been the industry's rubber stamp—the epitome of predictability. If carriers went to the ICC for a general rate increase or suspension of an independently set rate, they could count on a favorable reception. But in the late 1970s, when the commission pulled up the welcome mat, predictability went the way of fifty-cent-a-gallon diesel fuel.

Industry attacks on the ICC stressed the dangers of regulatory uncertainty. The commission's policy of "uneven and ill-considered administrative deregulation" had imposed an "intolerable burden of uncertainty" on carriers, testified the ATA, and had produced a "chilling effect" on the industry's ability to plan for the long range, obtain adequate financing, and recruit and retain top managerial staff. As some of the big carriers began preparing elaborate contingency plans in anticipation of deregulation, one complained that the commission was "cutting off our tails an inch at a time" when it "would be easier to lose it in one fell swoop."

Advocates of deregulation shared the industry's concern about the adverse effect of uncertainty on investment and financing decisions. Shippers especially desired more predictability so as to make their own long-range transportation plans. But whereas the industry sought to end the uncertainty with legislation that would turn back the clock, deregulators sought a statute that would spell out rules calling for greater competition.[37]

Reflecting what sentiment the two sides shared, congressional spokesmen stressed that a primary aim of trucking legislation was to reduce uncertainty. "Legislation is desperately needed to clarify the existing regulatory uncertainty that plagues the industry and those who care about it," said Howard Cannon on the floor of the Senate. "We simply cannot tolerate another year of indecision and change of policy as we have this past year."[38] Earlier Cannon had promised that his bill, if enacted, would "allow the transportation industry to know the ground rules in advance and [would give] explicit direction to the commission. . . ."[39]

The two sides ceased to share a desire for certainty, however, after their initial tests of strength in Congress. Once the truckers realized that any legislative compromise would call for significant decontrol, they preferred to keep unfavorable provisions as ambiguous as possible.

The ATA was not altogether unsuccessful in that regard. The Motor

Carrier Act of 1980, both truckers and reformers could agree, went quite far in spelling out the ground rules by which the ICC and industry would be expected to play. Yet the two sides disagreed markedly on just what some of those rules said—both cause and consequence of the uncertainty that still existed.

One source of uncertainty was the provision on antitrust immunity. The act clearly stated that antitrust immunity for single-line ratemaking would end on January 1, 1984 (with a possible six-month extension). However, the act also called for an independent study commission to investigate collective ratemaking and report to Congress *prior* to the date when immunity would end. The effect of that provision was to suggest that the issue wasn't really settled, as the ICC's analysis of a similar provision in the original Senate bill cautioned:

> Such a study seems out of place in light of the fact that one of the purposes of this legislation is to reduce the uncertainty felt by the trucking industry regarding the direction of regulation. We think that this provision only adds to the confusion by saying on the one hand that Congress intends to eliminate [rate bureau] discussions and then on the other, that it wants to study the matter.[40]

The trucking industry, much more than deregulators, found room for uncertainty and ambiguity in that provision. Deregulators would have preferred that Congress not reexamine an issue once it had outlawed it. But the statutory requirements for size, makeup, and appointment of the study group were such that deregulators saw little danger that it would make anticompetitive recommendations. The ATA, by contrast, felt that the prospect of a study commission made the future of antitrust immunity far less certain—so uncertain, in fact, that it could tell its members that the bill did not really do away with collective ratemaking after all.

The ATA's Desire for Uncertainty

The ATA opted to preserve uncertainty about the ground rules for reform partly in the hope that the political climate would improve and some future Congress would cancel them before they took effect. That strategy necessarily denied trucking firms the certainty that the ATA had initially said was essential for planning and investment decisions. But like someone who declines five dollars in cash in favor of a lottery ticket on a sweepstakes, the trade group preferred the possibility of getting more to the assurance of getting less.

Uncertainty also served the ATA's internal need to sell the compromise to members. The more ambiguous the bill, the more convincingly the trade group could claim that the compromise was actually a victory for the industry. ATA critics dubbed that the "George Aiken strategy," after the former Vermont senator who once proposed how the United States could end its doomed involvement in Vietnam without losing face: "Declare victory and get out," he advised.

The provision on antitrust immunity occasioned the ATA's most blatant use of the George Aiken strategy. During the Senate's consideration of the trucking bill, when the ATA was still trying to mobilize its members, it treated as laughable the idea that Congress would mandate a study of something—namely, collective ratemaking—that would have already been scheduled to end. (Sen. Ernest Hollings, the truckers' most ardent defender, likened it to the story of the "great French playwright Voltaire who, when advised that his lifelong enemy and adversary had died, said, 'He was a fine man and a great civic leader—that is, assuming he is dead.'") Study or no study, to abolish antitrust immunity would devastate the industry, ATA officials maintained.

However, once the ATA recognized that it did not have the votes to preserve its antitrust protection, the prospect of a study commission took on sudden importance. That prospect, together with the extension of immunity until 1984, gave ATA officials an excuse to deny defeat.

Deny it they did. Many ATA spokesmen predicted confidently that Congress would see the light and reverse itself on the issue of antitrust protection once it received the recommendations of the study commission. Some claims went even further. The rate bureaus prepared a brochure for ATA members entitled, "Collective Ratemaking Reapproved: The Motor Carrier Act of 1980."

The George Aiken strategy extended to the bill as a whole, not just the antitrust provision. ATA president Whitlock told one trade journal reporter that the industry got "90 percent" of what it sought. Another top ATA official told audiences around the country that the 1980 act was a "reaffirmation by the Congress of the need for economic regulation of the industry."

The ATA's announcement of the newly passed act to its members cleverly went beyond merely declaring the industry's success in Congress and denying press reports to the contrary. In addition, the group identified a scapegoat that members could blame if the bill-as-implemented proved not to their liking:

> If the press reports in your community were anything like they were here, I imagine you have difficulty accepting this appraisal. The news reports and interpretations I saw made it look as if regulation had just about been wiped out. This is not the case. The basic principles are preserved; the structure

remains intact; Congress has laid down guidelines and provided machinery to make certain they are observed. *It is now up to the Interstate Commerce Commission to carry out the will of Congress* [emphasis added].[41]

By predicting that the ICC would try to undermine Congress's reaffirmation of regulation, the ATA protected its own claims to victory and, at the same time, staked out a continuing role for itself as the indispensable industry protector:

> Frankly, the record of the Commission over the past year or so has been so hellbent for deregulation that I will not be surprised at any effort that might be made to thwart the intent of Congress. I assure you we will continue to keep on top of the situation and will meet it with whatever ethical and legal means are required.[42]

The Value of Uncertainty

In a political vacuum, the best transition plans are admittedly those that reduce uncertainty the most. But when the desired transition is to a change opposed by a powerful lobby, allowing room for uncertainty may be a politically expedient strategy. In addition to reducing transitional obstacles to change—knowing the rules are not cast in concrete is a comfort to those who fear a destructive transition, for example—uncertainty is useful in political bargaining, where other obstacles arise.

First, uncertainty gives interest groups an escape hatch. Continually faced with the free-rider problem, interest groups often exaggerate the magnitude of enemy threat in an effort to mobilize members' opposition. But once having done this, if the group must concede on issues that it has steadfastly told members are nonnegotiable, it needs a face-saving way out. Uncertainty and ambiguity in the compromise make possible a George Aiken–style declaration of false victory. While this by itself is not desirable, it tends to compensate for the group's initial exaggeration of the threat. Insofar as the effect of declaring false victory is to shorten the battle or get opponents of change to settle for less than they otherwise would, it may be a desirable charade.

The danger of making it easier for interest groups to overstate their performance is that their members will feel that nothing has changed—it's business as usual. The ICC worried that trucking firms would not adapt themselves to the more competitive environment if they accepted the ATA's reading of the bill as a reaffirmation of regulation. But in a subsequent speech to truckers, ICC chairman Gaskins cited the action of many motor carriers in writing off the values of their operating rights as evidence that they saw through the charade. "These write-offs show that motor carrier managers, who know their industry best, are unconvinced by ATA bluster about a rollback of regulatory reform," said Gaskins. "They know that Humpty-Dumpty is never going to be put back together again, and they are adjusting their books accordingly."

Second, a strategy of uncertainty capitalizes on the sincerity of those resisting change. Many opponents of desirable change are quite sincere in maintaining that their position is in the public interest. But if reformers agree to build in some ambiguity—in the form of oversight, further study, or opportunities for appeal—then opponents are able to accept change with the belief that it is only temporary and that, ultimately, the "truth will out."

Finally, whether or not opponents of change think they're on the side of truth, they will accept a greater degree of reform if they feel there is some chance of reversing it in the future than if the change seems irreversible. If those who resist change are justified in believing that future conditions will be more favorable to them than existing ones, then strategic uncertainty is a poor risk for reformers to take. But if reformers have superior knowledge that tells them their opponents are foolishly optimistic, then enduring some uncertainty about the future may be an expedient way to achieve more change in the present.

As an illustration, when the ATA agreed to the bill, its optimism about preserving antitrust immunity reflected a calculation that the industry could get a favorable majority appointed to the study commission. But when the appointees were named, it appeared that the ATA seriously underestimated the amount of control the administration would have—and knew all along it would have—over the appointment process. Thus the study commission was a low-risk concession for deregulators to grant the truckers.

Techniques for Introducing Uncertainty

To political practitioners, the notion of using uncertainty and ambiguity to grease the wheels of compromise is so commonplace that it's rarely made explicit. Nevertheless, one can identify certain common methods of introducing uncertainty into the policy process.

The example of the study commission on antitrust immunity illustrates one way of introducing uncertainty—by *creating opportunities for policy reversals*. Providing for congressional oversight or further study is another example of that method.

A second approach is to *keep language vague*. If two sides can't agree on how to be clear, they can often agree to be ambiguous. The 1976 railroad reform act illustrates this approach and the problems it can cause. Aimed at giving railroads freedom to set their own prices, the act gave the ICC authority to overrule rates as "unjust and unreasonable" only if the railroad possessed "market dominance." But "market dominance" was one of several crucial terms reached in the course of political debate and compromise that had no clearly identified meaning. As a result, the ICC as implementor of the bill was able to define the term so broadly as to undermine the intent of Congress.

The ultimate in vagueness is silence. If Congress intentionally says nothing about a particular issue, and in effect defers consideration of it to the courts, that may allow sufficient uncertainty to reach political compromise. The trucking bill was silent on the important issue of whether private carriers could haul for hire on their return trip. Deregulators saw that as a victory, since a lower court had ruled in favor of private carriers already. But the trucking industry could find some reason for hope as well, since the case was still on appeal.

A third method of allowing for uncertainty is the "classic two-step"— which involves explicitly *deferring controversial decisions to some other forum.* Typically, Congress identifies a policy goal upon which there is general agreement (step one) and then defers to an executive agency (step two) to make decisions that will occasion dispute. For example, the airline-deregulation act explicitly called for labor compensation but left it to the secretary of labor to make the crucial determination of what percentage of prior wages would be used as the basis for severance pay. Airline pilots were no doubt shocked when they saw what a low ceiling the regulations placed on monthly payments.[43]

Delay is still another way of allowing for uncertainty about future ground rules. The inevitable is somehow easier to accept if it is not imminent. Moreover, postponement is often enough to give victims some hope for reprieve. The 1984 termination date for antitrust immunity, particularly in combination with the provision of a study commission, made possible a compromise on an issue the truckers viewed as nonnegotiable.

Conclusion

The "rational, problem-solving approach" to policymaking calls for transition schemes that minimize uncertainty. But allowing for uncertainty about the ground rules can be an expedient way to overcome opposition to socially desirable change.

The role of special-interest groups is key. As noted repeatedly in this chapter, these groups have their own organizational agendas to serve, a condition that causes leaders to oppose change even more fiercely than members do. Interest groups are really no different from many other bargaining agents in that regard. Labor and other negotiations are always sensitive to the need for bargaining agents to sell the compromise to their followers. The allowance for uncertainty and ambiguity in the compromise is a standard way of meeting that need.

Also key is the recognition that those who resist desirable change are often convinced of their rightness, overconfident of their ability to regain political control, or both. A strategy of uncertainty—in this case, a transition plan that leaves room for future reappraisal and reversal of the ground rules—can be a low-risk way of getting them to accept more change now.

Finally, in addition to its importance in bargaining, where the aim is to outmaneuver opponents, a strategy of uncertainty can get at the very source of the opposition by easing fears about the transition to change.

This strategy has serious drawbacks, however. When interest-group members are misled by George Aiken–style claims of false victory or by their own foolish optimism, they don't respond properly to the changes occurring around them. At the time when members should be getting the most advice from their leaders as to how to prepare for change, they're being told that it's business as usual. That is inevitable, no matter how explicit the compromise, but legislation that builds in uncertainty only compounds the problem.

Transition Strategies: Conclusion

Economists' proposals to compensate truckers and thereby gain their acquiescence and avoid a political fight came to naught. The ATA did secure tax relief for its members to compensate them for their devalued operating rights, but only after the industry lobby had fought for the most favorable legislation it could get. Other, more traditional strategies proved more effective at softening political opposition: the phasing in of deregulation was useful chiefly as a way to reduce the economic loss to regulated truckers and Teamsters, and allowance for ambiguity in the new ground rules, above all, allowed the ATA to sell the compromise legislation to its members.

Judging from the widespread use of monitoring, ambiguity, and techniques of gradualism and delay, the legislative process is inherently sensitive to political obstacles to transition. The infrequent use of explicit compensation and insurance does not reflect oversight on the part of legislators and their staffers; those strategies are simply less compatible with the political and institutional setting in which legislation is shaped. The legislative process is not inherently sensitive to efficiency considerations of transitions, however. Thus, what distinguished the airline and trucking fights was the simultaneous attention by key political players to the expedient *and* efficient management of the transition.

Above all, that reflected the potential for deregulation to produce transitional distortions. To assure a successful transition, the three essential features of proposals for trucking deregulation—reforms in the areas of entry, antitrust immunity, and pricing flexibility—had to be synchronized. Letting one get out of step with the others could well have rendered deregulation ineffective or, worse yet, counterproductive. The prospect of those outcomes—and the danger that they would increase pressure on Congress to reregulate before decontrol was completed—made it imperative to coordinate closely the various elements of reform.

The attention to expedient and efficient management of the transition also reflected who was in charge. Alfred Kahn was a highly respected academic economist and author of a two-volume text on the theory and application of regulatory economics who had also gained practical experience as chairman of New York's public utility commission from 1974 to 1977. He thus brought to his appointment as CAB chairman an unusual concern for the practical problems of "getting from here to there," and in 1979, he addressed the American Economic Association on that very topic.

Darius Gaskins displayed the same close attention to transitional concerns as ICC chairman. A Berkeley economics professor-turned-policymaker, Gaskins was instrumental in deregulating five industries in addition to trucking, including airlines when he was an assistant to Kahn. His concern for the problem of transition was ever visible—from his congressional testimony on the motor carrier bill to an academic paper on managing the transition to deregulation, written as the trucking battle raged.[44] Gaskins's oft-repeated message about the proper sequencing of reforms ("the amount of ratemaking freedom in this legislation should be *exactly commensurate* with the measures taken to increase competitive behavior in the industry") was picked up and echoed in Neil Goldschmidt's testimony for the administration, and later in the Senate committee report on the trucking bill.

As professional economists who sought to apply theory to practical policy decisions, Kahn and Gaskins were the most self-conscious about the problems of transition in general and transitional synchronization in particular. In addition to them were key staffers and lobbyists, lawyers most, who likewise understood the need for, and the economics of, a well-managed transition. Kahn and Gaskins were interested foremost in bringing an economic perspective to the political debate; others—like Stephen Breyer—in bringing a political perspective to the economic debate. The result was a marriage of political and economic skills that, as chapter 7 will argue, was also a defining characteristic of the reformers' bargaining effort and a key to their success.

7

Political Leverage:
The President as
Strategic Bargainer

Strategy—in [an important] sense . . .—is not concerned with the efficient application of force but with the exploitation of potential force.
—Thomas Schelling, *The Strategy of Conflict*

There are two ways to win a poker game. One is to have a good hand. The other is to make your opponent think you have a good hand. Unable to change the objective dimension of power, one can directly attack an opponent's subjective perception of power by bluff and other tactics. This is strategic bargaining—the art of manipulating information and managing impressions so as to reflect *and transform* the basic power relationships that underlie a conflict of interest.

Because bargaining power is subjective—and thus to some extent contrived—strategic bargaining holds the answer to the question of how a president (or other reformer) can gain the necessary leverage with Congress to defeat an entrenched client group. Lacking a power base that is objectively as strong as that of the group, the White House must create the appearance of superior power through bargaining.

This is at least possible because dependency and uncertainty characterize bargaining. Two opposing parties bargain because they mutually perceive that some range of dispute settlements is better for both than no settlement at all. That area of interdependency is never known to either bargainer, however; it must be inferred. And every move one party makes affects the range as perceived by the other party.

The "settlement range" is itself somewhat fluid. It has as its limits the minimal demands that each side expects a settlement to satisfy, and a party's limit (conflict point, minimum disposition, bottom line) is based on his perception of the costs and benefits of agreement versus disagreement. Though reasonably stable, those perceptions are subject to limited tactical manipulation within the bargaining process.

Far more sensitive to manipulation, however, is an opponent's estimate of the bargainer's limit, since that is based largely on cues provided by the bargainer. These cues come not only from the explicit negotiation that takes place but also from the tacit process in which, according to Thomas Schelling, "adversaries watch and interpret each other's behavior, each aware that his own actions are being interpreted and anticipated, each acting with a view to the expectations that he creates."[1]

Expectations are the key. At least in situations in which a better outcome for one means less for another, there is an element of "pure bargaining"—that is, "bargaining in which each party is guided mainly by his expectations of what the other will accept." Schelling elaborates: "With each [side] guided by expectations and knowing that the other is too, expectations become compounded. A bargain is struck when somebody makes a final, sufficient concession. Why does he concede? Because he thinks the other will not."[2]

In *Presidential Power*, Richard Neustadt wrote of the importance of expectations in political bargaining:

> In influencing Washingtonians, the most important law at a President's disposal is the "law" of "anticipated reactions." . . . The men who share in governing do what they think they must. A President's effect on them is heightened or diminished by their thoughts about his probable reaction to their doing. They base their expectations on what they can see of him. And they are watching all the time.[3]

The threat to veto unsatisfactory legislation is the most prominent tool with which the White House can shape the expectations of those who are watching. Traditionally, presidents have been sparing in its use, though Gerald Ford relied heavily on the threat of veto in his legislative strategy and succeeded in getting Congress to alter many bills to satisfy him.

Two problems limit its usefulness. Like any threat, it must be (or must appear to be) enforceable to be credible. Moreover, even if a president could sustain the veto, it's difficult to make opponents (and supporters) believe that he's not bluffing. That's so because some legislation is often better than no legislation at all. Schelling states the bargaining problem in more general terms: "There is some range of alternative outcomes in which any point is better for both sides than no agreement at all. To insist on any such point is pure bargaining, since one always *would* take less rather than reach no agreement at all, and since one always *can* recede if retreat proves necessary to the agreement."[4]

Some presidents have been more skilled than others at strategic bargaining. Eisenhower was "notable for his seeming lack of concern for or involvement in getting many of his programs passed," according to presidential scholar George Edwards. "He also frequently wavered in his support, providing potential supporters with inconsistent cues."[5] Nixon lacked follow-through, at least on one major program proposed by his administration. After going on national television to present the Family Assistance Plan (FAP), Nixon's program for reforming the welfare system, the president put down his sword, according to Daniel P. Moynihan, his chief adviser on welfare matters: "Initial thrusts were rarely followed up with a sustained . . . second and third order of advocacy. . . . The impression was allowed to arise . . . that the president wasn't really behind them."[6] President Johnson, by contrast, was a skilled legislative bargainer, as the following description by Edwards reflects:

> President Johnson believed that it was important for his congressional opponents to understand his concern for the passage of his policies. He wrote that during the battle for the 1964 Civil Rights Act, he took special care that leaders of the opposition understood his uncompromising attitude and commitment to the passage of a strong bill. He felt that the slightest wavering on his part would give hope to their strategy of amending the bill to uselessness.[7]

Johnson did not, of course, have a truly uncompromising attitude toward the Civil Rights Act or any other legislation he promoted. Only an irrational bargainer would rule out points of compromise that are better than no compromise at all. But as Johnson's strategy recognized, the more a president can create the impression of being uncompromising, the less he will have to compromise. The more convincing his veto threat, the less chance he will have to carry it out.

A bargainer's task, then, is twofold, whether the game is poker or politics: to convince his opponent that he controls resources that the opponent needs and that he is willing to use power to achieve his desired outcome.[8] The following pages examine the performance of the Carter White House as strategic bargainer with that standard in mind. The first two sections evaluate how well the White House created the impression that it controlled power and that it was willing to use it absent a desirable settlement. Section three looks at external forces that kept the White House from "caving in" and at voluntary tactics that rest on the paradox that, in bargaining, weakness often provides strength. Section three also considers how the White House gained bargaining strength from its reliance on substance and substantive people for making tactical judgments. Recognizing that President Carter was only one, albeit the most important, bargainer, the final section of the chapter briefly examines the contribution of other key players on both sides.

Appearance of Controlling Needed Resources

The situation changed radically this fall when the three new ICC appointees made it clear they support major reform action. . . . [T]his has scared the industry into deciding it needs *legislation.*
—White House Memorandum (Rick Neustadt to Stuart Eizenstat), October 23, 1979

The ICC—a powerful political resource—was the key to the administration's victory. Early commission reforms forced the trucking industry to seek legislative relief—that is, to bargain. Continued ICC decontrol and the threat of more to come led opponents to accept a strong reform bill in the belief that it was better than no bill at all. Thus the ICC—through successive real and threatened reforms, none of which produced the dire effects predicted by the industry—managed to "shift the center" of the political debate and the bargainers' settlement range.

Carter's appointment of A. Daniel O'Neal as ICC chairman soon after taking office was key. O'Neal was a reformer, not a deregulator, and the changes that he sought to implement seem mild in retrospect. But they were ambitious for their time. Given the makeup of the commission he chaired, O'Neal made impressive strides.

Major changes became possible, however, only after the White House succeeded in appointing the "three marketeers"—Darius Gaskins, Jr., Marcus Alexis, and Thomas Trantum—in late 1979. Even then, the ICC was not solidly proreform: after O'Neal left, only three of the seven commissioners were deregulators, and a fourth was persuadable. But the agency had a persuasive and aggressive chairman in Gaskins and considerable administrative discretion.

The support the ICC gave Carter was unusual coming from an independent agency. In part, it was explained by the same broad political and economic changes that created a favorable climate for deregulation in

Congress—in particular, persistent high inflation. But there were more immediate explanations.

O'Neal was both pushed and lured toward deregulation. Initially he hoped to defuse support for congressionally imposed decontrol by carrying out reforms administratively. Kennedy's hearings, which portrayed the ICC in a poor light, made internal reform all the more urgent. O'Neal eventually recognized that legislation was necessary and inevitable, but he still sought to lead the way—no doubt in hopes he could borrow a page from Alfred Kahn's bestseller: as CAB-induced competition produced record-low air fares, Chairman Kahn was becoming America's most popular bureaucrat.

The man who reportedly convinced Kahn that he couldn't be the perfect regulator—to deregulate instead—was Darius Gaskins. Gaskins was a fierce believer in the benefits of competition and a persuasive advocate of those beliefs. He was instrumental in decontrolling crude-oil pricing as a deputy assistant secretary of energy, and before that the airline industry when he headed the CAB's Office of Economic Analysis. "In the beginning, Fred [Kahn] had instincts that you could be a perfect regulator," according to CAB member Elizabeth Bailey. "Darius [Gaskins] converted Fred to the position that it's very hard to regulate perfectly; that imperfect competition wins out over imperfect regulation."[9]

The change in the ICC as a result of Carter's appointments represented a real increase in the administration's resources and, likewise, an objective loss to opponents' power base. The iron triangle was genuinely weakened. At the same time, skilled bargaining exploited that change and created the appearance of an even greater power shift than was objectively the case. For, aggressive though it appeared, the ICC could proceed only as long as Congress continued to tolerate its actions and the courts to uphold them.

The risk of repudiation caused the ICC and the White House to walk a fine line. The strategy was to move ever closer to complete deregulation but without going so far that the courts would reverse the commission or that Congress would "cut it off at the knees." Neither side knew where the courts would draw the line. Privately, the White House felt the ICC could have revoked antitrust immunity with its existing authority; but the mandate for other reforms—open entry and broadened exemptions—was much less clear. Equally uncertain was the limit of Congress's tolerance.

The ICC finally crossed that limit when it eliminated an entry restriction that was the very foundation of regulation. A retaliatory maneuver by Senate Appropriations chairman Birch Bayh nearly crippled the commission. But Sen. Howard Cannon saved the day with his "mad-as-hell" speech promising legislation by June 1. Cannon's pledge gave the bargaining situation what it previously lacked—a deadline. Moreover, his seemingly antagonistic directive against irreversible commission reform cleverly appeased Congress while keeping potent the threat of independent ICC action.

Just how much of a threat that was did not become apparent to the ATA for several months. By then Gaskins, Trantum, and others had convinced the truckers that they could be faced with the worst of both worlds: more competition as a result of recent entry liberalizations that were sure to continue, and more regulation as well through strict rate-of-return standards. By the time the trucking bill moved from the Senate to the House, the risk of independent ICC action had become too great. The ATA willingly relinquished the fight for permanent antitrust immunity in return for a bill that gave the industry considerable pricing freedom and some protection from an unrestrained ICC.

Appearance of Willingness to Use Power

The crunch will come next year, when we have to decide whether to fight or compromise. My preliminary view is that we should be tough for the next couple of months—even hinting about a veto—and delay cutting a deal, if at all *until late in the process. . . . This approach reduces the chance of getting a bill but increases the chance of making real progress, either through legislation or through ICC action.*

—White House Memorandum (Rick Neustadt to Stuart Eizenstat)
    October 23, 1979

Even with the ICC seemingly in Carter's camp, the ATA stood to get favorable legislation unless Congress perceived that the president was willing to use power to prevent that from happening—willing, that is, to walk away from a bad bill and unleash the ICC. Initially, the expectation in Washington was that he would not be. The White House will "roll over and take any compromise," the ATA was rumored to have said.[10] ATA officials may not have truly believed that self-serving prophecy, but they didn't expect particularly hard bargaining from the Carter administration over an issue that so few people cared about. And while deregulators in lobby groups and on Capitol Hill never believed the White House would take *any* compromise— the potential for attack by Kennedy, Carter's political nemesis, would prevent that—they did fear the administration would settle for a bill that was worse than no bill in their eyes.

To a point, deregulators outside and within the administration shared a common interest in getting legislation. First, there was the uncertainty about how much administrative reform the courts would allow. And even if the courts upheld the ICC, there was no guarantee that if Carter were defeated in 1980, his successor would not undo by ICC appointment the good that had been done.

The White House had an additional, electoral interest in legislation, however, not fully shared by other deregulators—namely the desire for political credit. Carter was an unpopular president who was seen as ineffectual with Congress. He needed legislative "victories" to point to in the 1980 campaign. The desire for Teamster votes was seemingly another reason for the White House to cut a deal on trucking reform.

Any president would have been suspect. But first-hand experience had led many of the deregulators to expect "cavemen" in the Carter White House. In particular they feared a repeat of what happened with Carter's 1979 railroad reform bill, which one coalition member described bitterly: "[DOT Secretary] Brock Adams introduced the bill and then sat back and watched it get clobbered, essentially saying the White House would take whatever the committee came out with. There was no sense of what the bottom line was."

Ultimately, two types of cues served to convince opponents and supporters that Carter would not take just any compromise. The administration's expenditure of vast organizational resources—firepower—on lobbying was a clear indication of Carter's priority for trucking reform. And explicit positional cues—hints of veto and rejections of compromise offers—signaled that his bargaining demands were reasonably firm.

Firepower: Persuasion and Proof of Commitment

The president's personal involvement in the trucking bill was considerable by Capitol Hill standards—meetings with Senator Cannon, telephone calls to senators on the Commerce Committee before and during markup, an Oval Office meeting with House Public Works Committee members Bizz Johnson and James Howard during the height of the Iran hostage crisis, a scheduled appearance at a gathering of coalition members. Carter referred to trucking deregulation in his 1980 State of the Union message, plugged it at Democratic gatherings, and issued presidential statements and letters to Congress before and after key votes. He heard the words "trucking deregulation" at least weekly and often daily.

Several of Carter's personal appeals on the trucking bill had direct strategic value. The Oval Office meeting was what it took to break a logjam in the Public Works Committee. As one Public Works staffer observed, "When two senior [Democratic] members go to the White House, how can they not say something the president wants to hear." Veterans of the airline-deregulation fight recalled how a similar session with the president brought quick results there. "Carter put his arm around Bizz Johnson and told him he'd be a great American if he went back and pushed the airline bill through," said one lobbyist. "That has a lot of impact."

Carter's personal involvement contributed more to strategy indirectly, however, as a symbolic indication of the high priority he attached to trucking reform. "The president made telephone calls on the bill," said White House aides and lobbyists almost without elaboration. It established their credentials instantly.

In keeping with Carter's (as well as their own) priorities, senior administration officials also gave trucking reform considerable personal attention. Vice-president Walter Mondale telephoned several senators before key votes. Anti-inflation czar Alfred Kahn, domestic-policy chief Stuart Eizenstat, and DOT secretary Neil Goldschmidt made frequent visits and calls to Capitol Hill—initially to deliver testimony and speeches, and later to talk with individual members of Congress. After following the floor vote from the vice-president's Senate office, Kahn and Goldschmidt emerged jubilant to join Cannon and Packwood in a winners' press conference. When Capitol Hill staffers came to the White House to be briefed on the trucking bill they were greeted by Eizenstat and Kahn.

It was a strong show of White House support by any measure. Before markup, every swing senator on the Commerce Committee received a call or visit from Kahn, Eizenstat, or Goldschmidt. In preparation for the floor vote, a senior administration official contacted every swing vote in the Senate (a representative from DOT or the White House contacted *every* senator or senator's legislative assistant). On the House side, where the political battle was largely confined to the subcommittee, Goldschmidt met six separate times with Chairman Howard, and Eizenstat attended several of the meetings as well.[11]

In addition to lobbying the Hill directly, the White House sought to apply pressure indirectly. The ad hoc coalition was the primary vehicle for that strategy and, as chapter 5 described, the administration worked closely with that group.[12]

Another vehicle for putting indirect pressure on Congress was the press. Support for deregulation in the press was strong even before the political battle heated up: the hundreds of editorials endorsing trucking deregulation that appeared in newspapers throughout the country were a key to making the substantive case for reform, as chapter 4 described. For gaining political leverage, however, the administration looked to a more precise tool—the targeted editorial. In an effort to influence Public Works Committee members, for example, the White House sent materials to—and then telephoned—editorial writers at some thirty-five newspapers in key districts, most of whom promised to publish sympathetic editorials within a week.

Timing was the key. The question was not so much what editorial writers would say as when they would say it. Perhaps no newspaper showed more sensitivity to that than the *Washington Post* when it admonished John Warner to hold his position on antitrust immunity in an editorial published the morning of the critical vote. That same vote occasioned the editorial in the *New York Times* the previous weekend that derided Representative Howard's initial bill as "limp." Such censure, coming from the most influential newspaper in Howard's New Jersey district if not the country, unquestionably put him in a more cooperative mood.

Functions of Lobbying

In sum, White House lobbying served the direct functions of persuading and pressuring members of Congress. Logical persuasion played no small part in the process, particularly in the Senate, where many members were electorally secure enough to look to the merits. Also important was political "persuasion." "Few men . . . are immune to the impulse to say 'yes' to the President of the United States," observed Richard Neustadt, an adviser to Truman, in his analysis of presidential power. "It grows harder to say 'no' when they are seated in his oval office at the White House, or in his study on the second floor, where almost tangibly he partakes of the aura of his physical surroundings."[13]

A popular president is considerably more persuasive than an unpopular one. But as the trucking battle illustrates, the prestige of the presidency is itself a weapon even under the worst of conditions. Carter was an unpopular president who had exhausted most of his political capital in Congress by the time he declared war on trucking regulation. Yet his personal appeals—telephone calls to senators, requests for cooperation from committee leaders—had clout. As one Senate staffer summed it up, "He was still the president."

Because "he was still the president," the message that "Carter is very committed" to the trucking bill carried a certain intrinsic weight—or at least White House aides believed that it did. "The speaker needs to know of our priority for this bill," said one memo. "Reaffirm our commitment to a strong bill," said another. But ultimately more revealing of Carter's commitment was the administration's devotion of vast organizational resources. Thus the expenditure of firepower was important to bargaining chiefly as a symbolic demonstration of the president's priorities.

Viewed as symbolic action, what made for effective lobbying was a high degree of visibility and political sacrifice. More than one Public Works

Committee member expressed amazement that Carter had called in Representatives Johnson and Howard to talk about trucking deregulation in the
midst of the Iran hostage crisis. The appearance of top-level officials like
Eizenstat and Kahn on Capitol Hill to lobby the trucking bill made an
important statement even before they uttered a word.

Short Lists

"If Carter had invested that much effort in other legislation, he'd still
be president," said one DOT staffer about the administration's campaign for
trucking reform. The observation was facetious. The limits of the organization—none more severe than that there is only one president—preclude
that. Short lists are necessarily short. What's more, the White House effort on
trucking deregulation was effective precisely because other legislation was
not as favored. Those who "are watching all the time" base their expectations on the administration's ordering—both explicit and implicit—of legislative goals.

The administration's lobbying effort on the trucking bill received its
share of criticism, some of it no doubt deserved. The fact that only three of
ten Democrats on the Senate Commerce Committee voted "right" on the
critical test indicates that the administration's selling job left something to
be desired, at least at that stage of the battle. Even critics, however, would
concede that the White House mounted a highly visible effort that represented a sizable investment of resources.[14]

No one showed more surprise at the amount of firepower the White
House put into the trucking bill than the ATA. In part, that reaction was
expedient. If anything the ATA exaggerated the magnitude of the administration's effort so as to spur its members to act. But posturing aside, ATA
representatives were genuinely surprised at what a massive campaign was
mounted to defeat them. "The average person doesn't *care* about trucking
deregulation," they said with puzzlement. "Eizenstat and Kahn perceived it
as a big issue that people really cared about," one lobbyist offered as an
explanation. "It was incestuous. They were talking only to themselves."

The ATA was half right. Eizenstat and Kahn did perceive it as a big
issue, but it was in part precisely because the average person didn't care
about trucking deregulation—a fact the White House knew all too well—
that they felt such a visible effort was needed.

Explicit Cues: The Appearance of Firmness

Sometimes a showing of strong commitment can actually weaken a bargainer. Commitment—in the sense of importance ascribed to the issues or

outcomes at stake—implies dependence; the more dependent one is on the opponent, the more bargaining power the opponent has. What generally offsets this is the greater tactical effort that high commitment motivates.

With presidential bargaining, a massive lobbying campaign is generally accompanied by a firm will. Nevertheless, the White House had to make that explicit. In so doing, it gave opponents one significant miscue, and it's arguable that the White House could have gotten a slightly better deal had it held out longer. But overall, White House actions created the impression that President Carter had high expectations and a reasonably firm resolve.

The sweeping Carter-Kennedy bill, S. 1400, represented the administration's initial bargaining demand. It did little to strengthen Carter's image as a weak bargainer, however, because there was little cost to demanding so much. The usual risk—not being taken seriously—was low here, since Cannon had already scheduled hearings on the administration's proposal, and since committee bills would ultimately be the vehicle for congressional debate. And when that debate came about, the White House was quick to correct the impression—perpetuated by opponents—that Carter would settle for nothing less than S. 1400.

One of the first explicit statements to come (informally) from the White House only confirmed opponents' expectations of a weak presidential will. William Johnston, a Domestic Policy Staff aide assigned to the trucking bill, privately gave Jim Howard the green light on a bill that would relax entry regulations but leave antitrust immunity untouched. "He loves doing deals," said another administration staffer of Johnston, who later moved from the DPS to a high-level position at DOT. "It's part of his personality. And he truly didn't know that the president was so committed."[15]

Whatever the reason, this early signal caused considerable damage. Howard's "limp" bill, General Motors' formation of a pro-ATA "Committee of Truck Shippers," the rumored message that the White House would "roll over and take any compromise"—all are partly explained by Johnston's miscue. When the White House later tried to counter the initial signals—most notably through testimony by Neil Goldschmidt that was sharply critical of Howard's bill—it encountered strong resentment.[16]

Combined with President Carter's earlier hints of veto, Goldschmidt's testimony left little doubt that the Public Works bill fell outside the range of outcomes acceptable to the White House. But it was uncertain to observers where the limit of that range was. (Goldschmidt's reply to a committee member's query—that S. 2245 was the minimum the White House could live with—clearly reflected posturing, since the DOT secretary had praised the Commerce Committee bill in testimony.) That was just as the White House wanted it. Internal memos repeatedly cautioned against spelling out which items were indispensable for fear that would lock in the administration and reduce the bargaining room it might later need.[17] Thus the essence of the White House strategy was a paradox characteristic of bargaining: Make clear that we have a firm bottom line, but don't reveal where it is.

In truth, even the White House didn't know precisely where its bottom line was. The basic elements of reform—entry, antitrust immunity, and pricing flexibility—were closely intertwined; getting more of one might justify accepting less of another. In addition, a lot depended on how much latitude the legislation would grant the ICC. Even Gaskins could not have turned a "lemon" into "lemonade," but a seemingly mild bill might have been acceptable had it given the ICC wide berth. Overall, the White House applied this standard: If a bill cuts ICC discretion, particularly on entry, it's bad. If it moves forward in some areas and is silent in others, then it's better than nothing. Why veto such a bill?

A New Threat

When deregulators experienced early triumphs in the trucking battle, the veiled threat of veto lost credibility. Cannon's introduction of an unexpectedly strong bill ("While we should seek improvements," said a White House memo, "the President certainly could sign this bill as a major accomplishment"), and the Senate's subsequent approval of it, made it highly unlikely that Congress would pass a regressive bill. Opponents of deregulation ceased to fear that a president in Carter's position—faced with a tough reelection campaign and with few legislative victories to point to—would veto or derail any trucking bill Congress would realistically produce.

What they did fear was getting no bill. The issue was so complex and controversial that industry supporters believed a House-Senate conference committee might well deadlock, leaving the ICC—whose full threat potential had only recently become apparent—free to deregulate just as would a veto. Thus compromise was essential, and the critical question with regard to bottom lines was this: How much must we give deregulators to assure a compromise and avoid carrying the fight to conference?

White House actions in the following weeks served to answer that question.[18] When Representative Howard proposed a compromise that essentially called for a trade-off of the hard-fought food exemption for antitrust immunity, the administration's initial reaction was negative. White House aide Ron Lewis, a deputy to Alfred Kahn, met with DOT and ICC representatives and then recommended that Eizenstat turn it down. Lewis advised that the best strategy was still to urge Howard to move quickly, using the Senate bill. That way Howard could fend off amendments by portraying it as middle-ground legislation that already had the Senate's imprimatur.

Meetings with Howard during the next week convinced the White House aides that the subcommittee chairman sincerely wanted to help but was caught in the middle. When Lewis met with the ad hoc coalition on April 30, he gave coalition members a discouraging appraisal:

> We've talked to Howard lots. I wish I could say it's been productive. He's genuinely trying to be helpful—for the first time. And he's committed to getting a bill on President Carter's desk by June 1. On the other hand, he's getting tremendous pressure from truckers and Teamsters. The [Public Works Committee] staff is not enthusiastic. . . . Every member is up for reelection. Howard looks at us in anguish and says, "Where are the votes?" The truckers are just overwhelming us. . . . We've resisted every compromise Howard has proposed. . . [but] we're faced with a "bad" committee and a "bad" subcommittee.

When a coalition member asked Lewis if Carter would make clear his intention to veto a poor bill, Lewis responded quickly: "Yes. He's said that [all along]. . . . And we're in constant touch with the ICC asking, 'What's your bottom line?' "

The Oval Office Meeting

That same afternoon, Carter met with Representatives Johnson and Howard in the Oval Office, with Eizenstat and Lewis in attendance. "Talking Points" prepared for Carter's use at the meeting indicate that the White House sought to use its leverage, not by threat, but by an appeal for the kind of "strong leadership [Johnson and Howard had] exercised on transportation matters in the past," and a promise of "strong support" by the president. Both sides made some compromises, and the meeting ended in agreement.

White House aides believed that speed was critical to their strategy. Thus in the Oval Office, when Howard promised to mark up a bill within two weeks, they were delighted. But Howard proved elusive. A week later, he decided that rather than mark up the trucking bill, he had to make a trip abroad to interest European bus manufacturers in taking over an abandoned assembly line in New Jersey (a trip one White House aide described as "eminently postponable"). Aides prepared to have Carter telephone

Howard on the rationale that further delay might cause significant political damage. In particular they worried that the threat of independent ICC action would lose some of its credibility after June 1 had passed.

The call from the president was never made. Instead, White House aides met with Representative Johnson, implicitly to ask for his help. Johnson was sympathetic, but he said that Howard viewed the European trip as essential to his primary race and there was no stopping him. However Johnson called Howard on the spot and got his firm commitment to hold subcommittee markup on May 20—two weeks away—a date that Johnson felt would still allow the House to meet the June 1 deadline for legislation.

The aides were less than pleased. Among other things, Howard's absence would create a leadership vacuum at a critical time. But at least the coalition was prepared to work hard, and Rep. Peter Rodino, chairman of the House Judiciary Committee, was pressing Howard and Johnson for a good antitrust provision, using his committee's potential claim to joint jurisdiction over S. 2245 as leverage. His threat had infuriated the Public Works Committee chief counsel, aides told Eizenstat, but it would help ultimately.

The "Disgusting Draft"

Following the Oval Office meeting, White House aides had begun working with Public Works staff members on a draft bill reflecting the agreement reached with the president. A week later Lewis told Eizenstat that key staffers continued to talk about "decent-sounding" provisions while taking their time about putting anything down on paper. He was concerned that they be able to agree on specific language with Howard before he left for Europe.

When administration aides were finally shown the staff's "discussion draft" on May 8, hours before Howard was to leave, they were surprised and disappointed. While it was significantly better than the committee's original bill and tracked the Senate bill closely in most respects, the differences were critical. Moreover, the draft departed from the agreement they felt had been reached in the Oval Office in key ways. When Lewis met with coalition members six days later to talk about the discussion draft—dubbed by them the "disgusting draft"—he said it appeared the committee staff "has taken on a life of its own."

Three provisions of the staff draft were objectionable. The draft delayed the phaseout of antitrust immunity until 1984—six months (and possibly a year) later than what S. 2245 called for. Lewis told the coalition that while the administration didn't like the date slippage, it was hard to draw the line, and the White House could live with that change. What was unacceptable was language preserving antitrust protection for *discussions* preceding rate-bureau votes even after 1984. Lewis said administration lawyers were firm in insisting that discussion—which was the "heart of the matter" when it came to such collusion—could not be immune.

Second, the staff draft "weakened the agricultural exemption to the point where it was not very helpful," in Lewis's words. Rather than exempting processed food from regulation altogether, the draft authorized one-truck owner-operators to haul regulated food. This excluded multi-truck independents and private carriers operating for hire altogether, but even qualified owner-operators were limited by language that said regulated food could account for only 50 percent of their annual haul. Lewis said the White House was urging Public Works to preserve the provision in S. 2245 or, at the very least, drop the 50 percent rule.

Also objectionable was the provision for a pricing zone indexed for inflation. Rather than initiating indexing when antitrust immunity ended, as S. 2245 did, the House draft started it nearly two years before then. (Public Works knew what we didn't like, said one coalition member, and they "rubbed our noses in it.") Lewis said the administration had drafted language that would leave it up to the ICC to initiate indexing, and the White House was pressing Public Works on that change.

The administration had never been as anxious about the indexing provision as shippers, believing that competitive pressures would inevitably keep carriers from raising rates to the maximum allowed. But the key was a strong entry provision. For that and other reasons, White House memos had said repeatedly that entry was a "live-or-die" item. Coalition members were unhappy with the entry provision in the staff draft, and the administration shared their skepticism initially. But closer examination convinced the White House otherwise, as Lewis told the coalition. With good language in the committee report, administration lawyers believed the Public Works provision could be even better than its Senate counterpart.

"A Bill Everyone Can Live With"

As White House representatives—primarily Lewis and Domestic Policy Staff member Rick Neustadt—continued meeting directly with the Public Works leadership, it became clear that the two GOP leaders were the real obstacle—in particular, Rep. William Harsha of Ohio, the ranking Republican. White House aides thought they could turn the markup into a partisan fight and come out winners. They asked Eizenstat to call Howard in Europe and, among other things, point out the advantages of making this a political fight, since it would make the GOP look hypocritical.

The committee was not about to succumb to partisan fighting, however. Historically, infighting is anathema to Public Works, a committee where more (pork) for one member need not mean less for another. More important, the committee was determined to write a bill that Cannon, Packwood, and the administration would accept so as to avoid carrying the fight to a House-Senate conference, which the ATA desperately feared would end in deadlock. The discussion draft had been the committee's first stab at a House-Senate compromise without a conference—something almost unheard of on Capitol Hill. With that as a basis, Public Works staffers began meeting with Senate aides, White House representatives, and other key groups to come up with a "bill that everyone can live with."

The unusual negotiation process went on for seven dramatic days. The committee made minor concessions and the White House made others, but Carter aides continued to hold out for three key changes in the draft— removal of antitrust protection for rate-bureau discussions, elimination of the 50 percent rule for owner-operators, and a delay in price indexing. After several days of stalemate, the impending deadline brought movement in the negotiations. The Public Works Committee agreed to the change in antitrust immunity but said emphatically it would concede no more. The White House, jointly with Cannon and Packwood, made the decision to accept the compromise rather than try for further concessions or fight it out in the markup and, ultimately, in conference committee. Coalition members learned of the agreement shortly after.

Too Soon?

Whether the White House settled too soon—whether it could have gotten more from the Public Works Committee either by refusing to compromise at all or by holding out for a better deal—is a question people involved in the trucking battle will debate for years. At least some coalition members were quite critical of the compromise, as chapter 5 described. The seeming glee with which the ATA accepted the settlement also gave the impression that the White House could have done better. The Lyndon Johnson adage, "If you win by more than one vote, you've given up too much," seemed altogether apt. But some of that was posturing by ATA officials trying to impress their members. Moreover, there were no real "losers." By the very nature of bargaining, a settlement makes both sides better off than deadlock.

Those explanations aside, there were substantive differences of opinion that produced inconsistent reactions. The ATA felt that the compromise entry provision was more restrictive than existing ICC policy, and many coalition members agreed; the administration firmly believed it was as liberal, if not more so. With such a good entry provision, the administration felt competition would prevent abuse of the indexed pricing zone, whereas the truckers (and many shippers) looked on the zone provision as a potential pot of gold.

Despite their pleasure with certain provisions of the bill, those who negotiated in sympathy with the truckers do not regard the White House as having caved in. One ATA lobbyist referred to Lewis, without affection, as "Attila the Hun." Public Works staffers shared that image, crediting the aggressiveness of White House aides in part to naivete: "Once our members were satisfied, that left the White House and the Senate Commerce Committee," said one committee aide. "Ron and Rick held out the longest. We had the feeling they didn't understand the politics of it."

If Lewis and Neustadt were initially naive, it was to the dynamics of the Public Works Committee's internal leadership on the trucking bill. They, as well as members of the coalition, felt that getting the cooperation of the Democratic leadership—Howard and Johnson—was the key. In truth, the ranking Republican on the committee, Rep. William Harsha, was far more antagonistic than either Howard or Johnson. And because he involved himself so thoroughly in the committee's handling of the bill, Harsha largely dictated its stance. His bottom line became the committee's bottom line.

In part because they overestimated Howard's and Johnson's leadership role, White House aides were less amenable to early compromise proposals than other deregulators. When the staff draft was released, Senate Commerce Committee members found it surprisingly good. ("We were extremely pleased," said one Commerce staffer. "It was much closer to our position than where we thought they'd start out. That's when we first felt that we might really have something.") White House aides, by contrast, were disappointed because the draft fell short of what they felt Carter had been promised in the Oval Office. A week later, as the two sides approached agreement, White House aides held out even after other deregulators had privately concluded that the Public Works Committee had conceded as much as it was going to.

It's difficult to separate the hard-line stance the White House took up until the end from an aggressive bargaining style that the Public Works Committee found offensive. "The White House at first came on like gangbusters, using strong-arm tactics," said one committee staffer. "Strong-arm tactics" included Goldschmidt's harsh criticism of Howard's bill and Rodino's threat of a turf battle if Public Works went easy on antitrust immunity. Overall the White House bargaining style was characterized more by threat than diplomacy—but quite intentionally so; aides felt they didn't have the votes to win any other way.

That their actions were so uncharacteristic of the usual, nonaggressive Carter style made them all the more effective, if risky. "It was very touchy," said one Public Works staffer, "because one wrong statement and Harsha would have said to forget the whole thing. He didn't think in his heart he was doing the right thing by deregulating."

Harsha was indeed a fighter. When ATA lobbyists told him they wanted to avoid a "bloodbath in conference," he reportedly said to them, "Who's afraid of a bloodbath?" But he was also a fierce advocate of the ATA, and he quickly understood the group's desperate need to reach a compromise. Thus one must wonder whether he—and therefore the committee—would not have conceded still more had that been the price of compromise.

The ATA's needs aside, Public Works wanted very much to compromise for purely selfish reasons. Reform was by then inevitable and a compromise would allow the committee to take some of the credit. Continuing to fight would only enhance the committee's "black hat" image in the press and the Senate. In addition, Public Works had a heavy work load, and it was more than eager to be rid of the trucking issue and the intense political heat that accompanied it.

Nevertheless, if the White House was correct in concluding that the committee had made its final offer, what would have happened had Lewis and Neustadt turned it down? To be sure, Public Works would have passed a limp bill in markup. (The ATA felt it had the votes to pass even Howard's original bill, though committee staffers weren't so sure. "When they couldn't control the Senate," said one, "[that meant] the same thing could have been true for the House.") And the House would have approved it: it is almost impossible to beat Public Works on the floor of the House because the committee controls the community pork barrel. Thus the fight would have come in conference.

Could the White House have gotten a better deal there than in Public Works? Under Cannon's influence, conferees on airline deregulation produced a "compromise" that was stronger than either bill they began with. The knowledge of that made the ATA extremely reluctant to go head-to-head with Cannon, not to mention Packwood, whose passion for deregulation would make him a formidable bargainer. Moreover, the fundamental strategic fact was that the ATA felt it *had* to have a bill, and that severely limited its ability to bluff.

At the same time, deadlock or delay was also a sizable risk to deregulators. It was May of an election year. The conference committee wouldn't begin meeting until June or July. There was a good chance of getting no bill at all while Carter was still president. A compromise with Public Works guaranteed deregulators a good bill and at least six months of aggressive implementation of it by a friendly ICC (a consideration that subsequent events proved wise).

Perhaps deregulators—the administration in particular—could have gotten more, either by tougher bargaining with Public Works or by fighting it out in conference. But if the existence of the ICC gave them the leverage to demand a reasonably strong bill, it also gave them the freedom to settle for a less than ideal one. Alfred Kahn expressed that sentiment at a briefing for Senate legislative assistants when one said to him, "You've made a great case for deregulation. Why support a bill that does so little of it?" Kahn replied that even if the bill represented only "two-thirds a loaf, or three-quarters of one . . . combined with an excellent ICC, that's all we need."

In sum, fears (and hopes) that Carter's need for a bill would lead the White House to cave in weren't realized. As one coalition lobbyist conceded, the final bill was surprisingly good, given how much Carter wanted it. Her remark reflected the paradox of bargaining—the more one needs an agreement, the less one will settle for—if also the cynicism of someone who had been burned by previous experiences lobbying with a White House that seemingly had no firm bottom line.

Strength through Weakness;
Strength through Substance

> *[Gaskins's special assistant] urged us to be very careful, because seemingly minor changes in the entry standard could cripple the Commission. I urge you . . . to check any proposal with him.*
> —White House Memorandum, (Rick Neustadt to William Johnston in DOT) April 16, 1980

The pressing need for a bill Carter could take credit for was only one way in which the campaign impinged on the administration's bargaining stance. An early strategy memo noted the potential for Kennedy's staff to "attack . . . us if we compromise."[19] And when White House officials requested Carter's permission to use the veto threat, they pointed out that they could do so without political harm "because the truckers and Teamsters . . . are already against us, and . . . even more passionately against Kennedy."[20]

However, as the general election approached and Kennedy ceased to be Carter's major threat, the political costs of alienating the Teamsters became more visible. The powerful union had not hesitated to endorse Republican presidential candidates in the past, and its 1980 endorsement choice could hinge on the deregulation issue.

White House deregulators shared the desire to appease the union in ways that would not compromise the White House position on reform. In late February, aides met with Teamster representatives and worked out an amendment to a motor carrier safety bill then in committee on truck cab length. But they drew the line there. Noting that other Teamster demands were totally contrary to President Carter's position, an internal White House memo concluded that "we are going to have to be very tough, and the Teamsters are going to be very unhappy with us."[21]

Teamster pressure on the White House increased when the battle turned. Immediately after their trouncing in Senate markup, then-union head Frank Fitzsimmons arranged to meet with President Carter. At the meeting, Fitzsimmons proposed a compromise on the Teamsters' chief concern—the issue of entry. The heart of the proposal was to "split the difference" on the burden of proof between the old system (burden on applicant) and the provision in S. 2245 (burden on protestant).

Several weeks later, at the request of Landon Butler, a White House staffer involved in the reelection campaign, two administration aides met with Teamster representatives to discuss the compromise. The representatives indicated that the union might well endorse Ronald Reagan absent the compromise. Administration aides were noncommittal.

A subsequent White House memo discussed the issue further. While the Teamster proposal could be written to let a progressive ICC approve most new entrants, the memo advised, the White House could not "*appear* to be caving on a fundamental issue"—particularly before the Senate floor vote, since the White House was committed to supporting the Cannon provision and since it had the support to pass. The House is another matter, the memo noted, and a compromise on entry might make sense there, apart from campaign considerations.[22]

Shortly before the Senate vote, White House aides met with a group of Pennsylvania Teamsters and discussed the compromise in detail. The discussions convinced them that the union's proposal would severely discourage new entrants and bog the ICC down in complex proceedings and litigation. In a subsequent memo, one aide said that ICC chairman Gaskins and many of the coalition groups would feel such a bill was worse than no bill. "Apart from the merits," the memo stated, "it is hard to see how we could accept such a deal without a torrent of criticism for selling out."[23]

The aide concluded that any compromise with the Teamsters was unlikely and that the only hope was that the internal policies of the union allowed it "to take a small gain and call it a victory." He recommended leaving the door slightly ajar, but cautioned the need to consult the ICC before agreeing to even minor changes in the entry standard.

As predicted, compromise with the Teamsters proved impossible, at least directly. The entry provision in the Senate bill was modified as part of the overall compromise with Public Works. While the White House felt the new standard was no worse, and possibly better, the Teamsters viewed it as a definite improvement. And, as the White House aide hoped, opponents were able to claim it as at least a small victory.

Strength through Weakness

While the White House gave the Teamsters little encouragement, the very fact that administration aides were meeting secretly with representatives of the union caused concern to deregulators who were aware of it. No damage was done, in part for reasons that contributed to Carter's firm bargaining stance throughout the trucking battle.

The Carter White House was vulnerable to attack by supporters if it sold out—either through a deal with the Teamsters or in some other way. Edward Kennedy, who favored strong decontrol, was a political rival. The coalition was unified and prepared to be vocal if the White House caved in. Finally, the press was following the trucking issue closely. (One White House memo said "we do not want newspaper stories about deals with the Teamsters.")

The White House knew it had to maintain a firm bargaining position to avoid "a torrent of criticism." Moreover, opponents of deregulation knew that too. In that respect, the White House drew bargaining strength from its own vulnerability.

Howard Cannon drew strength from weakness in much the same way. When the *New York Times* reported on the FBI investigation into possible illegal influence, ATA pressure on Cannon to dilute his bill quickly stopped. Knowing that the senator could no longer back down without looking bad, the truckers gave him up as a lost cause. Earlier his vulnerability to attack by Kennedy as a result of the jurisdictional fight limited Cannon's flexibility to compromise and altered opponents' expectations accordingly. Bennett Whitlock told ATA members that the Commerce Committee introduced such a strong bill partly because "they have a gentleman named Ted Kennedy looking over their shoulder."

Deregulators were not the only ones who found bargaining strength in weakness. The White House viewed Public Works Committee members as less amenable to its influence because they were up for reelection. Howard and Johnson faced particularly tough campaigns (when Howard went to Europe the week before markup on a trip he insisted was essential to his reelection, there was little the White House could say), which made White House aides feel they could push the two Democrats only so far. Howard's inability to control his subcommittee also gave him bargaining leverage with the White House once the administration recognized the problem.

The notion that weakness is often strength is fundamental to bargaining of all kinds. At a crowded four-way stop, which car proceeds first? Often the one with the most dents in it. Schelling offers other examples:

> The sophisticated negotiator may find it difficult to seem as obstinate as a truly

obstinate man. If a man knocks at a door and says that he will stab himself on the porch unless given $10, he is more likely to get the $10 if his eyes are bloodshot. The threat of mutual destruction cannot be used to deter an adversary who is too unintelligent to comprehend it or too weak to enforce his will on those he represents.[24]

An important class of bargaining tactics rests on the notion that weakness is often strength. These tactics involve the use of a "commitment" in the strategic sense of the term—a pledge to adhere to a line of behavior or a specific position made in such a way that retreat is damaging. In Schelling's words, the strategy of commitment rests "on the paradox that the power to constrain an adversary may depend on the power to bind oneself." The bank manager who swallows the combination to the safe is immune to threats by the robbers who hold him captive. The army that burns its bridges can't be forced to retreat.

Carter's veiled threat to veto an unsatisfactory trucking bill was an effort by the White House to bind itself—a voluntary sacrifice of freedom designed to make more credible its claim that the president was committed to getting a strong reform bill. The penalty attached to retreat was damage to Carter's reputation.

Carter was careful not to bind himself too much, however. The veto threat referred only to "appropriate legislation." As a result the commitment gave the White House little additional bargaining leverage. A bargainer's credibility is reduced when opponents recognize that ambiguity (or other conditions) will allow him to retreat with honor.

Other strategic commitments in the trucking battle were more effective. Cannon openly pledged himself to getting a bill acceptable to Packwood, whose passion for trucking deregulation was well known. The two senators played a good-guy-bad-guy game that not only relieved some of the pressure on Cannon, but also persuaded opponents that he would "hang tough." White House aides' prior commitment to support the Cannon bill on the Senate floor proved useful to them in resisting both internal and external pressure to compromise with the Teamsters.

Strength through Substance

The problem of internal pressure was no small one for White House aides. Soon after it was organized, Neustadt convinced the coalition to hire a coordinator in part so that he could show the "campaign people" that there was a dedicated constituency supporting the anti-Teamster reforms. In the final days of negotiation, Lewis and Neustadt came under intense pressure from others as well within the White House to settle rather than continue to bargain and risk getting nothing.

One protection against this internal pressure was the informal under-standing among White House deregulators to accept no bill that did not satisfy the ICC. High-level administration officials never questioned that legislation would have to meet Gaskins's substantive demands. And they recognized that seemingly small changes in key provisions could cripple the commission.

This commitment to satisfy the commission was no less important to bargaining that went on outside the White House. It was a source of encouragement to the coalition (and dismay to opponents) to hear Lewis say: "We are in constant touch with the ICC asking, 'What's your bottom line?'"

Alfred Kahn's active involvement in the trucking battle had somewhat the same effect. Though Kahn was politically astute, his primary function in the White House was to reduce inflation, and he made clear that he viewed trucking deregulation as a significant step toward that goal. (When someone said that trucking decontrol would only lower the short-term inflation rate by one-tenth of a percent, Kahn responded: "I'd gladly shed blood for one-tenth of a percent. And do daily!") As Kahn's deputy, Lewis shared a reputation for substantiveness that was immensely important to his political role as White House bargainer.

"Substance" with respect to trucking deregulation involved more than economics. Lewis was a lawyer, and it was primarily a legal judgment that the entry provision in the Public Works bill would not reduce the ICC's discretion. DOT Deputy General Counsel Mark Aron, who drafted the administration's bill, was routinely consulted about legal aspects of com-promise provisions. But what ultimately distinguished Lewis, Aron and other administration figures who were regarded as substantive was a pri-mary concern for the economic rather than the political consequences of the trucking bill.

The "political people" were no less important to the overall adminis-tration effort on trucking reform. And key individuals like Lewis played both roles. But when it came to bargaining, what made the administration effective was the degree to which substance and substantive people dictated strategic judgments. For shaping the expectations of both supporters and opponents, the White House could give no more important cue.

Six Sketches

When the blackbird flew out of sight,
It marked the edge
Of one of many circles.
    —from Wallace Stevens, "Thirteen Ways of Looking at a Blackbird"

The link between a bargainer's personal motivation and his effectiveness is strong because appearances are important in bargaining, and personal commitment is generally apparent. Individual skill is also important to bargaining as it is to any endeavor. This account of the trucking battle has consciously played down the role of individual motivation and skill in an effort to draw generalizations about bargaining. But individuals made a difference, so much so that one is tempted to conclude that the key to good bargaining is good people.

The need to take a single perspective—that of the White House—has also distorted and depersonalized the account of strategic bargaining somewhat. The role of other bargainers on both sides has necessarily been downplayed. Young committee staffers who would dominate the story as seen through other eyes—none more than Will Ris, Cannon's much-admired staff counsel—have been left out altogether.

A full account would describe the battle through the eyes of a half-dozen or more key players—a task that is beyond the ability of the author. The following pages, however, sketch lightly those parts of the picture that were omitted. There is no effort to link the description to models of bargaining or theories of legislative behavior. The aim is simply to fill out the canvas.

The Administration

The President really wanted this one. That in the end is what did it.
—Carter aide

Soon after Neil Goldschmidt was appointed DOT secretary, he went to the Oval Office carrying a yellow legal pad on which he'd written his "short list" of high-priority transportation issues.[25] The president asked to see Goldschmidt's pad, read over the list of issues, and then added another— "trucking deregulation." More than once, when shown a weekly legislative agenda by his chief lobbyist, Frank Moore, Carter drew an arrow from "trucking" to the top of the list.

By all reports, Jimmy Carter came to Washington genuinely hostile toward unnecessary economic regulation and personally committed to reform—in the area of transportation perhaps more than any other. In 1977, Carter's staff had to talk him out of taking on the trucking industry while the airline deregulation bill was still grounded. Other priorities delayed trucking reform legislation even after airline deregulation was well aloft, and absent the threat that Senator Kennedy would take the lead for good, there might have been further delays. Nevertheless, when the Carter administration finally turned to trucking reform, it went all out. "The President really wanted this one," said one White House aide, referring to the successful trucking bill. "That in the end is what did it."

Carter's attitude was both cause and consequence of a strong commitment to trucking deregulation on the part of other senior administration officials, most notably Alfred Kahn and Stuart Eizenstat. As an economist, Kahn was near-fanatical in his belief that trucking controls were "the most insane network of regulation that could conceivably have been devised by a paranoid." And as the president's chief inflation fighter, he regarded trucking legislation as the single most anti-inflationary bill before Congress. (That Kahn had earlier offered the Teamsters a milder bill in return for moderation in their wage settlement can only be a sign of how critical that labor contract was thought to be to the future of the administration's inflation guidelines.)

Stuart Eizenstat shared Kahn's philosophical distaste for trucking regulation. More than Kahn, the domestic policy chief had to be sensitive to the political costs of taking on the truckers and Teamsters. But his resolve to get a strong bill remained firm. That resolve, by one who was the main conduit between the president and those making day-to-day lobbying plans, assured the availability of vast organizational resources.

A third senior presidential adviser who came to care deeply about trucking reform was Neil Goldschmidt. Goldschmidt's commitment may have owed more to pragmatism than philosophy, but the effect was similar. Soon after he succeeded Brock Adams at DOT, "closet deregulators" came out of hiding and others were enlisted as the agency embraced the cause.

The trucking issue engendered personal commitment throughout the administration. The president's personal stance was a major reason. As one White House aide said, referring to the story of Carter drawing arrows on his legislative agenda, "When things like that happen, word gets around." The issue itself was another reason: the merits were compelling and the opponents obstinate. "It was not quite a cult issue," said one staffer, "but almost."

Personal commitment notwithstanding, the White House smelled a winner. In August 1979, when Carter asked aides to raise the priority of truck deregulation, there was in place an ICC whose disposition and independence to deregulate on its own gave the White House considerable leverage with Congress. Moreover, there was by then a great deal of interest in trucking reform on Capitol Hill, much of it due to the visibility Kennedy had given the issue.

By 1979, Carter was a relatively unpopular president who was seen as ineffective with Congress. He needed legislative accomplishments to point to in the 1980 campaign. The White House went full throttle for trucking reform, but only in the belief that a bill the president could claim credit for was at the end of the road. "Compared to other issues, the administration was ten times better," said a consumer lobbyist in the coalition. "They assigned more people, better people. They were willing to use more clout. There haven't been many issues where they did that. Of course, it was all predicated on their perception that they had a winner potentially."[26]

One of those "better people" was Mary Schuman McInnis, the White House aide initially in charge of trucking reform. A dynamic attorney on the Domestic Policy Staff, McInnis had previously directed the administration's campaign for airline deregulation and would be Washington lobbyists' choice for the single individual most responsible for passage of the airline bill. When McInnis left the DPS, just as the trucking battle was beginning to heat up, it was to become general counsel at the CAB, a job with finite tenure by her own doing.

McInnis's role in charge of trucking legislation was assumed by Ron Lewis, a young tax lawyer who left private practice to become a deputy to Alfred Kahn. In a setting where individuals involved in legislation are regarded as playing either a "substantive" or a "political" role, Lewis did both. His substantive understanding of the complex trucking legislation was topped only by that of the DOT attorney who wrote the administration's bill. That was a source of comfort to coalition members, among others, whose fate came to rest considerably on Lewis's ability to negotiate the fine points of a compromise bill in a politically charged atmosphere.

Lewis operated in a low-key, meticulous manner. He made no agreements without checking with DOT and the ICC for additional substantive input. That and his air of firmness under pressure—the product of years of bargaining experience in private practice—reassured lobbyists and committee staffers who lived in fear that the White House would "cave." Lewis was extremely well thought of by both Cannon's and Kennedy's staff members as someone who was knowledgeable, reliable, and able to tap quickly into administration resources and make things happen. Said one Commerce staffer, "If you wanted something done, [you simply had to] call Ron."

At the other end of the Old Executive Office Building from Lewis was the DPS office of Rick Neustadt, who codirected the White House effort on trucking reform. It was a route frequently traversed, by telephone if not on foot, as the two men worked closely and amicably.

Neustadt was regarded as one of the brightest young minds in the White House, if not as tough a negotiator as Lewis, though the two aides consciously played a good-guy-bad-guy game in dealing with Public Works. Neustadt's greatest contribution may have been his handling of internal politics and pressure to cut a deal, an accomplishment fully appreciated only by other deregulators within the White House.

Neustadt's responsibilities in DPS included communications as well as trucking, and he worked simultaneously on legislation to deregulate both industries. An attorney by training, Neustadt was a political writer for CBS television before he joined the Domestic Policy Staff in 1977. The White House was familiar terrain to him even then, since his father, Richard E. Neustadt, a professor of government at Harvard University, had been a member of Truman's staff and a frequent adviser to John Kennedy.

On matters involving congressional liaison, Lewis and Neustadt worked closely with Susan Williams, an assistant secretary in DOT's Office of Congressional Affairs. When Senator John Warner cast his unexpected vote to eliminate antitrust immunity, Commerce Committee staff members gave her much of the credit. Harrison Schmitt was another senator whose conversion from skeptic to deregulator owed much to Williams's persuasiveness. Ironically, Williams was initially unenthusiastic about trucking reform because the opposition seemed unbeatable; Schmitt's turnaround made a believer out of her.

Also closely involved in the White House effort was Mark Aron, Deputy General Counsel at DOT. Aron was considered the most knowledgeable person in the administration about the substance of trucking legislation, having authored Carter's 1979 bill. Largely for his role in trucking reform, Aron received the government's maximum award of $20,000 for meritorious service in 1980.

The other substantive expert who was brought into the day-to-day political decision making was James Voytko, special assistant to ICC chairman Gaskins. (Although the ICC is technically not part of the administration, there was full cooperation throughout the trucking battle.) The communication process worked like this: If the Public Works Committee proposed a compromise on the food exemption, for example, Lewis would contact Aron. They in turn would call Voytko for the ICC perspective. Finally, Susan Williams was brought in so that the "political people" stayed informed of substance. This whole process—which produced a counteroffer in the case of a compromise—took less than thirty minutes.

The smooth coordination between Kahn's White House office, the Domestic Policy Staff, DOT, and the ICC set the administration's effort on trucking apart from many others it undertook. (Carter's 1979 cabinet shakeup was in part a response to complaints from Capitol Hill about the lack of coordination among the administration's component parts.) In the course of the trucking battle, close personal ties developed between the handful of administration and ICC aides who worked intensely on it. "It was a very, very nice relationship," said one. "Everyone who went through it has the warmest feelings for one another."

Howard Cannon

*After listening carefully to the comments and stinging criticisms by some
interest groups concerning this legislation, I am now willing to admit
that I was wrong. . . . I have determined that the Judiciary Committee
actually does have jurisdiction over this matter!*
— Cannon's opening statement at a hearing on S. 2245, February 21, 1980

Few things shocked the truckers and Teamsters more than the tenacity with
which Howard Cannon, one of the most senior and powerful members of
the Senate, ultimately fought for strong reform.[27] Proponents of deregulation—who earlier had tried to keep Cannon from taking jurisdiction over
trucking legislation in the belief that he would bury it—shared that surprise.
And for seemingly good reason.

Cannon was in many respects an old-fashioned Democrat who believed in the virtues of government intervention. No advocate of airline
deregulation initially, he came to support it only after being persuaded of its
merits for the country at large and for his own state of Nevada. But trucking
deregulation was stridently opposed by one of the most important constituencies to a Nevada Democrat—the Teamsters. Add to that Cannon's reputation as a "military man"—a committee leader who protects his members—
and it's no wonder truckers and deregulators alike felt he would oppose a
no-win issue like motor carrier reform.

The truckers blame the media reports of the FBI investigation for
Cannon's tenacity. "Cannon was talking compromise," say ATA lobbyists,
and other evidence confirms that he was wavering. Apparently unsure that
he had the votes to eliminate antitrust immunity, Cannon had indicated that
he might be flexible on that critical provision of his bill. After the news
reports appeared, "Cannon absolutely would not change a comma," Bennett Whitlock later told ATA members.

Whitlock exaggerated only slightly. Cannon agreed to minor industry-
favored changes in his bill prior to markup, but on the all-important issue
of antitrust immunity, he became resolute. "There's no doubt about it," said
one committee aide. After the news reports, "Cannon became more solid.
That's a fact of life."

That "fact of life" relieved Commerce Committee staff members, even
as they lamented the shadow cast on Cannon's reputation. "It made life so
much easier," said one about the publicity. "There was no way [Cannon]
could back down then [on the bill] without looking bad. It took lots of
[deregulation opponents] off his back. They said, 'He's a lost cause'."

But the unfavorable publicity still doesn't explain the fact that Cannon introduced an "unexpectedly tough" bill to start with. Or does it? When the *New York Times* story appeared on February 6, five days after the bill was introduced, some people speculated that Cannon somehow knew about the investigation and made his bill strong so as to remove suspicion.

While the question is best left to historians, there's no evidence to support that theory. The FBI maintains that its investigation of Cannon—part of a larger operation looking into political corruption that included what came to be known as ABSCAM—was highly secret. And Cannon would have had to know about it in early January, which is when a draft of his bill first circulated. Moreover, Commerce Committee aides say that Cannon's decision to make the bill so strong came in a watershed meeting the previous December.

Those who observed Cannon closely throughout the summer and fall of 1979—Senate Commerce Committee staffers and administration aides— agree that he made virtually the same odyssey on the trucking issue that he had on airline deregulation. After initial skepticism he was genuinely open-minded to the substantive arguments, and gradually he became convinced of the merits of deregulation.

Even so, committee staffers and others expected him to stop short of eliminating antitrust immunity. But when he met with his aides in December, just after the last field hearing, he decided to tackle that obstacle as well. At the meeting, aides outlined the three options in the rate-bureau area: leave antitrust immunity alone; undo it; or something in between. Cannon asked his staff if they saw any legitimate reason for keeping the immunity, and they said no. Cannon agreed. "I just can't see it. I just don't see the justification for rate bureaus," one aide recalled Cannon as saying. Soon after, Cannon told them to "go draft a bill."

Will Ris—"The Essential Player"

In the watershed meeting as well as on a day-to-day basis, a major influence on Cannon's thinking was William Ris, the young Commerce Committee staff counsel. Cannon had great affection and respect for Ris, as did nearly everyone who dealt with him, even trucking lobbyists, whose views had little in common with his own.

Ris was a young CAB attorney when he came to the Commerce Committee on temporary assignment to the airline deregulation bill. Alfred Kahn had selected Ris for the legislative job himself. "It was a sacrifice for us to lose him," recalled one then-CAB economist, "but it illustrates the importance of agencies not hoarding their best people." Ris stayed on at the committee permanently after the airline bill passed, and he began work almost immediately on trucking legislation. Two years later, he was the focal point of a legislative battle that made the airline struggle look like a friendly spat.

"I guess everyone has his own perspective and sees himself as being the essential player. The only one who can legitimately say that is Will." That appraisal, by Ron Lewis, would evoke little disagreement from anyone involved with the trucking bill.

The physical setting in which Ris operated was inauspicious enough—a small office in the Richard Russell building shared by several desks, telephones, and typewriters, all generally in use. Ris's own corner was decorated with photographs of his young son—born in December 1979, just as Ris was beginning to draft S. 2245. ("The bill would have happened sooner," he said more than once, "but . . . I was writing it between diaper changes.") On his desk was a metal spike on which he had speared his pink telephone messages over the preceding months. The two-inch high, neatly impaled stack was part objet d'art, part reminder of just how much hinged on what Ris did.

Trying to describe Ris's impact on the trucking bill is like trying to describe the contribution of Rostropovich to the Washington National Symphony. It was pervasive. "He simply controlled the whole process," said Mark Aron, the DOT counsel who wrote the administration's bill. "There were so many opportunities to water down the bill. Had Will not been there, there would not have been [an acceptable] bill."

One reason Ris was so effective is that he was extremely well liked by people on both sides of the fence. "One gem of a person," is how a colleague described him. In a setting where veiled maneuvering can become an end in itself, Ris's openness and sincerity were disarming. At the same time, his discretion gained him trust all around.

He found humor in everything. Farm lobbyists recalled one visit with Ris regarding the provision to deregulate certain fruit and meat. As they left, he called out to them, "May your bananas always be exempt!" The opening statements Ris wrote for Cannon brought laughter to somber committee proceedings. At a hearing on S. 2245 held shortly after the publicity implying that Cannon had been paid to steer the trucking issue into his committee, the senator began by announcing that "upon agonizing personal reflection, . . . I have determined that the Judiciary Committee actually does have jurisdiction over this matter!"

Perhaps Ris's greatest contribution, the influence he had on Cannon, is the hardest to pin down. "The genius of Will Ris," said one Senate staffer who was closely involved, "is that he [convinced] Cannon that S. 2245 wasn't a very radical bill." Presumably Ris could have made that argument by presenting it as legislation that would merely codify reforms that the ICC had already implemented with no resulting chaos and confusion. Whatever his approach, Ris likely influenced Cannon in a continuous, straightforward manner on the many occasions when, having heard the arguments all around, Cannon no doubt asked, "Now Will, what do you think about this?"

"The Great Deregulator"

"It wasn't all Will," remarked a White House aide who appreciatively characterized Cannon as a "bulldog" on the trucking issue. "Cannon made some very tough choices." Carter lobbied Cannon hard, and Packwood and Kennedy also served to push him in the direction of strong reform. But, ultimately, Cannon made those tough choices voluntarily.

An appealing explanation is that Cannon's elevation to chairman of the Commerce Committee in 1978 served to inspire him to adopt a less parochial outlook on legislation—a not uncommon phenomenon. "This was the biggest issue the Commerce Committee would do under his leadership," said a committee staffer. "That brought about a whole change in his approach. Being made chairman really makes a difference."

That this was the Commerce Committee in particular may have contributed to that transformation. Under Warren Magnuson's thirty-year tenure as chairman, Commerce had gained a reputation as a highly innovative and productive committee. "Cannon wanted to carve out something in his own mold," said a White House aide. "Regulatory reform was the obvious area."

The fact that Cannon's first regulatory reform—airline deregulation—proved successful is important for explaining the Nevada senator's support of trucking decontrol—even more so because Alfred Kahn was a strong advocate of both reforms. "Kahn led [Cannon] through airline deregulation, which proved very good for Nevada," observed Kahn's deputy, Ron Lewis. "[As a result of that experience] Cannon had an enormous fondness and respect for Kahn; it was palpable."

Whatever the reasons, Cannon's "bulldog" stance was a courageous one by Capitol Hill standards. He alienated a critical Nevada constituency, the Teamsters, not to mention the powerful trucking industry. And he went against his own (Democratic) majority in committee, in denial of his reputation for proceeding only when it was politically safe.

While he was able to hold the votes of only three of his nine Democrats on the key committee markup vote, Cannon's support was a critical source of political leverage from start to finish in the trucking battle. "The three marketeers" were confirmed to the ICC only with strong backing by Cannon. His "mad-as-hell" speech set a deadline for legislation and put the onus on the House to act. And his subsequent introduction of S. 2245 marked the turning point in the battle when deregulators began to take seriously the possibility of getting a very good bill. Several months later that possibility was realized, in good part due to Cannon's able leadership in the Senate.

Nowhere was Cannon's skill as a legislator more evident than in the speed with which the trucking bill moved—from Cannon's desk to Carter's in five months, a remarkably short time for major legislation that controversial and complex. Cannon believed that a no-win issue like trucking deregulation, which subjected members to scorching heat in an election year, had to move quickly. His most effective maneuver toward that end was to impose a deadline for getting a bill to Carter. Though the deadline was completely arbitrary, it took on a life of its own.

A *Business Week* article in September 1980 described Cannon as the "father of airline deregulation." It was an ironic but not inappropriate title for the senator who had at one time appeared to be an obstacle to that reform. The trucking battle was in many ways a replay of the airline fight, beginning with the struggle between Cannon and Kennedy over who would hold hearings and control the issue. White House aides scoff at the allegations that Cannon waged the jurisdictional fight with Kennedy so as to help the Teamsters. It was a turf battle, one maintained. "Cannon went after the trucking deregulation issue in the same [evenhanded] methodical manner as he did airline deregulation. And that's the only way we could have won it—with that appearance of fairness."

If Cannon's goal was in part to further the reputation of the Commerce Committee, he succeeded. His tenure as chairman ended when the Republicans won control of the Senate just months after the trucking bill was enacted, and he was narrowly defeated in 1982, due largely to adverse publicity surrounding the trial (and subsequent conviction) of Teamster president Roy Williams and others for conspiracy to commit bribery. Nevertheless, Cannon established a reputation as a highly productive committee leader. "His record is as impressive as Magnuson's," said the Carter aide. "He's 'the great deregulator'."

Robert Packwood

There is no reason why we should be controlling capitalistic acts by consenting adults.
        —Packwood, at the markup of S. 2245, March 11, 1980

While Cannon was open-minded about trucking deregulation, Packwood was passionate.[28] His motives were less enigmatic than Cannon's, though likewise inconsistent with the common view that members of Congress maximize their chances of reelection. Faced with a tough campaign in which such a position could well do him more harm than good, Packwood nevertheless declared war on trucking regulation. A primary reason: He believed passionately in the cause.

Packwood, like Cannon, adopted a less parochial attitude toward legislation when he became the ranking member of his party on the Commerce Committee. Previously, he had been relatively inactive on the committee; those issues he pursued—protection of marine mammals, the bottle bill—were of interest to his constituents in Oregon. He had supported airline deregulation, but not actively.

In early 1979, when Packwood succeeded James Pearson of Kansas as the ranking Republican on Commerce, he set about developing a new legislative agenda for himself. He had his staff director, William Diefenderfer, survey the issues that fell within the committee's jurisdiction and recommend several candidates for his attention. Of the recommendations, trucking deregulation had the most appeal. It was a "big, tough issue" and one that fit with Packwood's basic Republican belief in the free market. In addition, pressure from Kennedy and the White House made it inevitable that the committee would have to deal with the issue. For those reasons, according to Diefenderfer, "that's where [the senator] thought he'd make his mark."

"Educate Me"

When Packwood settled on trucking deregulation as his issue, he went about studying it with gusto. In response to Packwood's request to "educate me," the minority staff counsel, Matthew (Matt) Scocozza, put together a 186-page "memo" describing the industry. It was compiled in a three-ring binder with tab markers for easy reference to the major headings—Rate Bureaus, Private Carriers, Recent ICC Decisions, and the like. According to Scocozza, Packwood read it all. He took notes. He dictated memos filled with detailed follow-up questions: How many of the ICC's "39 recommendations" were ever implemented? What's the organizational structure of a rate bureau?

Packwood became something of an expert on regulation of the trucking industry. (Industry representatives probably wouldn't go that far, but they did concede that Packwood was one of the few highly knowledgeable members of Congress.) "It's the only time I've seen senators—Packwood [in particular], to some extent Cannon—know an issue better than many staff members," said Scocozza. "Packwood doesn't do this with every bill, but when he decides to take one on as his own [he's tireless]. No one chopped Cannon or Packwood down [for not knowing] the merits."

Packwood's request for information from his aide came in the course of a dialogue between the senator and Scocozza that was in some ways the reverse of that between Ris and Cannon. Unlike Will Ris, Scocozza was no deregulator initially. But through Packwood's influence, he came to "see the light." "When I first started talking with Packwood," said Scocozza, "I was still somewhat of a regulator. I would caution him about what deregulation would do to the health of the industry. He would say—Let the inefficient carriers go down; why should the government subsidize them? I was three-quarters of the way there [toward favoring deregulation]. Packwood drove me the [rest] of the way."

Scocozza worked as an ICC attorney in the mid-1970s, and it was there that he developed a bias toward regulation, particularly strict enforcement, his bailiwick at the commission. He never lost his belief in strict enforcement, much to the dismay of deregulators. One coalition lobbyist, complaining about the paperwork requirements imposed on private carriers in the 1980 bill, said he and the carriers he represented had been "Scocozza'd."

In other respects, however, Scocozza was a positive force for deregulation and, together with Cindy Douglass, the assistant staff counsel, formed an effective team that was highly regarded by the coalition and the White House. Scocozza got down on his knees for the cause, literally. During the markup, he moved from senator to senator on his knees, pleading for support on a critical vote. Douglass was every bit as much an advocate. Her passion for the issue was tempered only by a sharp sense of humor and a Kansan's ability to see the bright side of every situation.

Packwood's substantive approach to the trucking issue made him occasionally impatient with the shortage of hard statistical evidence. At one hearing, he criticized the administration over the COWPS estimate that deregulation would save $5 billion—a figure that even many deregulators suspected of having come off the back of an envelope. "He played bad guy because he wanted hard evidence," said a Packwood aide. "Statistics were very important [to him]."

That hard evidence is what Packwood used to persuade his fellow Republicans on the Commerce Committee. To be sure, he used political devices as well: While there was little if any trading on other bills, Packwood agreed to language changes and amendments to win votes. But even those concessions were generally to members who were persuaded by Packwood on the merits but had to appease a vocal constituency.

Packwood's persuasiveness may have been the single most immediate reason that S. 2245 survived the Commerce Committee and the full Senate. His success was most visible in markup, where he had the support of all seven Republicans on key votes. Not only was the bill not significantly diluted, it was markedly strengthened through the addition of Stevenson's food amendment. In the full Senate as well, Republican support was largely the basis for deregulators' victory.

Packwood's Bottom Line

Throughout the trucking battle, Packwood set high standards for acceptable legislation. In the fall of 1979, when the majority and minority staffs began meeting to develop the outline of a committee bill, Scocozza and Douglass had instructions to get the strongest bill possible, with elimination of antitrust immunity seen as a crucial issue. They were initially not optimistic that Cannon would agree to a strong bill. Eager to have Packwood prod Cannon, at the same time they wanted the working relationship between the two newly ranking senators to get off to a good start, a concern that Cannon's staff shared.

Packwood's aides soon overcame their pessimism as it became clear that Cannon was no laggard on the deregulation issue. ("In our meetings with Will," recalled Douglass, "we'd say we want X and Y, and Will would respond by saying—Well, how about X, Y and Z!... Then he'd say—Let me check this with Cannon, and Cannon would okay it. Cannon never cut us back even a little.") But Packwood's influence was in no small part responsible for that. Cannon stated on many occasions that he was committed to getting a bill that Packwood could live with. That commitment was sincere; the relationship between the two senators had developed very well, to the relief of committee staffers. At the same time, Cannon's statements were tactical in nature. Since Packwood's passion for deregulation was well known to opponents, Cannon was able to play a good-guy-bad-guy game using Packwood as the willing villain.

Packwood's demanding bottom line became especially important in the final negotiations with the Public Works Committee, when he and Cannon agreed to forego a conference only if the House produced a fully acceptable bill. Packwood's determination was reflected in the remarks of one of his aides: "Whenever you give up anything in negotiations, it's gone. We felt we were on the side of God. We wanted 100 percent, not just 85 percent."

In the end, Packwood's championing of trucking reform may have done more good than damage to his successful reelection campaign. The Teamsters in particular worked hard to defeat him. But newspaper editorials praised Packwood for his pivotal role in the deregulation battle, and the Oregon senator capitalized on the victory in his own campaign publicity. One aide described how Packwood's television commercials played up the senator's role in "getting government off the back of industry." The aide added with a smile, "Never mind that industry didn't want government off its back!"

Edward Kennedy

While I am sure this legislation does not go nearly as far as [Ted Kennedy] would like . . . , he is clearly to be credited for raising the consciousness of the Senate with respect to the issue.
　　—Howard Cannon's closing remarks on the Senate floor,
　　　　after passage of S. 2245, April 15, 1980

While Packwood pushed Cannon to support strong reform once trucking deregulation became a committee priority, the two senators might never have tackled the issue in the first place had it not been for another goad— Edward Kennedy.[29] Kennedy's attempt to take the lead on trucking reform forced the committee to act. Cannon won the turf fight, but with the clear understanding that the Commerce Committee would "diligently and thoroughly consider" the Kennedy bill that session.

In the same fashion, Kennedy's aggressiveness kept the White House "honest." Trucking deregulation might have stayed on the administration's back burner even longer than it did absent the threat that Kennedy, not Carter, would get the credit for reform. Once Kennedy challenged Carter for the Democratic presidential nomination, the threat became even greater.

Kennedy's motives were no less political than Carter's or Cannon's. But Kennedy had more to gain and less to lose from supporting trucking reform. As chapter 5 discussed, deregulation was an ideal issue for the Massachusetts senator in that it served to counter his image as a liberal even as it furthered the goals of his liberal constituents.

Not only did the competition with Kennedy force Carter and Cannon to put trucking reform on their front burner, but it caused them to prepare a dish that was far more tasty to deregulators than it otherwise might have been. The jurisdictional fight served to put great pressure on Cannon. He may not have felt compelled to eliminate antitrust immunity in order to disprove his critics' claims of industry favoritism, as some deregulators argue, but the effect of the fight was certainly to move him in that direction. Similarly, any temptation the White House may have had to go easy on the truckers and Teamsters was checked by the knowledge that Kennedy was watching.

In reality, the watchful eyes were those of Kennedy's aides on the

Judiciary Committee. When Kennedy lost the jurisdictional fight, his personal role in the trucking issue decreased substantially. He was not even in the Capital for the dramatic Senate vote on S. 2245; he was in Pennsylvania campaigning for the presidential primary. Nevertheless, Kennedy's staff—in particular his counsel Jay Steptoe—remained active.

Tall and rail-thin, Steptoe was the embodiment of the rod that Kennedy symbolized to many deregulators. Steptoe's self-confident manner only reinforced the image. He was quick to joke—he told a Capitol Hill symposium on trucking that a vote for Kennedy would get them the only president who'd know what LTL means—but Steptoe was also intense and often judgmental on the subject of deregulation, as when he scolded several coalition members for their failure to be team players. Even in victory, he kept the rod poised. At the last coalition meeting, when asked how he felt about the victory, Steptoe refused to indulge the group, and by implication the administration, in praise. A five-word pat on the back—"We disproved the conventional wisdom"—was followed by an admonition to get to work on railroad deregulation.

Despite Kennedy's ongoing role as the goad, and continued bitterness between Kennedy and Carter over the nomination fight, friction between the senator's office and the White House over the trucking issue was minimal. Kennedy's staff members expected the administration to cave in; they were pleasantly surprised when that didn't happen. Moreover, key individuals were compatible. "There was a personal chemistry between Ron Lewis, Will Ris, and myself," Steptoe observed. "And I say this as an antagonist."

In addition to keeping the rod poised, Kennedy brought visibility to the trucking issue. His hearings on rate bureaus, like his earlier investigation of airline regulation, drew considerable publicity in the press and helped to establish the credibility of deregulation. In early 1979, when Kennedy announced his bill in the company of the Nader-to-NAM contingent, *Time* magazine devoted a full page with picture to the event, which it described as evidence of Kennedy's "consummate political showmanship." The turf fight that ensued was followed widely in the press, thus increasing the pressure on Cannon to act and to act progressively.

Kennedy's star quality alone guaranteed publicity for legislation he championed. But his office also had good connections with individual members of the press. Deregulators gave Kennedy much of the credit for the extensive coverage of the trucking battle in the *Washington Post*. And when a *New York Times* editorial described the final trucking bill as "only a nibble," they suspected that Kennedy's office was behind it.

The "nibble" editorial notwithstanding, publicity worked to deregulators' advantage, and the White House was quick to try to capitalize on

Kennedy's star quality. An internal memo in August 1979 stressed the need for media attention to bring trucking deregulation off the back burner and recommended using Kennedy as a "centerpiece." Nine months later, as the White House prepared for a Rose Garden signing ceremony, the administration's desire for national television coverage was one argument for giving Kennedy a prominent role in the event.

There were other arguments as well—giving Kennedy credit would assure his support for the compromise; and, strategy aside, Kennedy rightfully deserved much of the credit. In a memo to Stuart Eizenstat, Rick Neustadt set out these arguments and urged the White House "to reach out to Kennedy."

The White House did invite Kennedy to the Rose Garden ceremony, where Carter was generous in praising his rival:

> Although the coalition which was finally successful in passing the bill was really organized effectively about a year ago . . . there was one senator who worked on this legislation for at least two years or more prior to that, sometimes alone, sometimes facing discouragement, but never giving up on the concept.

And the event did get television coverage—all three networks featured it on their evening news. Kennedy's presence was doubtless the key, the more so because the ceremony marked the first time Carter and Kennedy had appeared together in public since a birthday party for House Speaker Tip O'Neill seven months earlier.

It was an ironic setting for their reunion. In his bid for the Democratic nomination, Kennedy had taken to criticizing Carter for campaigning from the Rose Garden because the president wouldn't "come out" and debate the Massachusetts senator on television. Kennedy's opening quip—"There's no debate on trucking deregulation"—captured the irony. It was a humorous reference to the strains of competition between politicians, and a true statement about a policy—trucking reform—that was furthered by that very competition.

Public Works Committee

It's the all-American Committee, [some have] said. There's no Democratic, no Republican side; just members trying to do what's good for the country.
—Aide to a Public Works Committee member

The Public Works Committee and the trucking industry have been allies since 1956, when Congress decided to build a massive interstate highway system.[30] Public Works needed the trucking industry's support in order to raise highway user taxes to pay for the proposed system, and the bond that formed proved mutually convenient. By 1974, when House jurisdiction over motor carrier regulation switched from the Interstate Commerce to the Public Works Committee, the relationship with the trucking industry was well established.

With that change in jurisdiction, Public Works became one leg of a classic iron triangle—a political ménage à trois between industry, Congress, and the regulatory agency. The ATA began courting committee members systematically, and the committee started hiring staff members from the ranks of ICC regulators.

Thus when the ICC broke out of the triangle and began rolling back regulation administratively, and later, when Kennedy and Carter proposed deregulation legislation, there was little sympathy for either among the Public Works leadership and staff. Committee members, particularly those on the Surface Transportation Subcommittee, were also generally proindustry, with the notable exception of a young Pennsylvania Democrat, Allen Ertel, who was a hero of the airline deregulation fight and an enthusiastic spokesman for trucking reform.

Sympathy with the industry aside, deregulation was precisely the kind of issue the Public Works Committee dislikes. Public Works is largely a pork barrel committee; its members are happiest when dispensing federal funds for dams, highways, bridges, and government buildings. Trucking deregulation offered no pork. Worse, the issue was ideological and highly controversial. Said an aide to one of the committee leaders, "You had coalitions of groups that normally won't sit in the same room with one another. That always astounded [the congressman], and he took it as a sign that this issue was something to stay away from."

Strategy

The committee's first reaction to deregulators seemingly was to fight—behavior for which it received much criticism. Representatives Johnson and Howard censored the ICC by letter and were themselves pilloried for doing so. When they introduced the committee's bill, H.B. 6418, they were roundly criticized again—by the president indirectly through Goldschmidt's testimony, and in widely read press editorials.

"Clearly they called it wrong," said one House staffer, referring to H.B. 6418, and it would seem that, rather than setting out to write a regressive bill, the committee misjudged the political climate for deregulation. Miscues from White House aide William Johnston may be one reason for that. Poor advice from the committee's own staff is another possible explanation.

Whatever the reason, compromise became the alternative that eventually offered the Public Works Committee the most political mileage and leverage. The Senate's passage of S. 2245 made it clear that significant reform was inevitable. By compromising sooner—in their own committee—rather than later in a conference with the Senate, Public Works members could get some of the credit for reform. What's more, a reasonable compromise would satisfy the truckers who themselves wanted to avoid a conference and the danger that a deadlock between conferees would free the ICC to deregulate independently.

The Leadership

The ultimate compromise was presented to the members of Public Works as a fait accompli. The committee's position was negotiated solely by its leadership and a handful of staffers. That position was itself the product of compromise between the four leaders—the two ranking members of the full committee, Chairman Bizz Johnson and Representative William Harsha, and their counterparts on the Surface Transportation Subcommittee— Chairman James Howard and Representative Bud Shuster.

Deregulators had always assumed that Jim Howard would be their greatest obstacle. None of the four was viewed as friendly, but if the experience in the Senate was any guide, the Democrats would be especially troublesome. And, as subcommittee chairman, Howard was in a position to do the most harm. But Howard proved far less antagonistic than Harsha—a Republican. Moreover, Harsha's close involvement in the bargaining process gave his views disproportionate weight. "Harsha was the key," said an ATA lobbyist, an assessment with which few would disagree.

What motivated Harsha to back the ATA's position so staunchly? Harsha had announced his retirement, and the trucking bill represented his last opportunity to put his mark on a major piece of legislation. He had long been a champion of highway safety, and aides say he feared that easing entry into the trucking industry would put more trucks on the road and jeopardize safety. Both in committee markup and on the floor of the House, he told of a tragic accident involving a school bus and a careless truck driver.

The trucking bill also represented Harsha's last opportunity to "carry water" for the trucking industry. One ATA lobbyist described Harsha as "an old school politician—when he makes a friend, he takes care of it." The ATA had in turn taken care of Harsha over the years in its way. Many deregulators suspected that an additional incentive was at work on the trucking bill: Harsha planned to work as a private lawyer and lobbyist in Washington, D.C., when his term expired, and highly visible support for the ATA would assure him an industry clientele. (Soon after he retired, Harsha began lobbying for the ATA on a consulting basis. When a transportation reporter in Washington said over drinks to an ATA staff member, "Hey, I hear

Harsha's working for you guys now," the ATA staff member responded, "He's been working for us for twenty years, but he's finally collecting his pension!")

Whatever his motives, Harsha made his presence felt. His demands for the bill served to set the committee's bottom line. One Public Works aide described him as "iron-fisted." When the committee leadership reached a compromise with the Senate and the administration, junior committee members, who had hardly been consulted, caucused. According to one Public Works aide, "Harsha made clear that the draft bill had been worked out between interested parties and [that] members had better support it." Earlier, when Packwood asked to speak with junior Republicans on Public Works, Harsha refused.

Harsha's influence was probably a major reason the junior GOP leader on the trucking bill, Bud Shuster, was also an obstacle to reform. "Shuster *should* be good on this issue," deregulators said repeatedly, referring to the fact that he had chaired a transportation commission whose final report recommended more reliance on competition. He was not "good." Among other things, Shuster pleaded the truckers' case for compensation for operating rights during the committee markup, thus making it part of the legislative history of the act.

Harsha's influence aside, Shuster had his own ties to the ATA. "Bud Shuster is very ambitious," said an ATA lobbyist. "He wants to be president. First he wants to be minority whip. We help him along [financially]." A year after the trucking bill passed, Shuster's niece joined the ATA payroll.

The irony for deregulators was that the two Democratic leaders in Public Works—at least one of whom they assumed would be a real obstacle to reform—were in the end far less antagonistic than their Republican counterparts. Committee chairman Bizz Johnson had longstanding ties to the ATA in his home state of California. He was also in a tough reelection fight—he ultimately lost in a close vote—which made him especially vulnerable to ATA pressure. But while Johnson was no advocate of deregulation, neither was he a serious obstacle. He stayed largely out of the fight, and even tried to cooperate with the White House in the final weeks of negotiation.

If Harsha was the key to the ATA's House strategy, Howard was the weak link. "We're playing him very delicately," said one ATA lobbyist shortly after Howard had abandoned his proposal for total deregulation in favor of a plan (also later abandoned) to mark up the Senate bill. "That's why we haven't pushed him as to which bill to use in markup."

By all reports, Howard was a highly political individual who wanted an easy way out of a tight squeeze. He was receiving intense pressure from both sides in the deregulation fight—no picnic for a man with a history of heart trouble. And, like Johnson, he was battling for his political life at home.

Howard's most dramatic move in the trucking fight—to propose calling for total deregulation—is best explained as an act of self-preservation. The trucking lobby was not behind it, as deregulators initially thought. "We were consulted, but we didn't inspire it," said one ATA lobbyist. Nor was the Republican leadership on Public Works in agreement with Howard, as Bennett Whitlock's remarks to an ATA executive committee meeting revealed:

> [Harsha and Shuster] called us in and said it put the Republicans in a tremendous political bind if Howard were to use his total deregulation proposal as a markup [vehicle]. They said that Republicans would have a very difficult time because of the party's general philosophy of being opposed to government regulation, that it would be very difficult to hold the Republicans in line on such a proposal and that we had better go talk to Mr. Howard and try to get a different vehicle.[31]

If anything, Howard may have been trying to scare the truckers, since they too had criticized his bill. But his primary aim seems to have been to quiet the critics on the other side and put an end to their portrayal of him as the villain of the deregulation story.

As the battle grew more heated, Howard did his best to avoid it—he was in Europe when the "fragile compromise" was reached—and to defer to others, with Harsha eager to fill the void. One administration representative who met with Howard said he would "play with his little computer that sings songs to him—anything but talk about the substance" of the bill. During proceedings in committee and on the floor, he let Harsha—who was more knowledgeable about the legislation—handle substantive matters.

The Committee Staff

In part because Howard avoided the trucking issue, the committee staff played a very central role. Staff members were probably no more independent than their counterparts on the Senate Commerce Committee—it only seemed that way to deregulators, who found the views of the Public Works staff to be much like those of the leadership—antagonistic.

The lead staffer—Will Ris's counterpart—was Jack Fryer, the subcommittee counsel. Prior to joining the Public Works staff in 1975, Fryer had worked for twelve years as an ICC attorney. While he conceded that traditional entry controls were overly restrictive, he still believed in the need for regulation and resisted major reforms out of a fear of chaos in the industry.

The minority counsel, Jack Schenendorf, opposed deregulation even more strongly than Fryer. That was in keeping with his role as Harsha's representative on the staff. It also reflected his personal belief that "when a system is in place, and it's something as vital as trucking," any change should come slowly.

There were other key staff members—the most colorful was Richard (Dick) Sullivan, the chief counsel, who facilitated the negotiations. But with only one exception, they were not sympathetic to deregulation. The lone reformer was Pamela Garvey, a young attorney on temporary assignment from the ICC to provide technical assistance to the committee. (Garvey had a 360-degree view of the trucking battle because she performed the same function for the Senate Commerce Committee during the weeks that legislative activity was most intense there. After the election, with offers from both committees, she left the ICC to rejoin the Commerce Committee staff.)

The staff's sympathy with the ATA, combined with its practice of keeping information close to the vest, made deregulators ever suspicious. When the Public Works staff issued a discussion draft that differed in crucial ways from what White House aides felt had been agreed to in the Oval Office, they feared that the committee staff (the same group that had earlier sent a turkey tagged "S. 2245" to the Senate Commerce Committee) had "taken on a life of its own."

The staff members had other explanations for why their draft differed from the administration's expectations. "It's like *Rashomon*," said Dick Sullivan, referring to the Japanese play about perspective. "Everyone had their own perception of what [occurred]. It happens all the time." "Also," he added, "things get garbled in translation." Other staffers noted the tendency for members to underestimate what's involved in making seemingly minor changes, particularly when they're unfamiliar with a bill. "Howard and Johnson may have said something without realizing the implications of what they'd agreed to," said one.

These explanations are not inconsistent with still another—namely Harsha's influence. Whether or not Harsha was specifically responsible for the surprises in the staff draft, he certainly involved himself in the staff's work at many points. And given his views, what deregulators saw as antagonism by the staff exceeding that of the Democratic leadership more likely reflected the unretiring influence of the soon-to-retire Republican.

Legislation by Consensus

When the Public Works Committee set out in earnest to write "a bill that everyone could live with," it was more qualified for the task than most. For a variety of reasons, the Public Works Committee typically operates by consensus, at least within its own walls. Unlike other committees, where Republicans and Democrats are strong adversaries, Public Works has a tradition of bipartisan cooperation. As one committee member's aide remarked, "It's the all-American committee, [it's been] said. There's no Democratic, no Republican side; just members trying to do what's good for the country."

The nature of the committee's work is the major explanation for this. Dispensing pork need not be a zero-sum game, where more for one group necessarily means less for another. Since the supply is effectively unlimited, a consensual approach can mean more for everyone.

What's more, the Public Works Committee leadership and staff have encouraged the natural tendency for cooperation and compromise, even as congressional "reforms" have discouraged dealing and horse-trading elsewhere on Capitol Hill. Dick Sullivan, who managed to remain chief counsel to the committee under five successive chairmen, typifies their attitude. He likes to refer to Sidney Kingsley's play, *Detective Story*, about an uncompromising detective for whom everything is black and white. "Nothing is black and white," says Sullivan, "especially in this business."

While Public Works is accustomed to operating by consensus among its own members—an approach that almost guaranteed approval on the floor of the House—the challenge of the trucking bill was to make it acceptable to the Senate as well. The successful result—a major bill that passed both houses without a conference—was highly unusual.

The Delicate Balance

When coalition members nominated Harsha for the "Karl Wallenda award for maintaining a delicate balance," they were bitterly sarcastic. Harsha's stress on what a "fragile compromise" existed was an expedient tactic that allowed him to reject additional procompetitive amendments outright, on the ground that they would upset the "delicate balance." But Public Works staffers maintain that the compromise really was tenuous. "That bill could have fallen apart at any point," said one.

What made the compromise—however fragile—possible here? The most obvious reason is that both sides wanted it. (Individual groups in the coalition preferred to fight rather than compromise, but the administration overruled them by maneuver.) "No one knew what he had or where he was going," said Dick Sullivan. A compromise strategy minimized the risk all around. What's more, the alternative—a fight in conference—was totally unacceptable to the ATA. That gave the Public Works Committee, which was in the best position to orchestrate a compromise, added incentive to do so.

If incentives were at work, so was skill. Perhaps the ultimate proof of a well-crafted compromise was the scene at "Bullfeathers," a Capitol Hill watering hole, the night the House passed the trucking bill. Representatives of nearly every group—ATA, owner-operators, and deregulators—were celebrating victory at different tables in the room. (The Teamsters were there, too, but their mood was less than celebratory.) The wife of one ATA lobbyist, herself a House staffer, asked why the people from DOT and the White House were celebrating. Deregulators asked themselves the same question about the ATA table. And everyone ordered another round of drinks.

"It's a real art—compromise—and one that isn't respected enough," said Dick Sullivan. It wasn't that way when Sullivan came to Capitol Hill in 1956, having gained his political instincts ringing doorbells and delivering speeches for the Bronx Democratic machine. But procedural "reforms" and other changes have made old-fashioned compromise much less common, in Sullivan's view.

If compromise is viewed as an end in itself, then perhaps it deserves its declining status. The belief that every political group is (equally) legitimate leads to bad public policy, as chapter 1 argued. But as a practical matter, achieving a well-crafted compromise—one that manages to give every group more than it expects—is an art, and one that's alive and well in the Public Works Committee.

The American Trucking Associations

Chickens may be an exempt commodity, but then the trucking industry has never been run by chickens. So we will continue to stand our ground and fight.
—Former ATA Chairman Lee R. Sollenbarger, June 17, 1976

Anyone who has tangled with the ATA has a favorite story to illustrate why that group has traditionally been viewed as one of the most powerful and effective lobbies in Washington.[32] One such story involves the coat worn by President Abraham Lincoln on the night he was assassinated in Ford's Theatre. The coat is now displayed at the Ford's Theatre Museum in Washington, D.C.; a plaque beside the display lists the American Trucking Associations as a contributor. Washington old-timers recall that the ATA bought the coat from a descendent of a White House servant for $25,000; a member of Congress whose favor the ATA sought to gain was a Lincoln buff, and the coat was given through him to the museum!

The trucking industry is proud of its reputation for clout on Capitol Hill, and when the ICC abandoned its long-standing role as industry protector, it was natural that the ATA turn to Congress for help—and with considerable optimism that it would be rescued. "We have insisted over the years that we've got great political muscle [and] the media gives us credit for having great political muscle," Bennett Whitlock told the ATA Executive

Committee on the eve of the Senate Commerce Committee markup of S. 2245. "Well, gentlemen," Whitlock said, "this will be the time to tell whether we really have that political muscle or not."[33]

Three weeks later, Whitlock informed industry members that the Commerce Committee had approved a bill that "cuts the heart out of regulation." The ATA recovered some of its losses in the House but, overall, the outcome raised serious questions about the trucking lobby's effectiveness.

What went wrong? Granted, deregulators waged a skillful offensive battle, as the pages up to now describe. But that's not to say that a better defense wouldn't have changed the outcome.

Two hypotheses merit brief consideration. According to the first, the ATA's mistake was not compromising earlier, at a point when industry critics' expectations for reform were modest. The second hypothesis argues that, given its decision not to compromise, the trucking industry should have devoted far more resources than it did to the fight. Both explanations point to a misassessment by the trucking industry of the potential strength and commitment of the opposition.

Bend in the Wind versus Don't Give an Inch

Shortly after President Ford sent his motor carrier reform bill to Capitol Hill, a Texas carrier warned fellow members of the ATA's executive committee that they should compromise now to avoid a worse fate later:

> Political animal[s] . . . don't get too far out in front of their political groups, and so [the call for] deregulation did not come out of the ivory tower. [It] came about because there is an ever-growing demand for some form of regulatory reform. [We] as a regulated industry . . . had better come up with some solutions to our problems or somebody is going to come up with [them] for us.[34]

Few regulated truckers shared that view: the carrier who expressed it had a self-interest in seeing ICC controls relaxed (three years later, he testified in favor of S. 2245). A much more prevalent attitude was that of the carrier who responded that "any crack in the door [to allow for more entry] weaken[s] the position of ATA."

ATA officials recognized the political need for some degree of compromise. In 1975, they outlined the industry's strategy as one of enlisting shipper support against the enemies in DOT and the White House. To do that—and ultimately to defuse the movement for deregulation—the industry had to answer the growing criticisms of shippers with a "positive program" of reform. "If we can get nearly 17,000 shippers across this land, plus our own efforts, with a positive program on regulation," one industry leader advised, "we will just jerk that rug right out from under that administration."[35]

But the trucking industry agreed to only half of the ICC's "39 recommendations"—a modest agenda for change that had strong support from shippers and their association, the NIT League. Later on, the industry conceded more in writing its own regulatory reform bill, but the concessions were still largely symbolic, and the bill alienated shippers in large numbers. "As long as the issue was 'deregulation,' the ATA had shipper support," observed one NIT League official. But once the ATA came onto the field with its own status quo bill, that cleared the board for reform. Trees have to bend in the wind if they're not to be uprooted."

Once the battle lines were drawn, deciding whether or not to compromise involved a different set of calculations for the ATA. With 20-20 hindsight, some deregulators maintain that the ATA should have cut a deal with the Carter administration in 1979 or earlier—before Howard Cannon introduced S. 2245—when trucking deregulation was still seen as a losing cause.

That view is less than convincing, however. Given the tremendous political uncertainty at that point, industry members had no rational reason to concede even partial antitrust immunity without a fight, and it's unlikely that the Carter administration—pessimistic though it was—would have agreed to any compromise that offered less. Moreover, the ATA had no guarantee that a compromise would be honored in the future. If the political climate for deregulation continued to improve, Congress could well decide to take the issue up anew.

Political strategy aside, there was substantial economic value to the industry and its employees in delaying deregulation. Even by 1979, with significant ICC reforms in effect, delay was probably worth several billion dollars a year to Teamsters and regulated carriers.[36]

In sum, a more flexible stance by the ATA—particularly at a time when shippers were still afraid of "deregulation"—might have successfully defused the reform movement. But given the high cost of compromise—that is, the economic benefits of delay foregone—and the possibility that Congress would reconsider the issue in the future, the industry's decision not to compromise was reasonable.

Too Little, Too Late

Deregulation didn't sneak up on its victims. If anything, the ATA saw it coming even before it was a real threat. That's not surprising: Lobby organizations often invent or exaggerate a crisis both to justify the group's existence and to offset the tendency for members to free-ride.

When President Ford sent his motor carrier reform bill to Congress, the industry responded with heavy lobbying and public relations. Deregulators were amused by the ATA's seeming overreaction to Ford's futile gesture toward reform. But the chief lobbyist warned industry members not to relax their guard just because the Ford bill went nowhere: "The seeds have been planted, and . . . regardless of who the next president of the United States is, we are still going to have this fight. . . . Don't let your guard down. The mere fact that we do not have hearings this year does not mean that we are home free. All we are doing is buying time."[37]

Two years later, when Edward Kennedy challenged Howard Cannon for jurisdiction over the trucking issue, the industry overwhelmed reformers with its show of lobbying force. (Some Capitol Hill offices reported receiving 4,000 letters, telegrams, and calls from truckers and Teamsters.) But victory left the ATA only cautiously optimistic. "[While] we won a crucial first round," an ATA news release told industry members, "we're not out of the woods yet."

In keeping with that cautious attitude, the ATA hired the world's largest public relations firm and set about raising the $2.4 million necessary to finance the first year of a media campaign directed largely at shippers, small communities, financial institutions, and truck dealers and suppliers. And on another front, ATA lawyers fired off round after round of ammunition in an effort to halt administrative decontrol by the ICC.

One could hardly accuse the ATA of not taking the threat of deregulation seriously, it would seem. And yet, as the battle progressed, there were signs that the industry underestimated the opposition. Most significant was the Senate's confirmation of "the three marketeers" in the summer of 1979. While the truckers and Teamsters put up a fight, their resistance was mild considering what was at stake.

More generally, the ATA allocated too little, too late in the way of lobbying resources. This was particularly damaging in the Senate, where several Commerce Committee members committed themselves to supporting reform before they were seriously approached by the other side. When the truckers and Teamsters finally brought out their heavy ammunition, the sound was near deafening; Senate staffers said the lobbying that took place just before and during committee markup was the most intense ever seen on Capitol Hill. But perhaps no amount of firepower could have changed things at that late stage, given the simultaneous barrage coming from the White House.

Why the miscalculation? An important reason, no doubt, has to do with Howard Cannon. Even if ATA leaders did not expect Cannon to be an active ally, they never anticipated such a determined foe. More generally, ATA leaders underestimated the commitment of deregulators as a whole—especially Jimmy Carter. They were amazed that an issue so few voters cared about could inspire such a show of presidential support.

Other factors may help explain why carriers, as distinct from their leaders, underestimated the threat of deregulation. One was members' confidence in the ATA lobbyists based on past performance. Bolstering that confidence was a sincere belief shared by many industry members that regulation had served the public interest. ATA executive committee meetings resounded with the heartfelt statements of hardworking carriers who maintained that if they could explain their case to Congress rationally, support would surely follow.

The industry was not far off in its assessment of enemy strength. Key votes were extremely close; absent flukes—such as the drafting error in the Hollings amendment on the Senate floor—they would have been even closer. And had President Carter not all but twisted the arms of swing senators, the committee markup would likely have been a victory for the ATA.

But the assessment was off nonetheless. While the figures on industry expenditures sound high—several million dollars on public relations; hundreds of thousands of dollars on campaign contributions—they pale in comparison to what deregulation would cost the industry. "Given the stakes, the truckers should have been willing to spend enough to buy all of us [deregulators] off," said one administration official tongue in cheek. "They should have been willing to set me up on a farm in the Virginia countryside."

Conclusion

Despite his reputation as a poor bargainer and his need for legislative accomplishments to cite in the 1980 campaign, Jimmy Carter secured a reasonably strong trucking deregulation bill. Had the White House held out longer in negotiating with Public Works, or fought it out in conference committee, the resulting legislation might have been even stronger. But the decision to compromise when it did assured the administration a solid bill and six months of implementation by an aggressive ICC chairman.

While the ICC gave the administration the freedom to settle for a less than ideal bill, it also provided the leverage to demand a reasonably strong one. Early ICC reforms eliminated the strong defensive advantage that the ATA (like most client groups) enjoyed—namely the ability to subvert reform by delaying or derailing legislation to change the status quo—and forced the ATA to go on the offensive seeking legislation that would restore the status quo. Continued administrative changes and the threat of still more ultimately forced the ATA to accept legislation embodying substantial reform.

While the actions of the ICC meant that Congress didn't need to take affirmative action in order to bring about deregulation, merely approve administrative changes already in place, legislation to undo those reforms was a distinct possibility. Vague hints of veto and visible lobbying by senior administration officials, including the president himself, helped convey Carter's unwillingness to accept a regressive bill. Once the risk of getting such a bill disappeared, White House bargaining focused on getting the most progressive bill possible. Several of Carter's appeals on the trucking bill had direct strategic value, but Carter's personal involvement, and that of his senior officials, contributed more to strategy indirectly, as a symbolic indication of the high priority he attached to trucking reform.

To some extent, Carter was a strong bargainer because he was politically weak. Vulnerable to attack by Edward Kennedy, or members of the press who were following the trucking issue closely, Carter couldn't cut a deal with the Teamsters or cave in to Public Works, even if electoral considerations so dictated. But the administration's bargaining strength also derived from the fact that decisions about what constituted an acceptable compromise were made in collaboration with ICC economists and other substantive experts.

White House resources and commitment—the focus of this chapter— were only one source of deregulators' bargaining strength. Howard Cannon, though initially skeptical, came to believe in the merits of trucking reform and proved a skillful advocate for reform. He successfully kept Congress at bay while the ICC moved closer to deregulation, thus increasing the industry's need to strike a bargain. Robert Packwood, a passionate believer in trucking decontrol, brought large numbers of Republicans to his side both in committee and on the Senate floor, and he made ambitious bargaining demands that Cannon committed himself to achieving. Edward Kennedy gave the trucking issue visibility and then goaded Cannon and Carter into action—roles he had also played in the airline-deregulation contest.

Truckers' and Teamsters' strength in Congress was concentrated in the House Public Works Committee. Though deregulators anticipated getting the most resistance from the Democratic leadership in Public Works, the Republicans—especially William Harsha—proved to be the hardest bargainers. Once Public Works and the White House had struck a deal, Harsha resisted virtually all efforts by deregulators to strengthen the bill on the grounds that it would upset "the delicate balance."

While the ATA preferred the compromise struck by Public Works to no compromise, it was a far cry from what the industry group set out to obtain from Congress. Had industry been willing to compromise several years earlier, truckers would have had to give up much less to satisfy reformers, but they would also have foregone substantial monopoly profits during that time and with no assurance that Congress wouldn't legislate more ambitious reforms later on. Thus it's hard to criticize their bargaining strategy on that score. An earlier and stronger show of commitment on industry's part would probably have reduced the losses in the Senate and possibly have reversed one or two key votes. The industry's failure on that score reflects its underestimation of both the strength and commitment of deregulators, a serious miscalculation.

8

The Elements of
Political Strategy

In war and politics, there is a natural tendency for the losing side to rationalize its loss as the inevitable result of uncontrollable forces, and for winners to credit victory to their own skill, hard work, and careful timing. The truth is usually somewhere in between, and that was certainly the case with trucking deregulation. While this analysis has focused largely on strategy, the enormous impact of exogenous political and economic forces is inescapable. It's no coincidence that Congress deregulated airlines, air cargo, buses, financial institutions, and trucking all within the space of a few years. Strategy aside, structural changes in government and the economy served to erode the symbiotic tie that traditionally linked Congress, the regulatory agency, and the regulated industry.

Most important to understanding why widespread deregulation occurred when it did, rather than ten years earlier or ten years later, is the inflationary *economic climate* of the 1970s and early 1980s. In previous decades, proposals to eliminate government subsidies had little appeal; increasing prosperity and productivity meant that there were greater gains to be made from trying to increase the size of the national economic pie than from trying to divide the pie more efficiently and equitably.[1] As chapter 4 discussed, "efficiency" was something of a pejorative to many congressmen because it implied loss of jobs and bankruptcies. By the late 1970s, persistent high inflation and declining productivity had changed that calculation.

Shipper support for trucking decontrol was a direct response to changing economic conditions. For many years, motor carrier regulation had been a costly nuisance to corporate shippers—but not a strong candidate for political action. When fuel prices soared in the mid-1970s, however, trucking deregulation became a priority to shipper groups like NAM and NFIB. Farm groups, whose members were also burdened by higher shipping costs, responded similarly.

Inflation also made trucking deregulation an appealing issue to consumer groups, but less because of the potential savings to members than because of the prospect for improving the image of consumerism. As chapter 5 discussed, the consumer movement lost favor in the late 1970s, when its traditional goals became linked in the public's eye with increased government and inflation. Trucking deregulation represented an anti-inflationary issue on which consumer groups could work with business— their major critic—to reduce the size of government.

Most important, economic problems led to a change in the White House calculation of the political costs and benefits of deregulation. Presidents Kennedy, Johnson, and Nixon all were dissuaded from pursuing motor carrier decontrol because the potential political gains were slight relative to the costs of alienating industry and labor. But during the Ford administration, double-digit inflation, the energy crisis, and increased public distrust of government combined to make deregulation good presidential politics.

Carter's inflation czar Alfred Kahn viewed trucking deregulation as the single most important anti-inflation reform before Congress, and the White House assigned its resources accordingly, as chapter 7 indicated. But the important thing was not the direct impact trucking reform would have on the rate of inflation, as Darius Gaskins observed. "The important thing was that [deregulation] gave something concrete to point to at a time when there were few attractive anti-inflation alternatives. It gave Carter a chance to win credits with conservatives by attacking bureaucracy, and simultaneously win liberal support by playing the Teamsters and truckers as fall guys."[2]

Deregulation was not the only possible response to inflationary pressures; increased regulation was a plausible alternative. That politicians and ICC commissioners opted for less rather than more regulation reflects a profound change in the *intellectual climate*. "Forty years ago," observed Darius Gaskins in 1980, "the hostility of intellectuals toward the market system appeared so strong . . . that [Joseph Schumpeter] accorded it a major role in his scenario for the breakdown of capitalism." But gradually, intellectual attitudes shifted, and the competitive market ideal again became academically respectable. As a result, wrote Gaskins, "the critical view of regulation that only a short time ago was considered heresy now has assumed the status of conventional wisdom."[3]

This shift in intellectual attitudes has had considerable impact on the political and legal environment surrounding regulation. In part, this has come about through the teaching of academic economists. Law school graduates—many of whom were exposed to economics during their legal training—have gone on to work for congressional committees, regulatory agencies, and judges making high-level regulatory policy decisions. A large number of these judges have themselves received some training in economics in recent years.[4] Members of Congress have also become increasingly sophisticated in their understanding of economics in general and economic regulation in particular.

The impact of academic thinking on the political environment has come about even more directly as a result of the increasing number of economists, and policy analysts trained in economics, who have moved into government jobs in the last decade. It's no coincidence that the most aggressive administrative deregulation occurred in agencies directed by economists: airlines under Kahn; trucks, buses, and to some extent railroads under Gaskins. More generally, economists and analysts have become a key part of what Hugh Heclo describes as "issue networks"—the "specialized subcultures of highly knowledgeable policy watchers" that have come to play a major role in the policy process.[5]

While deregulation efforts benefited from the shift in intellectual attitudes toward the competitive market, they also contributed to that shift. Kennedy's dramatic hearings on the CAB served to educate the press and politicians as to the problems inherent in regulating a naturally competitive industry (Stephen Breyer, who orchestrated the hearings, subsequently published a text on the economics of regulatory reform). Alfred Kahn's visible success in decontrolling the airline industry ("laissez faire and half fare") was visible proof of economists' claims for the market. Trucking deregulators took advantage of the growing movement toward competition that airline decontrol spawned and in turn added to that movement through their own success.

In sum, deregulation is testimony to the power of ideas. John Maynard Keynes' oft-quoted claim for social science seems written for the occasion: "The ideas of economists and political philosophers, both when they are right and when they are wrong, are more powerful than is commonly understood. . . . I am sure that the power of vested interests is vastly exaggerated compared with the gradual encroachment of ideas."[6]

Linked to the shifting economic and intellectual climate were changes in the *organizational climate* favorable to deregulation. The emergence of public-interest groups in the 1960s and early 1970s served to give consumer interests representation on certain issues and reduce somewhat the advantage enjoyed by client groups. Though less well funded than the groups they battled, public-interest lobbies benefited enormously from friends in high places—especially Congress and the media. The passage of major safety and environmental regulations during that period was testament to the power of that movement, as were the actions of regulatory agencies, where, as James Q. Wilson observed, a "political market" emerged that was as strong—or stronger—than the economic market:

> Why this political market . . . emerged . . . has much to do with the arrival of a political elite that has absorbed the neopopulist outlook fostered by the 1960s: the suspicion of institutions, the criticism of business enterprise, the interest in speaking on behalf (or so they think) of unorganized consumers, and the conviction that such an outlook is not only morally correct but politically useful.[7]

The beating it took in the press, Congress, and regulatory agencies such as the Federal Trade Commission in turn galvanized business. The Business Roundtable, founded in 1972, whose CEO members lobbied Congress directly, symbolized the priority and legitimacy of political action by business. Buoyed by the faith in business and markets of increasingly influential economists, business rode in on a wave of concern over inflation and excessive government regulation that simultaneously swamped the consumer movement. Deregulation was the rare issue that served the needs of both the descendent consumer and ascendent business lobbies.[9]

Strategic Action

As recently as this time last year, the conventional wisdom had it that regulatory reform of the trucking industry was a hopeless cause—a grandiose monument to unpopular economic theories put together, brick by hypothetical brick, by theoretical dreamers with no knowledge or experience in the real world. That was last year.
—DOT Secretary Neil Goldschmidt, January 17, 1980

These structural forces—persistent inflation and declining productivity, the growing influence of economic thinking, and the rise of a public-interest movement followed by the politicization of business—were necessary but not sufficient to bring about deregulation. As late as 1979, well after they were in place, trucking reform was still viewed as a "hopeless cause." Implicit in this case study is the belief that strategic action by reformers—much of which was carried out in 1979 and 1980—is a significant factor in explaining the favorable political outcome.

Explanatory aims aside, this case study focuses on strategy in an effort to gain insights applicable to other policy-reform battles. Whereas structural change is exogenous, strategy is subject to reformers' control. Thus, even if strategic action accounts for only a small part of a political outcome, it is disproportionately important to policymakers because it can be influenced.

Despite its importance, political strategy is a notoriously difficult subject about which to generalize. What succeeds in one political setting—a divide-and-conquer tactic, for example—may be entirely inappropriate in another. No two policy battles are alike. Moreover, what appears to be "the" winning strategy is often just one part of a larger game plan.[10]

In an effort to be both more general and more comprehensive, this case study has examined four generic elements of strategy: use of analysis to make a strong case on the merits; formation and maintenance of a diverse coalition to lobby actively; transition schemes to reduce uncertainty and cushion the blow to losers; and presidential (or other executive) bargaining to gain sheer political leverage. These four elements were the key to trucking (and airline) deregulators' success, but they also provide a more general recipe for terminating a client policy, be it at the federal, state, or local level; be it a price support, tax subsidy, or protective tariff.[11]

Recipes for success aren't hard to come by in the legislative arena, but the ingredients are. Basic impediments to producing them in part explain their scarcity. The experience of trucking deregulators sheds light on both what those obstacles are and possible ways to get around them.

Demonstrating the Merits

In our political system, the burden of proof is on those who advocate major change, especially when that change risks disruption and dislocation. To meet this burden, a case to Congress on the merits must demonstrate that something is seriously wrong with the existing system and reduce uncertainty about the possible ill effects of policy change. To accomplish these goals, it must be understandable to politicians and sensitive to political factors.

The fact that an existing policy is economically inefficient has not traditionally been seen as a serious problem in the eyes of Congress. When an inefficient policy produces meat shortages, gas lines, and other crises of scarcity, Congress is responsive. But special-interest policies like economic regulation cushion the system against shortages, bankruptcy, and other such problems. While the cost to consumers is excessive, they aren't complaining; hence, until recently, politicians rejected economists' claims that a problem existed.

One way to demonstrate that a problem exists is to link the inefficient policy to one or more major national concerns. In the late 1970s, with inflation seen as public enemy number one, the link to that concern was a natural one to draw. Even if the reform won't noticeably reduce the national concern, legislators can appear to be doing something about it. (The growing concern with U.S. competitiveness and productivity may systematically ease the task of portraying inefficient policies as problematic; conversely, it may stimulate and strengthen protectionist sentiments.)

Demonstrating that there's a problem requires empirical evidence with strong scholarly credentials—evidence able to withstand direct attack as well as comparison to misleading counterevidence. Evidence of a supportive consensus among experts is also key, because the existence of a small number of deviant views is enough to neutralize even a strong case on the merits before a jury of legislators. But while empirical evidence helps to establish reformers' credibility, concrete examples and anecdotes are important for making the case dramatic and bringing it close to home. (The less persuasive the empirical evidence, the more important anecdotes are.) Under any circumstances, anecdotes and concrete examples are useful for trial-by-media.

Use of "soft" evidence to complement more scientific data is also key to reducing legislators' uncertainty about possible ill effects of policy change. (Theoretical arguments—still a third form of ammunition—have limited value in a political setting, except insofar as they appeal to common sense and intuition.) Academic studies of settings where the reform has been successfully implemented (or where the special-interest policy was never instituted) are generally persuasive. However, anecdotal evidence gathered from a particular region or state may provide a more satisfying answer to the inevitable question, But how will it affect my district? Such evidence serves both a substantive function, by persuading genuinely skeptical congressmen, and a symbolic function, by giving would-be supporters "something to hang their hats on." Another symbolic function it serves is to reduce opponents' ability to postpone reform by calling for further study—a common ploy.

Qualitative evidence that addresses the How-will-it-affect-my-district? question, unlike scientific data on aggregate effects, is tailored to the policy debate at hand—a major advantage. A second way of tailoring the case to Congress is with evidence that addresses the specifics of a realistic reform bill. Since academic studies tend to view reform in its theoretically pure form rather than as a coarse product of political compromise, this tailored evidence is useful in the debate.

Tailoring the substantive case to the policy debate at hand requires close coordination between the analytic shops and the political front line. Timing is critical in the release of both affirmative and rebuttal evidence. Moreover, statistics must at times be carefully crafted so as to fight fire with fire.

Close contact between analysts and political players produces a sensitivity not only to timing and number-crafting but also to the kind of evidence needed. Economists in the heat of fire are more likely to recognize the strategic weaknesses of theoretical reasoning and the value of anecdotes, "three-week studies," and simplicity of argument.

Ultimately, strategic use of analysis requires a marriage of political and economic skills and perspectives. That union may take place within "a multidisciplinary team or a multidisciplinary head," to use John Mendeloff's phrase.[12] In either form, it's a first step to defeating a powerful special interest.

Forming and Maintaining a Coalition

While analysis and anecdotes provide one measure of the merits, interest-group support provides another. To elected officials, a broad coalition is convincing evidence that its crusade is in the public interest. The more active the coalition, the more likely a congressman is to feel that he can vote against the opposing client group without suffering significant electoral damage.

Two fundamental problems confront an embryonic policymaking coalition. The first of these—the free-rider problem—discourages political action of any kind by an organization when the issue at stake is a collective good. This explains why private firms generally stay out of politics: Their individual stakes are small, and they will receive the economic benefits of collective action even if they're silent. Not only is there no economic incentive for a private firm to speak out, but there are costs to doing so, because political visibility can jeopardize the firm's basic mission of doing business. The exceptions—the paying riders in any given policy debate—are firms whose stakes are not small.

A political organization faces altogether different incentives. While members will receive the economic benefits of collective action in any event, the organization must participate in order to receive the noneconomic benefits that enhance its image in the eyes of existing and potential members—namely, visibility and opportunities for claiming credit. Organizations that exist largely to give political expression to the ideological and other policy beliefs of their members have the strongest incentive not to free-ride, since they must be visible, and at least occasionally successful, in order to survive. Organizations that exist largely to provide individual material benefits to their members can also benefit from receiving visibility and credit for legislative success. But overall, they behave more like private firms, participating in political battles that will have a very direct economic impact on their members and often lobbying for narrow provisions designed to provide specialized benefits.

While groups as groups benefit from being politically active, there are disincentives to joining a coalition to pursue that activity. Joining *any* coalition requires a sacrifice of independence and autonomy that groups are hesitant to make. Particular coalitions raise other problems as well, especially for ideological groups, which risk offending their purist members by associating with organizations of a clashing political stripe.

Despite these drawbacks, most Washington lobbyists feel that coalitions are an extremely efficient and effective way for interest groups to share information, coordinate lobbying activity, and overcome the inherent limitations of any single member group. Thus, even groups that officially avoid coalitions in fact work closely with them, and groups that once eschewed cooperative lobbying as a threat to their emerging identities now prefer to lobby as part of a coalition.

The decision to join a particular coalition—that is, the choice of an issue—reflects a variety of considerations, few more important than the likelihood of success. But beyond that, the presence of individual political organizations in coalitions is explained largely by one or more of five factors:

1. *The will of the membership.* The organization's membership virtually mandates support of particular issues, because it accords with members' private interests or with their privately held conceptions of the "public interest." Organization memberships are rarely homogeneous, however, and the existence of even a splinter element may be enough to inhibit group action.

2. *Flank covering.* Many small or nascent groups face what one lobbyist called the "What-do-we-put-in-our-next-newsletter?" problem. Group leaders need to justify their existence and cover their flanks with the membership. Hungry for issues, they'll take almost any one that's plausible.

3. *Political signalling.* An organization's lobbying agenda is a signal as to the group's political identity. Thus groups, like politicians, sometimes embrace an issue in an effort to change an undesirable image or appeal to a broader audience of potential members.

4. *Staff interest and expertise.* An organization's paid staff or top leadership (paid or unpaid) has special talents, interests, and ambitions that make them want to lobby certain issues for largely personal reasons. Staff members have the most discretion to select issues in public-interest groups and ideological groups, since they are characterized by a centralized decision-making structure.

5. *Selective benefits.* Even when the issue at stake is a collective good, there may be opportunities for legislation to provide individualized ben-

efits to particular groups ("curb service"). Such opportunities explain the support of certain interest groups—typically economic ones.

These five factors help explain the sheer presence (or absence) of particular organizations in a coalition. Harder to explain is their degree of individual involvement, since that is more dependent on what other claims are competing for a group's resources simultaneously. Staff discretion is the most immediate explanation, but that reflects indirect factors—opportunities for group credit-taking, members' stake in the issue, the need for defensive positioning to avoid being sold out by other groups—as well as the sheer interest and commitment of staff members.

Precisely because groups come to an ad hoc coalition with such varying motivations for political involvement, internal compatibility is difficult to achieve. Two related but distinct substantive problems threaten the unity of such a group: disagreement over *what* to seek in the compromise, and disagreement over *how much* to settle for. "What" problems are of two types. The first involves a direct conflict of interest: some members of the group favor a provision that others oppose. The second type involves a conflict over what weights to assign different provisions: faced with the need to choose between multiple goals, groups disagree as to their priorities.

Even allied groups with identical priorities can face the "how much" problem, if one group feels that a compromise containing A and B is satisfactory, while others insist that any settlement that doesn't contain A, B, and C is worse than no settlement at all. Similarly situated groups may well disagree about how much to settle for, simply because they perceive the bargaining situation differently. But the disagreement will more likely reflect inherent differences between the groups. The coalition player whose motives are primarily electoral will tend to settle for less than players driven by economic gain will—at least when the legislation is of the type that, at best, will provide only diffuse benefits to voters. Thus representatives of the president are often viewed as "cavemen" by others in the coalition. Other motives—primarily the need to satisfy an ideological membership—drive a coalition player to take an unreasonably demanding bargaining position.

While it's difficult to generalize, the trucking experience suggests that direct conflicts of interest will be the least troublesome for ad hoc coalitions: Groups that coalesce to support a particular reform generally agree on at least the basics. Conflicts over priorities are apt to be more of a problem, particularly between groups with differing economic interests. Diverse ideological perspectives will tend to produce conflicts among political organizations over how much a compromise should contain.

These observations illustrate how a political cartel differs from an economic one. For profit-maximizing firms that form a cartel in order to keep prices above the competitive level, there is an optimal price and a single measure of the utility of both the individual firm and the cartel as a whole. When any firm prices below this optimal level, that triggers retaliatory price cuts by the others, and everyone in the cartel, including the initiator, is worse off.

In policymaking cartels, by contrast, there is no single measure of utility. One member's aim is to maximize electoral benefits, another's is to maximize the savings to consumers. Thus, whereas independent action by a profit maximizer is clearly self-defeating, that is not the case for coalition members, since one member's maximization may be inconsistent with another's.

Several conditions in addition to capable leadership work to inhibit these conflicts and maintain the internal compatibility of a coalition. One is the *"KISS"* requirement—the need for lobbyists to keep their arguments and wish lists simple in accord with the generally low level of information on Capitol Hill about specific issues and the competing demands for congressmen's time and interest. Coalition members who can agree on the basics may never have to resolve their differences on more subtle concerns.

The faster an issue moves through Congress, the greater the need for simplicity. Thus *speed* is another unifying force. Speed is especially important once coalition members accept a tentative compromise. The longer it takes to ratify, the more likely individual groups are to find something unacceptable in the agreement.

Staff discretion is a third boon to coalition unity. The more freedom group representatives have to act on behalf of their memberships, the easier it is for them to make politically expedient accommodations and work out a compromise to their ideological and economic differences with other coalition members.

Coalition members can't always resolve their differences, no matter how much discretion they have. But a member organization is less likely to secede over internal disagreements if the coalition has an *informal structure*. A formal coalition is viewed as speaking with a single voice, and members who can't fully endorse that position are more likely to feel they must break away from the alliance (or never join it in the first place). Then the coalition must spend considerable effort appeasing the group—effort that could otherwise be directed against the opponent. This need to maintain unity is critical because when a coalition is formally organized, its internal politics more than its policy demands become the focus of outside attention, and any friction receives undue and damaging publicity.

The price a coalition pays for harmony-through-informality is reduced clout. As is true for individual organizations, the more cohesive the members appear to be, the more deference legislators will grant to the group's views.

Whether a coalition is formal or informal, the process of internal bargaining and maintenance is ongoing. The experience of the trucking-reform alliance suggests that four broad phases characterize this process. During the first phase, organizations with a mutual interest in some issue meet to share information and explore the possibility of coordinated action. One or more groups begin to emerge as leaders even at this early stage. Having decided to coalesce on some more permanent basis, members proceed to elaborate their goals and minimal requirements for legislation (phase two). This elaboration process leads to establishment of internal procedures for operation—including choice of permanent leadership and a decision as to how tightly to structure the organization—and to development of a strategic plan of external action. Applying that plan, coalition members begin to lobby actively during phase three, and based on that interaction with the "outside," they reformulate their goals and strategies. Tests of strength (committee markups, floor votes) lead to additional modifications of the coalition's aspirations and minimal disposition. Alliance members are at their most unified as they prepare for these tests of strength. Once they are over and legislative opponents begin to compromise (phase four), independent action by individual coalition members—especially those with an incentive to compromise prematurely—becomes a significant problem. The closer opponents get to a compromise, the more splintering there is, as coalition members try to secure provisions responsive to their individual needs.

Transition Strategies

Economic arguments and evidence can allay some concerns about possible adverse effects of policy change; interest-group support consistent with those arguments can ease concerns still more. But where "brute sanity" leaves off, transition strategies can often pick up.

A strategy of *compensation* is theoretically the most powerful. The threat of economic loss represents the greatest source of opposition to efficient policy reform. But in theory, no one need lose. Since the gains from an efficient change outweigh the losses, gainers can compensate losers fully and still be better off.

In practice, however, a compensation strategy runs up against the organizational needs of client groups and their leaders. These groups—like all interest groups—thrive on political conflict, which generates feelings of group pride and dependence on the leadership. Thus any effort to buy off an opposing client group and preempt the fight altogether is anathema. This holds whether the offer is one of compensation or concessions on policy.

Even if it is made late in the battle, an offer of compensation will be less attractive to client-group leaders than equivalent concessions on policy, because the substantive concessions imply some ongoing need for the organization, whereas compensation (in return for the termination of the inefficient policy) eliminates that very need. Concessions will also be more attractive if the client group perceives that its members can receive compensation independently, arguably as an equity remedy for their losses due to a "change in the rules." In sum, if a compromise involving compensation occurs at all, it will occur after a prolonged battle, but a compromise is more likely to take the form of concessions on policy.

There are situations where a strategy of compensation holds more promise. One involves potential losers who have benefited only indirectly from an inefficient policy: their political agents—unlike client-group leaders—have no vested interest in continuing the policy. Another involves workers: unlike owners of capital, workers have no property rights reflecting their monopoly position and hence are more likely to seek contingent compensation as part of the political compromise rather than in subsequent legislation.

Political feasibility aside, the design of a compensation scheme that is efficient—i.e., nondistorting—requires several very difficult determinations: who are the gainers, since they should pay for the compensation? Who are the losers, and how far removed must the injury be before it need not be compensated? And what is the magnitude of losses? Implementation of a compensation strategy raises still other potential problems—for example, in the case where payment is contingent on unemployment, it may prolong the duration of that unemployment. In addition, a compensation strategy may do more to subvert the goal of equity than to serve it. In sum, though it is in theory a powerful notion, in practice, compensation is problematic from the standpoint of equity, efficiency, and political expediency.

A variation on the strategy of compensation avoids some of those problems. If payment is contingent on some harm that reformers predict will not occur, the result is an *insurance* policy more than a compensation scheme. An insurance strategy is potentially quite effective at reducing fear of the unknown, a powerful obstacle to change. In an adversary system, opponents exaggerate the risks of change; the policy equivalent of a money-back guarantee can reduce unfounded fear at virtually no cost in some situations.

In other situations, insurance may create more of a problem than it solves, however. The guarantee may actually lend credibility to the client group's prophecies of disaster by making it appear that a crisis is anticipated. Moreover, in the course of giving the other side ammunition, an insurance scheme complicates the political debate—a serious drawback in a game with a strong defensive advantage. Finally, since insurance policies amount to contingent compensation, they will encounter some of the same resistance as buy-off schemes from client groups concerned about organizational survival.

A third transition strategy—*going slowly*—avoids many of the problems of compensation by making payment implicit rather than explicit. The advantages of this approach are several. Interest-group leaders prefer it since, unlike explicit compensation, it implies a continued role for them. Interest-group members and other skeptics value delay beyond its worth as compensation because it simultaneously reduces their fear of the unknown. And others, who view compensation as a deal with the devil, look on gradualism as the responsible management of change.

In addition, implicit compensation through gradualism or delay avoids virtually all the design and implementation problems of an explicit payment scheme. By delaying the harm, a slow transition automatically compensates all those who would be directly or indirectly hurt by policy change. Likewise, a strategy of postponement automatically "taxes" gainers and only gainers by delaying the benefits they receive.

By delaying these benefits, a lengthy transition offers political expedience at the expense of economic efficiency. In addition, the process of phasing in policy change sometimes creates its own market distortions. Distortions or no distortions, major policy reforms will likely be accompanied by a long transition period. For whether the obstacle is the threat of economic loss, uncertainty, or fear of chaos, it seems there's no general strategy more well suited to reducing transitional opposition to change.

This trade-off between political expedience and economic efficiency, basic to any transition strategy, is perhaps best illustrated by the example of uncertainty. From the standpoint of efficiency, maximum certainty about the ground rules governing change is desirable; it allows client-group members to adjust more rapidly and effectively. But since those individuals generally don't want to adjust, preferring a continuation of the status quo, some degree of uncertainty or ambiguity may be strategically useful.

Uncertainty and ambiguity—through delay, vague (or nonexistent) legislative language, congressional deferral of decisions to another forum, and inclusion of opportunities for appeal and policy reversal—are politically expedient for several reasons. First, they allow client-group leaders to "sell" a compromise to their members. If the leaders have been forced to concede on issues that, for purposes of bargaining, they insisted were nonnegotiable, ambiguity allows for a face-saving way out. Second, ambiguity in the form of oversight, further study, and opportunities for appeal allows client-group members who sincerely feel they're on the side of truth to accept change with the belief that, eventually, the "truth will out." Third, whether or not they feel truth is on their side, client-group members will accept more change if some ambiguity about the ground rules allows them to believe that the change may be reversed in the future. Finally, where opposition to change represents genuine fear of chaos and instability, ambiguity in the form of flexible ground rules can help reduce that opposition.

The drawback to strategic uncertainty and ambiguity is the loss in efficiency. When interest-group members are misled by their leaders' false claims of victory or by their own foolish optimism, they don't respond properly to the changes occurring around them. At the time when members should be getting the most advice from their leaders as to how to prepare for change, they're being told that it's business as usual. Some of that is inevitable, no matter how explicit the compromise, but legislation that builds in ambiguity only compounds the problem.

Presidential Bargaining

For the sheer political leverage necessary to overcome a powerful client group, there is no substitute for executive support. "Support" alone, however, is not enough; lacking a power base superior to that of the client group, a president must contrive one. Strategic bargaining holds the key, because bargaining power is subjective power. A skilled bargainer can convince his opponent that he controls resources the opponent needs and that he will use power absent a satisfactory settlement to the dispute.

While bargaining is the key to gaining political leverage against a powerful client-group opponent, the president-as-bargainer has a notable handicap to overcome—the expectation on the part of opponents and supporters alike that he will "cave in," or compromise prematurely. Any bargainer faces the problem of appearing firm to an opponent who recognizes that many points of settlement are better for the bargainer than no settlement at all. But the problem is more serious for a president because of the widespread preception that virtually *any* legislative settlement will serve his needs better than deadlock.

The basis for this perception has to do with the different "accounting systems" that bargainers use. At each potential settlement point, bargainers decide whether to compromise or not based on the perceived costs and benefits to them of doing each. A bargainer's bottom line is the point where the net value of settlement precisely equals the net value of nonsettlement.

For an economic interest group—either the client group or an opposing lobby—those costs and benefits are largely monetary. But for a president, the economic incentives are indirect; electoral incentives tend to dominate. A president wants to defeat a client group primarily to enhance his public image as an effective leader. Because the average voter can't distinguish between a poor legislative settlement and a good one, the White House has less incentive than an economic actor to bargain hard.

This description does not fit all presidential battles. In a highly visible fight with Congress, the president may reap direct support from taking an uncompromising stance on a popular issue. In addition, when there is a direct link between the economic effects of legislation and the president's popularity, the White House has political incentive to bargain for legislation that it believes is economically optimal (as illustrated, for example, by President Reagan's hard bargaining on his 1981 budget bill).

But in a low-visibility battle against a special-interest group, where the economic benefits to individual voters are highly diffuse, hard bargaining—which risks getting no settlement—holds little political reward for the White House, or so it would seem to those who are watching. Thus a determined president must overcome expectations that he will cut politically expedient deals.

Statements that "the president is committed to getting a good bill" carry a certain intrinsic weight. Commitment is an overused word in Washington, however, and a president's proclaimed intent may have little to do with practical action. Sooner or later, his commitment is judged by the administration's willingness to make sacrifices and incur costs.

The expenditure of firepower on lobbying represents an important and visible sacrifice, since organizational resources are severely limited and other legislative goals must thus be neglected. Harsh criticism of would-be congressional supporters represents another clear sacrifice, since that risks loss of future support on other legislation. Alienation of constituent groups entails a visible electoral cost.

Even a demonstration of strong commitment is no guarantee that the White House will not abandon its position on major aspects of legislation, however, since to remain firm entails the greatest cost of all—the risk of getting no settlement whatsoever. Explicit cues as to the president's position are important. But because they are often dismissed or discounted as posturing, the ultimate demonstration of commitment by a president is a strategic "commitment"—a pledge to adhere to a line of behavior or a tactical position such that the bargainer is penalized if he retreats.

In political bargaining, one inevitably stakes his reputation on fulfillment of a commitment. When a president threatens to veto unsatisfactory legislation, he does just that, since retreat would make him appear weak and reduce his future leverage with Congress. But a veto threat must be nonambiguous to be credible, and that is not always practical given how much uncertainty exists prior to initial tests of strength (votes) in Congress.

The trucking battle illustrates an alternative way to create the appearance of firmness while preserving bargaining flexibility. The effect is to anchor one's bottom line to other groups or individuals who appear more demanding. The White House did this when it pledged to satisfy the ICC, whose chairman applied economic rather than political standards to proposed compromises. Cannon did it when he committed himself to satisfying Packwood, whose passion for deregulation was known to both sides.

The advantages of anchoring oneself to another person rather than to a particular position in political bargaining are two. First, the connection allows flexibility. If bargaining conditions change dramatically, the anchor person adjusts automatically, whereas the pledged position is stationary. Second, while flexibility reduces credibility, this is less true when one is committed to a person compared to an ambiguous position because the discretion is with that person rather than with the bargainer.

This anchoring takes place to some extent whether a president likes it or not, in that he must satisfy his supporters or risk their criticism. This points up an important function of (unified) ad hoc coalitions—to keep a presidential bargainer "honest." Congressional supporters serve the same function.

That function is important even with a genuinely committed president, because the White House is not a single-minded organization. Inevitably, there are internal pressures to compromise brought to bear by individuals whose primary concern is reelection. Honest disagreements over what constitutes an acceptable compromise compound the problem.

Reelection is important even to individuals in the administration whose primary concern is policy reform—but more so to some than others, depending largely on their functional position. In the eyes of observers, administration aides and officials are either "substantive" or "political" in orientation. That distinction is crucial for bargaining because substance generally demands a better outcome than politics.

Given the "caveman" expectations that a president must overcome, a key to bargaining, then, is the reliance on substance and substantive people for making tactical judgments. The integration of substantive judgments makes good policy sense for its own sake. But it also serves as an important cue for shaping expectations.

Common Threads

Each of the four elements of strategy—a case on the merits, an ad hoc coalition, transition schemes, and presidential bargaining—makes a necessary and unique contribution to overcoming a powerful client group. Common threads run through them nonetheless. Briefly described, these threads or themes represent essential tasks for policy reformers.

   a. Attending to the symbolic functions of political action. Appearances are all-important in Congress. In part because the link between actions and results is difficult to demonstrate in the policy area, legislators are often judged by the positions they take rather than the effects of those positions.

   Harmful special-interest policies are inevitably disguised in language that gives supporters the appearance of furthering laudable social goals. Transportation regulation was enacted in the 1930s in the name of safety and economic stability.

   Similarly, efforts to undo such policies must give reform a flattering "face," to use Graham Allison's term for the way in which people see an issue.[13] Reformers successfully linked deregulation to inflation reduction, energy conservation, and control of government-gone-haywire. The actual contribution of reform to those goals was less important than the appearance of one.

   Perceptions of facial beauty change over time. DOT deputy undersecretary John Snow was probably right when in 1975 he warned deregulators not to play up the potential for aggregate social savings because such savings implied an adverse impact on capital and labor. Five years later, with inflation running at 18 percent annually, that potential had become a political asset instead of a liability.

   Saying deregulation will produce savings does not make it so. Evidence and analysis are necessary to give form to the face chosen for an issue. Intellectual persuasion—of legislators who can "afford to be statesmen"—is a direct and important function of analysis.

   Also important, however, are the symbolic functions of analysis. Even if they're never examined, the sheer existence of scientific studies is a sign that reformers have done their homework and can thus be trusted. Establishing this trust reduces opponents' ability to delay reform by calling for further study. In addition, the studies provide "cover" for would-be supporters who are vulnerable to political pressure from opposing groups or skeptical constituents.[14]

   The form that the substantive evidence takes is itself a symbolic statement. Among other things, anecdotal information gathered from going out into the field serves to counter the politically harmful appearance of ivory-tower naivete.

   Evidence and analysis—both scientific and anecdotal—are not the only sources of cover for a legislator worried about appearances. Interest-group support serves a similar, symbolic function; hence the congressman's oft-heard plea to lobbyists to "get constituent mail up here so I have something to hang my hat on." For the legislator free to be a statesman, interest-group support provides a proxy measure for the merits, and team lobbying—when the team represents a broad range of organizations—is a dramatic symbol of policy worth.

White House lobbying has a large symbolic dimension to it as well in that it provides a cue as to how important an issue is to the president as bargainer. When the president telephones senators in the midst of an international crisis, winning their votes may be no less important a result than communicating to others in Congress—those who are "watching all the time"—the depth of White House commitment.

b. Keeping it simple. Symbols serve to simplify. Symbolic action is central to politics in part for this reason. In an environment where countless organized groups compete for severely limited legislative resources and public attention, the need to reduce complexity is great.

No feature of Capitol Hill life is more important to strategy than the low level of information on individual issues. Important distinctions between groups with the same name—owner-operators who work independently versus those who work for regulated carriers—are not perceived. At the same time, subtle distinctions in terminology—"deregulation" versus "regulatory reform"—are extremely important because they have largely symbolic significance to those who are poorly informed.

Given this lack of information, simplicity of argument is essential. Sophisticated economic reasoning is lost on the average member of Congress who—confronted with a great many policy issues—can devote only minutes to thinking about any single one. Even if the member understands a complex argument, he must be able to explain his decision to constituents. And if opponents can simplify them in unflattering ways, complex arguments may even prove counterproductive.

Simplicity is also the key to maintaining unity within a diverse coalition. So as not to "overload the circuits," lobbyists typically press for only a few items. Thus if coalition members can agree on one or two basic aims—and limit their collective demands to those—they may never have to resolve their differences on more subtle concerns. In this respect a successful coalition is like an interest group that follows the lowest-common-denominator rule of choosing issues so as to avoid internal dissension.

While the keep-it-simple requirement helps to unify a coalition by making certain internal disagreements moot, complexity can aid the task of coalition formation. Provisions that offer selective benefits are a carrot to groups that might otherwise free-ride. The need for simplicity also tends to work against transition strategies. An insurance scheme, which promises restitution in the event a policy reform goes awry, complicates the political debate and, in so doing, can even lend credence to opponents' predictions of disaster. Buy-off strategies involve their own transactions costs in the form of delay and added complexity necessary to work out an explicit compensation arrangement. A go-slow strategy is superior in this respect in that it provides compensation implicitly and hence automatically.

c. Playing interest-group politics. Delay and complexity were only partial explanations of why compensation didn't take place in the trucking deregulation battle. More central reasons had to do with interest-group politics and organizational survival—the importance to group leaders of political fighting as an end in itself, and the incentive to preserve a regulatory system that was the organization's reason for being. Similarly, the success of other transition approaches had to do with their sensitivity to organizational factors: a go-slow strategy implies a continued role for the economic interest group; allowing for vagueness and uncertainty about the ground rules of change gives the group an escape hatch—a face-saving way to "declare victory and get out."

Playing interest-group politics is as important for coalescing supporters as for dealing with opponents. Any political organization has a life of its own. Its survival needs determine which issues—and hence which coalitions—the group will select. Look for winners. Avoid issues that will cause even a slight splintering. Seek causes that will enhance the group's public image.

While the survival drive is shared, in other respects, not all political organizations are alike. Ideological groups behave in ways that are predictably distinct from those of economic interest groups. Nascent groups are systematically different from established groups. This has implications for how groups choose issues, how hard they bargain with opponents, and how effectively they interact with others on the same side.

Even a coalition organizer who is sensitive to organizational politics can control only a few of the factors that determine a group's choice of issue. Offering selective benefits may draw in specific organizations. Casting the issue in one light rather than another may make it more generally appealing to potential supporters.

Internal unity—perhaps more than size—depends on factors a coalition leader can control. Following a lowest-common-denominator rule of lobbying helps avoid internal conflict over points that are likely to be moot. Keeping the group informal in structure reduces the likelihood that members will secede for symbolic reasons and lessens the damage done even if they do—though at the expense of a certain degree of political clout. Finally, knowing when and how to soothe fragile institutional egos helps ease conflicts that have little to do with substance.

   d. *Combining political and economic perspectives.*   Sensitivity to interest-group politics isn't always an asset. Robert Behn has observed that the infeasibility of change is often overrated among those who are keenly alert to organized constituencies. Leading to a "mythology of power," the "influence . . . of interest groups is often sustained through an unwillingness to challenge a reputation rather than by a frequent and serious testing."[15]

   In contrast to political actors, economists set their priorities for reform based on the relative economic damage of various existing policies. The virtue of this approach—its indifference to the distorting influence of organized constituencies—is also its liability, as Behn observes: "[Economists] are often blind to the opposition that will, quite predictably, challenge any effort to change these arrangements and . . . oblivious to what must be done to overcome or placate these opponents."[16]

   Ideally, the agenda-setting process for reform can incorporate both perspectives. Many politicians who supported regulatory reform nevertheless viewed the trucking industry as unbeatable. Less sensitive to political reputations, economists felt that trucking regulation should take priority as a target for reform because of its extraordinary cost to consumers. The final agenda represented a de facto compromise: reformers first tackled the airline industry, a politically weaker lobby than trucking, and then used their political and economic success with that experiment in decontrol to win over remaining skeptics.

   In other respects as well, efforts to eliminate harmful special-interest policies benefit substantially from the linkage of political and economic perspectives. To be persuasive, a case on the merits must be politically informed—tailored to the debate at hand, a debate that inevitably centers on practical questions of implementation rather than on matters of academic theory; sensitive to timing and the need for simplicity of argument; alert to the symbolic functions of issues themselves and of the analysis used to promote them; and open to the use of anecdotal data to complement more scholarly evidence. Such a case is best made by either a "multidisciplinary team or a multidisciplinary head."

   In the same way that the analytic effort improves by becoming more political, strategic bargaining—traditionally carried out by political actors—benefits from the incorporation of "substantive" players. When a reform promises diffuse benefits to a large population, there is no closely attentive audience, and politicians tend to compromise prematurely rather than risk getting no settlement at all. In such a bargain, where economics demands a better outcome than politics, visible reliance on substantive people for making tactical judgments is effective—both for easing internal pressure to compromise and for shaping opponents' expectations of what settlement will be acceptable.

Finally, the design of ways to get from Here to There, which is itself part of the bargaining process, is ideally an intramural activity. Political expedience calls for a sensitivity to what, if anything, can be done to soften opposition to change—that of both client-group members and their leaders, who mediate the bargaining process. But lest the promised economic savings be sacrificed to expediency, efficiency considerations must also guide the transition.

No more important lesson can be drawn from the trucking story than the value of linking political and economic skills and perspectives on policy reform. Others have pointed out the need for such a linkage. "The policy game [ought not be] a relay," advised Behn, "with the analyst running the first (analytical) lap and then turning the baton over to the politician to run the last (political) leg while the analyst watches passively (if painfully) from the sidelines."[17] The success of trucking deregulators confirms the wisdom of that advice.

Recognizing the Limits of the Self-Interest Model

While the deregulation experience drew political actors and economists together in the advocacy arena, it seemed to widen the gulf between economists and other scholars of politics and policy in the realm of academe. At issue is the role of self-interest in explaining political behavior.

The belief that individual behavior is narrowly self-interested—or utility-maximizing—underlies all neoclassical economic theory. It was implicit in economists' prediction that deregulation of the trucking industry would lower prices as (economically rational) firms competed for a larger share of the market and (economically rational) shippers purchased the most efficient service. It was explicit in economists' rejection of the "small-town blues" argument on the grounds that truckers were not currently serving small towns unless it was economically profitable.

So powerful was the utility-maximization model in explaining purely market behavior that, starting in the 1960s, economists began to apply it systematically to political behavior as well. Lacking the measuring rod of money to represent utility, they assumed that elected officials sought to maximize their chances of reelection. That simple assumption, combined with the traditional assumptions about economic actors, produced a number of parsimonious yet powerful explanations of political behavior. One of those explanations, the "economic theory of regulation," maintained that regulatory agencies were *created* to serve the industries they benefited, a view contrary to the old, "public-interest" theories of agency origin as well as the more recent "capture" theories.[18] While the economic theory did not account for the subsequent creation of such agencies as OSHA and EPA in the late 1960s and early 1970s, nor the deregulatory activities of the CAB and ICC in the late 1970s, its adherents were reluctant to abandon it for a theory with less predictive, if more descriptive, capability.[19] In his memorable closing paragraph to *The Politics of Regulation,* in which he concluded that "we must be struck at every turn by the importance of ideas" in explaining both regulation and deregulation, James Q. Wilson admonished economists everywhere: "It would be a pity if an excessive devotion to the assumption of utility maximization as an *explanation* of behavior led scholars to ignore the intellectual impact of the efficiency test as a basis for *evaluating* behavior."[20]

Though conceding that "ideas mattered too," Darius Gaskins was quick to point out that the trucking battle did nothing to undermine utility theory with respect to the regulatory appointment process: "Having noted President Carter's personal commitment [to transportation deregulation], I think it would be a mistake to think this was a case where ideology won out over self-interest. . . . I think the president simply found a higher priority political use for his ICC appointments than appeasing Teamsters and the ATA."

Nor was the theory undermined with respect to agency behavior, Gaskins maintained: "As in the case of the president, I think it is unnecessary to invoke altruistic or public-spirited motives to explain why [proreform ICC commissioners] acted in accordance with their convictions. . . . [T]here are many ways to advance one's career through regulatory reform."[21]

While theory testing was not the aim of this case study, certain strategic phenomena in the trucking battle were examined from a loose theoretical perspective. That examination process yielded several insights relevant to this debate.

Chapter 5 applied the "logic of collective action"—Mancur Olson's economic theory of why rational individuals fail to join organizations in pursuit of their common interest—to a policymaking coalition: an organization of organizations. Why would any firm or interest group join such a coalition, chapter 5 asked, when the policy reform sought is a collective, or nonexclusive, good? Some of the findings are fully explained by Olson's logic. Private firms join a coalition and speak out politically when their individual stakes are large; firms and interest groups also join in an effort to get selective economic rewards— "curb service." Other findings require an extension of Olson's logic: The process of seeking collective (economic) benefits for interest-group members yields noneconomic benefits to their leaders. These benefits—visibility and opportunities for claiming credit—

are important to the survival of the interest group itself. They are particularly important to groups whose members join in order to promote their ideology or some ad hoc conception of the public good.

Chapter 5 also used a theoretical framework to examine how a diverse coalition maintained internal unity. Analogizing a policymaking coalition to an economic cartel, the chapter examined the tendency for individual members (i.e., groups) to take independent action harmful to the alliance as a whole. The findings reveal a fundamental limitation in the analogy. For an economic cartel, there exists a single optimal outcome, and independent action (lowering price or raising quality) is ultimately self-defeating. For the members of a policymaking coalition, by contrast, no single outcome is necessarily optimal. Taking a strong ideological stand, for example, may be more important to certain organizations in the alliance than "winning." Since independent action is not necessarily self-defeating, unity is inherently harder to maintain in a policymaking coalition than in an economic cartel.

If the need to appear ideologically firm leads some groups in the coalition to break away, then other needs can tempt alliance members to cave in. Chapter 7 concludes that the president is perceived as an inherently weak bargainer because he is motivated largely by electoral considerations—the need for a list of legislative accomplishments to recite. And since voters can't judge a good bill from a mediocre one—at least when the economic benefits it confers are diffuse—virtually any legislative settlement is perceived to be better for the president than no settlement at all. This finding points up the distinction between political and economic "accounting systems" in bargaining, and the importance of this distinction for shaping opponents' expectations.

A final theory-based insight comes from chapter 6. Economic logic says that where resources are inefficiently allocated, there's room for a deal; by moving to an efficient allocation, gainers can compensate losers fully and still be better off. Thus, in principle, complete compensation should make the beneficiaries of an inefficient policy arrangement indifferent between the status quo and reform. While the findings do not dispute that theory, they reveal a major impediment to implementing it—namely, the organizational needs of special-interest-group leaders, who dictate tactical decisions. Even if members could be made indifferent by compensation, the leaders would be worse off because their raison d'etre—to perpetuate the inefficient policy—would disappear.

In sum, these findings are not fully explained by pertinent theories of strategic action, which have in common a view of actors as motivated by economic self-interest and behaving rationally in pursuit of defined goals. A more complete explanation requires a larger cast of players—one that includes interest-group leaders as well as members—and a broader conception of self-interest—one that includes noneconomic factors such as ideology as well as economic factors.

Though less systematic, "data" about individual political actors in the trucking battle is also relevant to the debate. Here too, a narrow model of self-interest explains a lot but by no means all. For Jimmy Carter, strong support of deregulation was no doubt consistent with the goal of reelection, given his need at least to appear to be reining in galloping inflation. Likewise for Ted Kennedy, championing deregulation was electorally useful because of the conservative credentials it provided him. Howard Cannon and Robert Packwood, neither of whom aspired to national office, at least in the near future, probably risked more than they gained electorally. Cannon's motivation—seemingly to enhance his reputation for policy innovation and leadership—while not selfless, was not electorally self-interested.

Among the rank and file in Congress, exceptions to the self-interest model were numerous on the trucking issue. To be sure, many of them— not facing imminent reelection—could "afford to be statesmen." But, as the phrase implies, such statesmanship was not without cost.

Self-interest is only a very partial explanation of the behavior of congressional staffers and lobbyists as well. In case after case, one is struck by the evidence of their personal attachment to—and even passion for—the cause of deregulation.

Ironically, individual economists like Darius Gaskins were among those most propelled by their vision of the public interest. Granted their behavior may have led to career advances, but that wasn't forseeable a decade earlier, when at least one of them risked his career, nor was that what motivated even the most prescient. Rather it was a commitment to a particular vision of the public interest and a belief that others—whether through intellectual suasion or political persuasion—would ultimately come to share it.

Notes

Chapter One

1. *New York Times*, November 26, 1981.
2. Ibid.
3. Lester C. Thurow, *The Zero-Sum Society: Distribution and the Possibilities for Economic Change* (New York: Basic Books, 1980).
4. William Greider, "The Education of David Stockman," *Atlantic Monthly*, December 1981, p. 51.
5. Mancur Olson, *The Rise and Decline of Nations: Economic Growth, Stagflation, and Social Rigidities* (New Haven: Yale University Press, 1982).
6. The "free-rider problem" plagues even relatively small organizations—trade associations and labor unions, for example—and they have been able to survive only by providing their members with selective benefits such as technical information or low-cost insurance. But as the size and heterogeneity of a group increases, so does the cost of organizing it.
7. Mancur Olson, *The Logic of Collective Action: Public Goods and the Theory of Groups* (Cambridge: Harvard University Press, 1965).
8. Arthur M. Okun, *Equality and Efficiency: The Big Tradeoff* (Washington, D.C.: The Brookings Institution, 1975), pp. 28–29.
9. Dennis C. Mueller, Robert D. Tollison, and Thomas D. Willett, "Solving the Intensity Problem in Representative Democracy," in Ryan C. Amacher, Tollison, and Willett (eds.), *The Economic Approach to Public Policy: Selected Readings* (Ithaca: Cornell University Press, 1976).
10. R. Douglas Arnold, "The Local Roots of Domestic Policy," in Thomas E. Mann and Norman J. Ornstein (eds.), *The New Congress* (Washington, D.C.: American Enterprise Institute, 1981), pp. 250–87.

11. Roger H. Davidson, "Subcommittee Government: New Channels for Policy Making," in Mann and Ornstein, pp. 99–133.

12. Douglass Cater, *Power in Washington* (New York: Vintage Books, 1964), p. 158.

13. Richard F. Fenno, Jr., *Congressmen in Committees* (Boston: Little, Brown and Co., 1973), p. xiv.

14. Ibid., pp. 1–14.

15. The term "reciprocal noninterference" belongs to E. E. Schattschneider.

16. Davidson, in Mann and Ornstein, p. 118.

17. Mueller, Tollison, and Willett, pp. 448–50.

18. Allen Schick, "The Distributive Congress," in Schick (ed.), *Making Economic Policy in Congress* (Washington, D.C.: American Enterprise Institute, 1983), pp. 257–73.

19. Ibid.

20. Aaron Wildavsky, *How to Limit Government Spending* (Berkeley: University of California Press, 1980), p. 67.

21. Thurow, p. 15.

22. Russell Hardin uses the word *hysteresis* to describe this perceived asymmetry between gains and losses, and cites sources from economics, philosophy, and literature (*You Can't Go Home Again,* by Thomas Wolfe) that treat it as self-evident. Hardin, *Collective Action* (Baltimore: The Johns Hopkins University Press, 1982), pp. 82–83.

23. James Q. Wilson, "The Politics of Regulation," in James W. McKie (ed.), *Social Responsibility and the Business Predicament* (Washington, D.C.: The Brookings Institution, 1974).

24. Charles L. Schultze, *The Public Use of Private Interest* (Washington, D.C.: The Brookings Institution, 1977), p. 23.

25. Robert A. Dahl, *A Preface to Democratic Theory* (Chicago: University of Chicago Press, 1956), p. 15.

26. Schultze, p. 24.

27. Ibid., p. 25.

28. E. E. Schattschneider, *The Semi-Sovereign People* (New York: Holt, Rinehart and Winston, 1960), p. 35.

29. Thurow, chapter 8.

30. Ibid., pp. 21–22.

31. Ibid., p. 212.

32. James Q. Wilson, "The Dead Hand of Regulation," *The Public Interest*, Fall 1971, pp. 39–58.

33. Robert P. Biller, "On Tolerating Policy and Organizational Termination: Some Design Considerations," *Policy Sciences*, June 1976, p. 136.

34. Eugene Bardach, "Policy Termination as a Political Process," *Policy Sciences,* June 1976, p. 128.

35. Abram N. Shulsky, "Abolishing the District of Columbia Motorcycle Squad," *Policy Sciences,* June 1976, p. 192.

36. Greider, p. 52.

Chapter Two

1. Nancy Lin Rose, "An Economic and Political Interpretation of Trucking Regulation: The Motor Carrier Act of 1935" (honors thesis, Harvard College, 1980), p. 86. The epigraph at the head of this chapter is drawn from Rose's thesis.

2. Ibid., p. 91.

3. Ibid., p. 94.

4. Ibid., p. 99.

5. Ibid.

6. Ellis W. Hawley, *The New Deal and the Problem of Monopoly* (Princeton: Princeton University Press, 1966), p. 232.

7. Ibid., pp. 232–33.

8. Rose, pp. 104–5.

9. Hawley, pp. 233-34.

10. Stephen Chapman, "Too Much: The ICC and the Truckers," *Washington Monthly*, December 1977.

11. U.S. Congress, Senate, Judiciary Committee, *Federal Restraints on Competition in the Trucking Industry: Antitrust Immunity and Economic Regulation*, 96th Cong., 2d sess., April 1980, p. 1.

12. Ibid., p. 34.

13. Sobotka and Co., and Mandex, Inc., "New Entry into the Regulated Motor Carrier Industry." Report prepared for the Office of Transportation Regulation, U.S. Department of Transportation, December 1979.

14. U.S. Congress, Senate, Judiciary Committee, p. 120.

15. American Trucking Associations, Inc., "1978 Financial Analysis of the Motor Carrier Industry," 1979, p. 6.

16. "The Byzantine World of Trucking Industry," *Washington Post,* March 2, 1980.

17. John W. Snow, "The Problem of Motor Carrier Regulation and the Ford Administration's Proposal for Reform," in Paul W. MacAvoy and Snow (eds.), *Regulation of Entry and Pricing in Truck Transportation* (Washington, D.C.: American Enterprise Institute, 1977), pp. 3–4.

18. Transportation Consumer Action Project, "Trucking Regulation and Consumer Prices," proceedings of a symposium held May 17, 1979, in Washington, D.C., p. xx.

19. U.S. Congress, Senate, Judiciary Committee, p. 46.

20. Congress's major purpose was apparently to reverse a Supreme Court ruling regarding railroad rate bureaus, and there was little attention to important structural differences between the rail and motor carrier industries that might make collective ratemaking inappropriate for the latter. U.S. Congress, Senate, Judiciary Committee, Subcommittee on Antitrust and Monopoly, *Hearings on Oversight of Freight Rate Competition in the Motor Carrier Industry,* 95th Cong., 1st and 2d sess., October 27 and 28, 1977; March 10 and 13, 1978, p. 2.

21. U.S. Interstate Commerce Commission, 1977, *Annual Report*, p. 113.

22. Chapman, p. 36.

23. U.S. Congress, Senate, Judiciary Committee, pp. 118–20.

24. Policy and Management Associates, Inc., "The Impact on Small Communities of Motor Carriage Regulatory Revision," report prepared for U.S. Congress, Senate, Commerce, Science, and Transportation Committee, 95th Cong., 2d sess., June 1978, p. 18.

25. Snow, p. 39.

26. James C. Miller III, "The Pros and Cons of Trucking Regulation," American Enterprise Institute Reprint no. 95 (Washington, D.C.: American Enterprise Institute, 1979), pp. 4–5. The epigraph below the subhead "Economic Objections to Regulation" is from this paper.

27. Clifford Winston, "The Welfare Effects of ICC Rate Regulation Revisited," *Bell Journal of Economics,* Spring 1981, pp. 232–44.

28. E. J. Mishan, "Second Thoughts on Second Best," *Oxford Economic Papers,* October 1962, pp. 205–17.

29. American Trucking Associations, Inc., "Accounting for Motor Carrier Operating Rights," brief and petition submitted to the Financial Accounting Standards Board of the Financial Accounting Foundation, 1974.

30. Transportation Consumer Action Project, "Trucking Regulation and Consumer Prices," p. x.

31. Thomas Gale Moore, "The Beneficiaries of Trucking Regulation," *Journal of Law and Economics,* October 1978, pp. 327–43.

32. James R. Snitzler and Robert J. Byrne, "Interstate Trucking of Fresh and Frozen Poultry under the Agricultural Exemption," U.S. Department of Agriculture, Marketing Research Division, March 1958; Snitzler and Byrne, "Interstate Trucking of Frozen Fruits and Vegetables under the Agricultural Exemption," U.S. Department of Agriculture, Marketing Research Division, March 1959; and J. C. Winter and Ivan W. Ulrey, "Supplement to Interstate Trucking of Frozen Fruits and Vegetables under the Agricultural Exemption," U.S. Department of Agriculture, Marketing Research Division, July 1961.

33. W. Bruce Allen, Steven Lonergan, and David Plane, "Examination of the Unregulated Trucking Experience in New Jersey," U.S. Department of Transportation, July 1978.

34. Dennis A. Breen, "Regulation and Household Moving Costs," *Regulation: AEI Journal on Government and Society,* September/October 1978, pp. 51–54.

35. Thomas Gale Moore, *Trucking Regulation: Lessons from Europe* (Washington, D.C.: American Enterprise Institute, 1976).

36. Monopoly profits—the result of setting prices higher than cost—represent a transfer payment from consumers to the monopolist. Reduced is the "consumer surplus"—the gain to consumers who would be willing to pay more for something than they are actually charged. From an economic standpoint, there is nothing intrinsically objectionable about this; it's a distributional, not an efficiency, matter.

But unless a monopolist is a perfect price discriminator (i.e., capable of charging each consumer the maximum he or she would be willing to pay), above-cost pricing leads to reduced demand and a deadweight loss to society equal to the value of the unexpressed demand minus the cost of producing the good or service. (In trucking, the deadweight loss came from some commodities not being shipped because of noncompetitive pricing by regulated carriers or being shipped by a method that, while cheaper to the shipper, was more costly to society.) Society also suffers a deadweight loss when regulation leads to unnecessarily high costs of operation. No matter what other misallocations exist (e.g., railroad regulation), it is still preferable to use as few resources as possible to produce a given service or product.

37. Miller, p. 9.

38. Moore, "The Beneficiaries of Trucking Regulation," pp. 331–32.

39. Ibid., p. 339.

40. A DOT study found that service—the desire for either more or less of it—was the major reason shippers turned to private carriage. U.S. Department of Transportation, Office of Transportation Planning Analysis, "Industrial Shipper Survey," September 1975.

41. Snow, pp. 15–17

42. Ibid., p. 18

43. Not captured by those estimates was the potential loss from lack of incentives to innovate. Thomas Gale Moore, "Deregulating Surface Freight Transportation," in Almarin Phillips (ed.), *Promoting Competition in Regulated Markets* (Washington, D.C.: The Brookings Institution, 1975).

44. Moore, "The Beneficiaries of Trucking Regulation," p. 342.

Chapter Three

1. See the following sources for information on the merits of, and the political battle for, airline deregulation: Bradley Behrman, "Airline Deregulation: A Test Case for Fundamental Regulatory Reform," honors thesis, Harvard College, 1978; Bradley Behrman, "Civil Aeronautics Board," in James Q. Wilson (ed.), *The Politics of Regulation* (New York: Basic Books, 1980), pp. 75–120; Rochelle Jones and Peter Woll, *The Private World of Congress* (New York: The Free Press, 1979), pp. 63–75; and Martha Derthick and Paul J. Quirk, *The Politics of Deregulation* (Washington, D.C.: The Brookings Institution, 1985).

2. *Washington Post,* November 8, 1977.

3. *New York Times,* May 9, 1978; *Washington Post,* May 9, 1978.

4. *Youngstown Vindicator,* September 6, 1978.

5. *Congressional Quarterly,* July 29, 1978.

6. *Washington Star,* November 17, 1977.

7. Ibid.

8. Ibid., February 4, 1978.

9. *Wall Street Journal,* November 7, 1978.

10. *Washington Post,* November 8, 1978.

11. Ibid., November 11, 1978.

12. *New York Times,* November 21, 1978.

13. *Wall Street Journal,* November 28, 1978.

14. *Congressional Quarterly,* December 9, 1978.
15. *Washington Star,* January 4, 1979.
16. *New York Times,* December 21, 1978.
17. *Congressional Quarterly,* February 3, 1979.
18. Ibid.
19. Ibid.
20. *New York Times,* January 25, 1979.
21. *Boston Globe,* January 31, 1979.
22. *Washington Post,* March 16, 1979.
23. *Congressional Quarterly,* April 7, 1979.
24. *New York Times,* April 16, 1979.
25. *U.S. News and World Report,* April 16, 1979; *Business Week,* April 30, 1979.
26. *Truck Line,* May 3, 1979.
27. *Congressional Quarterly,* May 24, 1979.
28. *Washington Post,* June 21, 1979.
29. *Congressional Quarterly,* June 23, 1979; *Truck Line,* June 22, 1979.
30. *Washington Star,* June 7, 1979.
31. *Congressional Quarterly,* June 23, 1979; *Washington Post,* June 21, 1979.
32. *Wall Street Journal,* June 27, 1979.
33. *Washington Post,* June 27, 1979.
34. *New York Times,* June 27, 1979.
35. *Washington Star,* July 27, 1979.
36. *Truck Line,* July 16, 1979.
37. *Washington Star,* September 6, 1979.
38. *Truck Line,* September 6, 1979.
39. *Washington Star,* September 6, 1979.
40. *Wall Street Journal,* October 18, 1979.
41. Ibid., October 23, 1979.
42. *Washington Star,* October 23, 1979.
43. *Washington Post,* October 29, 1979.
44. *Truck Line,* October 26, 1979.
45. *Washington Star,* December 7, 1979.
46. *Washington Post,* December 9, 1979.
47. *Washington Star,* December 18, 1979.
48. *Wall Street Journal,* January 31, 1980.
49. *Washington Post,* January 31, 1980.
50. Ibid., March 4, 1980; *Truck Line,* January 31, 1980.
51. *New York Times,* February 6, 1980.
52. Ibid.
53. U.S. Congress, Senate, Commerce, Science, and Transportation Committee, *Hearings on Economic Regulation of the Trucking Industry,* 96th Cong., 2d sess., pt. 5, February 21, 26 and 27, 1980, p. 1449.
54. Ibid., p. 1577.
55. *Washington Post,* February 29, 1980.
56. Ibid., February 27, 1980.

57. Letter from Whitlock to "All of Those Who Are Interested in the Survival of the Trucking Industry," March 14, 1980.

58. Stanton Sender, March 5, 1980, in a meeting of the ad hoc coalition.

59. These and other quotations from the Senate markup are taken from the author's own notes.

60. *Washington Post,* March 7, 1980.

61. Robert Knipe, March 6, 1980, in a conversation with the author.

62. *Congressional Quarterly,* March 15, 1980.

63. *Washington Post,* March 11, 1980.

64. Ibid., March 12, 1980; *Washington Star,* March 12, 1980.

65. Letter from Whitlock to "All of Those Who Are Interested in the Survival of the Trucking Industry," March 14, 1980.

66. *Congressional Quarterly,* March 15, 1980.

67. Ibid., April 19, 1980.

68. *Congressional Record,* April 15, 1980, S3604.

69. Ibid., S3605.

70. Ibid., S3607.

71. Ibid., S3633.

72. *Washington Post,* April 16, 1980.

73. Ibid., March 20, 1980.

74. *Congressional Quarterly,* April 19, 1980.

75. Ibid., May 24, 1980.

76. These quotations from the House markup are taken from the author's own notes.

77. *Washington Star,* May 23, 1980.

78. *Congressional Quarterly,* May 24, 1980.

79. *Washington Post,* May 23, 1980.

80. *Washington Star,* May 23, 1980; *Congressional Quarterly,* May 24, 1980.

81. *Congressional Quarterly,* June 14, 1980.

82. *New York Times,* July 2, 1980.

83. *Traffic World,* July 7, 1980.

84. Ibid.

Chapter Four

1. *Newsweek,* October 12, 1981. Sullivan, cited in the epigraph to this section, was a member of the National Committee for the Review of Antitrust Laws and Procedures.

2. Paul W. MacAvoy (ed.), *Unsettled Questions on Regulatory Reform* (Washington, D.C.: American Enterprise Institute, 1978).

3. Robert D. Behn, "Policy Analysis and Policy Politics," *Policy Analysis,* Spring 1981.

4. Charles L. Schultze, *The Politics and Economics of Public Spending* (Washington, D.C.: The Brookings Institution, 1968).

5. George Eads, "Economists versus Regulators," in James C. Miller III (ed.),

Perspectives on Federal Transportation Policy (Washington, D.C.: American Enterprise Institute, 1974).

6. Bradley Behrman, "Airline Deregulation: A Test Case for Fundamental Regulatory Reform," honors thesis, Harvard College, 1978, p. 229.

7. Donald L. Martin and Warren F. Schwartz (eds.), *Deregulating American Industry* (Lexington, Mass.: Lexington Books, 1977), pp. 67–68.

8. Stephen Breyer, *Regulation and Its Reform* (Cambridge: Harvard University Press, 1982), chapter 16.

9. All three quotes are from Shelby E. Southard, legislative director, Cooperative League of the U.S.A., personal interview, October 7, 1980.

10. See chapter 2, discussion of monopoly profits.

11. Congressional Budget Office, Inflation Impact Statement, March 26, 1980.

12. U.S. Congress, Senate, Commerce, Science, and Transportation Committee, *Economic Regulation of the Trucking Industry: Testimony by Nancy Drabble, Staff Attorney, Congress Watch:* 96th Cong., 1st and 2d sess. (hereafter *Commerce Committee Hearings*), pt. 1, March 28, 1979, p. 169.

13. Attachment to letter from Goldschmidt to Cannon, April 14, 1980, p. 2.

14. Other industry counterarguments were even less logically compelling. One was the claim that deregulation couldn't possibly save $5 billion, because total industry profits were scarcely equal to that. That argument carefully sidestepped two facts: Regulation produces monopoly rents for labor as well as for industry; moreover, high rates can reflect industry inefficiencies, which benefit no one, as well as monopoly profits.

15. *Commerce Committee Hearings,* pt. 5, February 21, 26, and 27, 1980, p. 1586.

16. Walter Miklius and Kenneth L. Casavant, "Stability of Motor Carriers Operating under the Agricultural Exemption," U.S. Department of Agriculture, August 1975.

17. W. Bruce Allen, Steven Lonergan, and David Plane, "Examination of the Unregulated Trucking Experience in New Jersey," U.S. Department of Transportation, July 1978.

18. Thomas Gale Moore, *Trucking Regulation: Lessons from Europe* (Washington, D.C.: American Enterprise Institute, 1976).

19. William T. Cassels, Jr., ATA chairman, in a speech before the Comstock Club, Sacramento, Calif., July 24, 1978.

20. Ann F. Friedlaender, "Hedonic Costs and Economies of Scale in the Regulated Trucking Industry," in *Motor Carrier Economic Regulation,* National Academy of Sciences, 1978. In other work sponsored by DOT, there was some evidence of limited economies of scale in LTL shipments, but deregulation proponents argued that even if those economies existed, they would long since have been exhausted by all but the smallest firms.

21. Transportation Consumer Action Project, "Trucking Regulation and Consumer Prices," proceedings of a symposium held May 17, 1979 in Washington, D.C., p. 103.

22. *Commerce Committee Hearings,* pt. 2, June 26 and 27, 1979, pp. 359–83.

23. D. Daryl Wyckoff, *Truck Drivers in America* (Lexington, Mass.: Lexington Books, 1979).

24. *Fortune,* June 18, 1979.

25. Attachment to letter from Goldschmidt to Cannon, April 14, 1980.

26. Virginia State Corporation Commission, Division of Motor Carrier Regulatory Planning and Control, "Deregulation of Motor Carriers—Is it in the Best Interest of Virginia's Rural Communities?" 1979.

27. Opponents of decontrol cited the airline experience every time they testified on the trucking bill. Senator Cannon, the sponsor of the airline legislation, finally tired of hearing their claims and began challenging them with statistics of his own showing that airline deregulation had on average increased air service to communities in every population category. As Cannon's figures reflected, most disruptions in air service following deregulation proved merely temporary.

28. Policy and Management Associates, Inc., "The Impact on Small Communities of Motor Carrier Regulatory Revision," report prepared for the Senate Committee on Commerce, Science, and Transportation, 95th Cong., 2d sess., June 1978.

29. Congressional Budget Office, "The Impact of Trucking Deregulation on Small Communities: A Review of Recent Studies," February 1980.

30. Karen Borlaug, et al., "A Study of Trucking Service in Six Small Communities," U.S. Department of Transportation, November 30, 1979, p. 22.

31. Speech by Neil Goldschmidt to a symposium sponsored by the Coordinating Committee on Truck Regulatory Reform, January 17, 1980.

32. California Public Utilities Commission, "Small Community Survey Preliminary Data," March 28, 1980.

33. In their analysis of the trucking contest, Derthick and Quirk reached the same conclusion. They note that senators from the most rural one-third of the states voted to pass the trucking bill by a ratio of more than three to two—a substantial majority, even though smaller proportionately than in the rest of the Senate. Martha Derthick and Paul J. Quirk, *The Politics of Deregulation* (Washington, D.C.: The Brookings Institution, 1985), p. 133.

34. Speech by Howard Cannon before the Regular Common Carrier Conference of the American Trucking Associations, February 3, 1979.

35. For example, the National League of Cities adopted a resolution opposing trucking deregulation in 1975 but then came out in support of the reform in 1979. DOT's small-community studies played a big part in the league's turnaround. Some shippers also joined the reform side once the small-community issue was put to rest.

36. It was feared that consumer groups would not find trucking reform as "sexy" an issue as airline deregulation, because the savings would be less visible. But these groups gave trucking a very high priority in the end, partly because of empirical evidence that the potential savings to consumers, albeit indirect, were several times greater than those from airline reform.

37. These figures were compiled by Jay Steptoe, Counsel, Senate Judiciary Committee.

38. Gary Broemser, Director, Office of Regulatory Policy, Department of Transportation, personal inverview, August 11, 1980.

39. Martin and Schwartz, p. 33.

40. Former Hill staffer James M. Verdier attests to the wisdom of this strategy: "Congressmen love numbers, but not in the same way economists do. Congressmen look for a single striking number that can encapsulate an issue and can be used to explain and justify their position. They have little use for endless columns and rows of unassimilated data." "Advising Congressional Decision-Makers: Guidelines for Economists," *Journal of Policy Analysis and Management* 3, no. 3 (1984): 432.

41. Richard Klem, Director of Motor Carrier Policy Analysis, ICC, Seminar at the Kennedy School of Government, Harvard University, February 18, 1982.

42. Frank Swain, lobbyist, National Federation of Independent Business, and Chairman, Coordinating Committee on Truck Regulatory Reform, personal interview, October 8, 1980.

43. As another example, when the ATA ran full-page newspaper ads implying that truck transportation accounted for less than 2 percent of the cost of groceries, DOT shot back with an explanation of how the ATA arrived at that misleading figure instead of the "best estimate" of 5 percent. ("What the ATA has done is take the transportation costs for a few high-priced items (coffee and steak) where transportation is a small proportion of overall costs, and not include the cost of transporting bulkier items, where the costs are significantly more.") Senate supporters in turn inserted DOT's rebuttal into the *Congressional Record.*

44. Letter from Goldschmidt to Cannon, April 14, 1980.

45. Michael R. Gordon, "The Profits and Perils of Progress in P.R.," *New York Times,* August 3, 1980.

46. Lana Batts, Director, Economics and Planning Department, American Trucking Associations, personal interview, September 8, 1980.

47. Wesley R. Kriebel, Managing Director, Research and Economics Division, American Trucking Associations, personal interview, September 9, 1980.

48. Batts interview.

49. Interstate Commerce Commission, Bureau of Economics, "A Cost and Benefit Evaluation of Surface Transport Regulation," 1976. An edited version of the ICC's analysis appears in Paul W. MacAvoy and John W. Snow (eds.), *Regulation of Entry and Pricing in Truck Transportation* (Washington, D.C.: American Enterprise Institute, 1977), pp. 47–91.

50. W. Bruce Allen and Edward B. Hymson, "The Costs and Benefits of Surface Transport Regulation: Another View," in MacAvoy and Snow, p. 105.

51. CBO's analysis was the work of Christopher Barnekov, a Ph. D. economist and price theorist. Tagged by some for his estimate as "the $8 billion man," Barnekov was a strong proponent of deregulation. He had worked for the government doing transportation regulation research off and on since 1971; he was in DOT's Office of Regulatory Policy directly before going to CBO.

Barnekov himself did not feel that there would be any short-term rate increases as a result of deregulation. But other CBO analysts favored a more cautious outlook, and the caveat was included to satisfy them.

In other respects, Barnekov's analysis is quite defensible. A few deregulation advocates even chided him for being overly conservative in his estimate, and there's something to that: He limited his analysis to the regulated sector and declined to estimate savings from deregulation in the unregulated sector.

52. Paul O. Roberts and James T. Kneafsey, "Traffic Diversion and Energy Use Implications of Surface Transport Reform," in MacAvoy and Snow, pp. 159–88.

53. Stephen Sobotka and Thomas Domencich, "Traffic Diversion and Energy Use Implications: Another View," in MacAvoy and Snow, pp. 189–212.

54. *National Journal,* May 14, 1977.

55. Christopher C. DeMuth, "A Strategy for Regulatory Reform," *Regulation: AEI Journal on Government and Society,* March/April 1984, p. 26.

56. An excellent analysis of this phenomenon is Steven Kelman's *What Price Incentives? Economists and the Environment* (Boston: Auburn House, 1981).

Chapter Five

1. Milbrath found that collaborative lobbying "usually communicates augmented power behind a proposal. Nearly all governmental decision-makers hesitate to decide against a strong coalition. . . . If the groups presenting a united front previously disagreed, the achievement of the front is in itself impressive." Lester W. Milbrath, *The Washington Lobbyists* (Chicago: Rand McNally and Co., 1963), p. 169.

2. Jeffrey M. Berry, *Lobbying for the People* (Princeton: Princeton University Press, 1977), pp. 253–56; Milbraith, pp. 170–71.

3. Mancur Olson, *The Logic of Collective Action: Public Goods and the Theory of Groups* (Cambridge: Harvard University Press, 1965).

4. James Q. Wilson has speculated that the "logic of collective action" may be even more applicable to coalitions of organizations than to those of individuals: "Individuals will often contribute to large organizations without receiving any specific material benefit from it; organizations rarely will. And when organizations do form coalitions, the largest or richest members of it tend to pay a disproportionate share of the cost. The United States, for example, pays a disproportionate share of the cost of the North Atlantic Treaty Organization and the United Nations. That is true, as Richard Zeckhauser and Mancur Olson have explained, not so much because the United States is foolish or other nations are irresponsible, as because the logic of coalition formation among rationally self-interested actors (which formal organizations are, I would argue, more so than individuals) gives the large nation an incentive to pay proportionally more than the small one." Wilson, *Political Organizations* (New York: Basic Books, 1973), p. 277.

5. Because internal conflict is so damaging, ideological compatibility is generally thought to be a requirement for participation in an enduring coalition. Drawing together evidence on size and ideological compatibility, Michael Leiserson has posited that coalitions which form will contain the minimal number of ideologically "adjacent" parties necessary to win. "Coalitions in Politics: A Theoretical and Empirical Study," Ph. D. diss., Yale University, 1966; cited in Wilson, *Political Organizations,* pp. 269–70.

6. Wilson, *Political Organizations,* p. 20.

7. *Congressional Quarterly,* July 29, 1978.

8. Robert C. Fellmeth, et al., *The Interstate Commerce Omission* (New York: Grossman Publishers, 1970).

9. *Wall Street Journal,* July 5, 1979.

10. B. Kent Burton, legislative representative, American Trucking Associations, personal interview, July 15, 1980.

11. *Congressional Record,* 96th Cong., 2d sess., vol. 126, no. 57 (April 15, 1980), pp. S3591–92; 3607; and 3619.

12. As part of an analysis of PAC contributions and legislative behavior, Frendreis and Waterman examined the effect on senators' support for trucking deregulation of four factors: party, ideology (Americans for Democratic Action rating), constituency (percent rural), and PAC contributions (1980 ATA contributions). They combined roll call votes on the three floor amendments (the Hollings amendment on food, and two amendments on entry restrictions) plus the final vote on the entire bill to produce a single, summated scale of support for deregulation.

Frendreis and Waterman found that senators who were Republican, conservative, from urban states, and who had received fewer (or no) ATA contributions were more likely to support trucking deregulation. Of the four factors, ATA contributions had the largest individual impact. That impact, which the authors characterized as "fairly strong" overall, was strongest for senators facing reelection in 1980 and monotonically decreased as senators' proximity to their next election increased. John P. Frendreis and Richard W. Waterman, "PAC Contributions and Legislative Behavior: Senate Voting on Trucking Deregulation," paper delivered to the Midwest Political Science Association, April 1983.

13. Either of these organizations would have added considerable clout to the trucking coalition. Founded in 1972, in the midst of inflation and consumerist pressure on Congress, the Business Roundtable is the preeminent political organ of big business. BR has no middlemen; its members—the CEOs of some two hundred Fortune 500 companies—set policy and lobby Congress directly. The Chamber of Commerce, "easily dismissed in the sixties as a feeble and discredited vestigial organ," according to former Federal Trade Commission chairman Michael Pertschuk, subsequently "took on new sheen and gloss." Between 1974 and 1980, the chamber doubled its membership and tripled its budget. However, the added size may have only made more cumbersome the process of policymaking by the chamber's sixty-five-member board. Pertschuk, *Revolt against Regulation: The Rise and Pause of the Consumer Movement* (Berkeley: University of California Press, 1982), p. 57; "Chamber's Ponderous Decision Making Leaves It Sitting on the Sidelines," *National Journal,* July 24, 1982.

14. See, for example, Andrew S. McFarland, *Public Interest Lobbies: Decision Making on Energy* (Washington, D.C.: American Enterprise Institute, 1976).

15. Wilson, *Political Organizations,* pp. 154–63.

16. As Wilson notes, "associations can often find similarity threatening, especially when autonomy is low. . . . Further jeopardizing one's weak autonomy by joining a coalition is not attractive to many organizations." Wilson, *Political Organizations,* p. 272.

17. Donald R. Hall, *Cooperative Lobbying: The Power of Pressure* (Tucson: University of Arizona Press, 1969), p. 80.

18. Michael T. Hayes, *Lobbyists and Legislators: A Theory of Political Markets* (New Brunswick, N.J.: Rutgers University Press, 1981), p. 80.

19. Hayes, *Lobbyists and Legislators,* pp. 78–79.

20. *Congressional Quarterly,* January 20, 1979.

21. This pattern is generally consistent with that observed elsewhere. Berry's study of public-interest groups concluded that such groups are characterized by staff domination and personalized decision making, and by a low degree of direct constituency influence. While factors like the group's organizational goals and its current resource commitments and capabilities indirectly influence the choice, issue selection often turns on personal interest and expertise. Berry, *Lobbying for the People.*

Studies of private-interest groups have found a similar lack of direct member influence, but with control by governing boards being more the rule than staff dominance. This locus of control lends itself to internal division—something rarely found in public-interest groups. Bauer, Pool, and Dexter, in their classic study of foreign trade legislation, wrote of the tendency of those trade groups that one would expect to be most active to be immobilized by internal division of the membership. Banfield found the same phenomenon among civic associations in Chicago: ". . . they were generally ineffective because of their preoccupation with their own mainte- nance. They avoided controversy in order to maintain themselves." Raymond A. Bauer, Ithiel de Sola Pool, and Lewis Anthony Dexter, *American Business and Public Policy* (New York: Atherton Press, 1963); Edward C. Banfield, *Political Influence* (New York: The Free Press, 1965), p. 297.

22. For a more theoretical discussion of this incentive, which Russell Hardin terms "asymmetry in the content of goods," see his book *Collective Action* (Balti- more: The Johns Hopkins University Press, 1982). George Stigler has also discussed asymmetry, in the context of tariff legislation, as a possible deterrent to free-riding. Stigler, "Free-Riders and Collective Action: An Appendix to Theories of Economic Regulation," *Bell Journal of Economics* 5 (Autumn 1974): 359–65.

23. See "Sideline Conflicts of Interest" (later in this chapter) for a brief discussion of this conflict.

24. The single-issue members of the coalition ultimately fared quite well. In the crunch, the ATA concentrated all its energies on the key provisions of the bill. The coalition was thus able to pick up some of its lesser priorities as "throwaway" items.

25. *Transport Topics,* October 13, 1980, p. 20.

26. Posner speculated that this would be true in the case of regulated airlines. Richard A. Posner, "Theories of Economic Regulation," *Bell Journal of Economics* 5 (Autumn 1974): 352.

27. Roland A. Ouellette, director of transportation affairs, General Motors Corporation, personal interview, September 8, 1980.

28. *Congressional Quarterly,* December 9, 1978.

29. The largest regulated carrier of all—United Parcel Service—was actually a member of the reform coalition. But UPS—called the "Brown Giant" because of the

color of its more than 50,000 delivery trucks—was unique. UPS was a specialist in small-package delivery with no general-freight operation; the U.S. Postal Service was its chief competitor. UPS didn't belong to a rate bureau and had never opposed any application for authority by another carrier.

UPS had systematically expanded its operating authority over the previous twenty-five years, but it was still restricted by the ICC from serving a belt of states in the Midwest and prohibited from accepting more than 100 pounds per day from any one shipper going to any one receiver. For these and other reasons UPS supported deregulation.

30. Bennett C. Whitlock, Jr., president, American Trucking Associations, in a speech to the Illinois Trucking Association, June 11, 1976.

31. *Traffic World,* June 7, 1976, p. 20.

32. In December 1979, Borghesani sent an eight-page single-spaced memo to all congressional-affairs representatives of PCC members exhorting them to speak out for legislative reform on the *Toto* issue. He didn't mince words: "[The *Toto*] decision gravely threatens the continuation of the virtual monopoly [ATA] members have had for forty-five years over the rates and service of the nation's common carriers. . . ."

"If [the ATA and Teamsters] are against it, you as shippers must be for it. Their interests and your interests are mutually exclusive!"

The memo apparently went out without authorization of the PCC's longtime director; he promptly sent out a disclaimer and there was talk of firing Borghesani.

33. These and other quotes to follow are from a personal interview with Callaghan, October 6, 1980.

34. Kennedy's subsequent and broader deregulation bill addressed all the contract carriers' needs. Callaghan recalled how that came about: "When Kennedy's aide was drafting the bill, he called me up and said, 'What do you want in it?' I answered. He said, 'Is that all?' That's how public policy gets made!"

35. *Traffic World,* June 28, 1976, p. 16.

36. The real damage of the contract and private carriers to the powerful common carriers was economic. But that was largely inevitable, defection or no defection from the ATA. The reforms that the dissident conferences succeeded in getting—including compensated intercorporate hauling and elimination of the "Rule of Eight"—will diminish the profitability of common carriage—significantly so, if one can judge by the vehemence with which the ATA resisted them.

By keeping the private carriers "on the reservation," however, the ATA at least reduced the losses to others members. The compromise on intercorporate hauling stopped short of what private carriers might well have gotten from Congress. The original Cannon-Packwood bill was more generous to private carriers than the final legislation; tradeoffs along the way, which the PCC was obligated not to oppose, yielded a provision identical to the ATA-PCC compromise.

37. William Ris, staff counsel, Senate Commerce Committee, personal interview, July 22, 1980.

38. Aside from their differing priorities, one issue—labor protection—put the Teamsters and the ATA directly at odds. The ATA strongly opposed any sort of

provision guaranteeing laid-off Teamsters the "right of first hire." The conflict never materialized, however, because the Teamsters were unable to get any meaningful labor-protection provision in the legislation.

39. The best and most thorough analysis of nonmaterial incentives is Wilson, *Political Organizations,* chapters 2 and 3. See also Robert N. Salisbury, "An Exchange Theory of Interest Groups," *Midwest Journal of Political Science* 8 (1969): 1–32; Hayes, *Lobbyists and Legislators;* and Berry, *Lobbying for the People.*

40. Wilson, *Political Organizations,* pp. 166–67.

41. *Congressional Record,* 96th Cong., 2d sess., vol. 126, no. 57 (April 15, 1980), p. S3619.

42. These findings contrast with what Bauer, Pool, and Dexter concluded in their classic study of tariff legislation. The one common finding has to do with organizational paralysis: in both the trucking and the tariff battles, major groups that "should" have been active weren't—NAM and the Chamber of Commerce on the tariff issue, the chamber and the Business Roundtable on trucking reform. But beyond that, Bauer, Pool, and Dexter found that their evaluations of self-interest were not good predictors of whether or not the heads of business groups made efforts to lobby on foreign trade legislation. Ad hoc groups were set up, but they suffered from lack of resources.

The nature of the issue is probably a major explanation for the difference in findings. With respect to the tariff issue examined by Bauer, Pool, and Dexter, the self-interest of lobby groups was often complex. Compounding this complexity was the fact that the debate centered, not on the granting of special-interest benefits directly, but rather on delegation of tariff-setting authority to the executive branch, which allowed for considerable obfuscation of the outcome. Trucking reform, by contrast, was so ripe as an issue that most groups had long since determined whether or not deregulation served their own self-interest. As the issue became one of Carter's major legislative priorities, and then one of the biggest political battles of the Ninety-sixth Congress, it was difficult for affected groups to stay out of the fray. Bauer, Pool, and Dexter, *American Business and Public Policy.*

Chapter Six

1. Raymond A. Bauer, Ithiel de Sola Pool, and Lewis Anthony Dexter, *American Business and Public Policy* (New York: Atherton Press, 1963).

2. U.S. Congress, Senate, Judiciary Committee, *Oversight of Freight Rate Competition in the Motor Carrier Industry: Testimony of John H. Shenefield, Assistant Attorney General, U.S. Department of Justice,* 95th Cong., 1st and 2d sess., October 27 and 28, 1977; March 10 and 13, 1978, p. 13.

3. Thomas Gale Moore, "The Beneficiaries of Trucking Regulation," *The Journal of Law and Economics,* October 1978, p. 339. Moore estimated that the combination of regulation and unionization resulted in gains to Teamster members of between $1 billion and $1.3 billion in 1972.

4. Charles L. Schultze, *The Public Use of Private Interest* (Washington, D.C.: The Brookings Institution, 1977), pp. 22–25.

5. Gordon Tullock, "Achieving Deregulation—A Public Choice Perspective," *Regulation: AEI Journal on Government and Society,* November/December 1978, p. 51.

6. *New York Times,* November 13, 1977.

7. For different views on the equity of compensation in this context see: Harold M. Hochman, "Rule Change and Transitional Equity," in Hochman and George E. Peterson (eds.), *Redistribution through Public Choice* (New York: Columbia University Press, 1974); and Steven Kelman, "A Case for In-Kind Transfers," *Economics and Philosophy* 2 (1986).

8. Tullock, p. 54.

9. B. Kent Burton, legislative representative, American Trucking Associations, personal interview, March 24, 1980.

10. Special executive committee meeting, American Trucking Associations, May 28, 1980.

11. Bartley M. O'Hara, legislative counsel, International Brotherhood of Teamsters, personal interview, April 11, 1980.

12. *Washington Post,* December 1, 1980.

13. The following summary draws from three articles: Robert S. Goldfarb, "Compensating Victims of Policy Change," *Regulation: AEI Journal on Government and Society,* September/October 1980; Kenneth Gordon, "Deregulation, Property Rights and the Compensation of Losers," American Enterprise Institute Working Paper no. 4, May 15, 1980; and Edmund W. Kitch, "Can We Buy Our Way Out of Harmful Regulation?" in Donald L. Martin and Warren F. Schwartz (eds.), *Deregulating American Industry* (Lexington, Mass.: Lexington Books, 1977).

14. Alfred Marshall once observed that the greatest return on monopoly is the quiet life. A regulated monopolist enjoys the same luxury.

The epigraph at the head of this section is from Charles L. Schultze, *The Politics and Economics of Public Spending* (Washington, D.C.: The Brookings Institution, 1968), p. 43.

15. *Congressional Record,* 96th Cong., 2d sess., vol. 126, no. 14 (February 1, 1980), p. S793.

16. *Washington Post,* May 23, 1980.

17. Robert P. Biller, "On Tolerating Policy and Organizational Termination: Some Design Considerations," *Policy Sciences,* June 1976, pp. 145–46.

18. *Congressional Quarterly,* November 5, 1977.

19. Deregulators did use other transitional devices to allay fears of small-town blues, including monitoring: the act called for a study of the effects of decontrol on service to outlying areas. But their most calculated tactic was to preserve the common-carrier obligation itself in the deregulation act—a ploy designed to beat the ATA at its own game.

To elaborate, the truckers had long insisted that the regulatory obligation to provide service to all those who desired it was the only thing that kept trucks rolling to small towns, most of which were unprofitable to serve, according to the industry. Deregulators had consistently countered that the common-carrier obligation was a paper tiger: The ICC had never enforced it and there was no evidence that carriers honored it voluntarily; to the limited extent that regulated carriers did serve small towns, it was because such service was profitable. Nevertheless, recognizing the appeal of the truckers' argument, deregulators provided in the bill for the continuation of the common-carrier obligation—an action inconsistent with the economic philosophy of deregulation, which aims to do away with internal cross-subsidization. The deregulators' ploy riled truckers but may have had some soothing effect on those who feared for small towns.

20. Martin and Schwartz, *Deregulating American Industry,* p. 106.

21. Ibid., pp. 101–2.

22. Alfred E. Kahn, "Applications of Economics to an Imperfect World," *American Economic Review,* May 1979, p. 12.

23. Ibid., p. 7.

24. Ibid., p. 5.

25. Ibid., p. 7.

26. Ibid., p. 10.

27. Ibid.

28. *Report to the President and the Attorney General of the National Commission for the Review of Antitrust Laws and Procedures,* January 1979, p. 213.

29. U.S. Congress, Senate, Commerce, Science, and Transportation Committee, *Hearings on Economic Regulation of the Trucking Industry,* 96th Cong., 1st and 2d sess. (hereafter *Commerce Committee Hearings*), pt. 5, February 21, 26 and 27, 1980, p. 1591.

30. *Congressional Record,* 96th Cong., 2d sess., vol. 126, no. 14 (February 1, 1980) p. S793.

31. Goldfarb, p. 27.

32. Ibid., p. 28.

33. Bruce M. Owen and Ronald Braeutigam, *The Regulation Game: Strategic Use of the Administrative Process* (Cambridge, Mass.: Ballinger Publishing Co., 1978), pp. 20–21.

34. One reason for postponing or phasing in reform is to allow time for an adjustment in people's expectations. But the delay need not wait until after the reform legislation is passed. The shift in expectations begins as soon as the political debate commences. So it's justified to deduct the time spent getting a bill from the total period of delay deemed desirable, much as a judge reduces a prisoner's courtroom sentence by the time already spent in jail.

35. Thomas Gale Moore, *Trucking Regulation: Lessons from Europe* (Washington, D.C.: American Enterprise Institute, 1976).

36. Darius W. Gaskins, Jr., and James M. Voytko, "Managing the Transition to Deregulation," *Law and Contemporary Problems,* Winter 1981.

37. Several of the Interstate Commerce Commissioners warned truckers that, if certainty was what they wanted, they should lobby to be rid of ICC controls. "Uncertainty is inherent in trucking regulation," one commissioner told them. "Will a route extension be approved? Will a deviation request be denied? Will a rate increase be cut back? Generally, there are few things more predictable than the unpredictability of a regulatory agency. [By contrast] the rules of the market never change" (*Washington Post,* March 6, 1980).

But if "uncertainty is inherent in trucking regulation," that is a recent development. Historically, regulatory agencies like the ICC have been highly predictable—consistently protective of industry. Even an agency that has abandoned that philosophy to take a competitive stance is arguably still more predictable than the free market.

38. *Congressional Record,* 96th Cong., 2d sess., vol. 126, no. 57 (April 15, 1980), p. S3586.

39. Ibid. (February 1, 1980), p. S793.

40. *Commerce Committee Hearings*, pt. 5, February 21, 26, and 27, 1980, p. 1868.

41. Letter from Bennett C. Whitlock, Jr., to "All of Those Who Are Interested in the Survival of the Trucking Industry," June 24, 1980.

42. Ibid.

43. Goldfarb, p. 30.

44. Gaskins and Voytko.

Chapter Seven

1. Thomas C. Schelling, *The Strategy of Conflict* (Cambridge: Harvard University Press, 1960), p. 21.

2. Ibid., pp. 21–22.

3. Richard E. Neustadt, *Presidential Power: The Politics of Leadership* (New York: John Wiley and Sons, 1960), p. 59.

4. Schelling, p. 22.

5. George C. Edwards III, *Presidential Influence in Congress* (San Francisco: W.H. Freeman and Co., 1980), p. 135.

6. Quoted in Edwards, p. 138.

7. Ibid., p. 134.

8. Samuel B. Bacharach and Edward J. Lawler, *Bargaining: Power, Tactics and Outcomes* (San Francisco: Jossey-Bass Publishers, 1981), p. 51.

9. *New York Times,* September 14, 1980.

10. Memorandum from Rick Neustadt to Stuart Eizenstat, January 22, 1980.

11. Working closely with the White House was the DOT Office of Congressional Affairs. As lead agency on the trucking bill, DOT carried the burden of lobbying (or "liaison," as it is described, since administrative agencies are forbidden by law to "lobby"). The White House relied on its own congressional liaison staff as well. For selective help, White House aides called on specific administration officials. At their request, Esther Peterson, head of the White House Office of Consumer Affairs, contacted proconsumer members of the key committees. The Secretary of Agriculture talked with senators on the Agriculture Committee; later his department contacted members of Howard's subcommittee about the food-exemption issue. Officials from the Department of Justice played a key role throughout the trucking battle.

12. In addition to lobbying the Hill directly, the White House sought to apply pressure indirectly. The ad hoc coalition was the primary vehicle for that strategy and, as chapter 5 described, the administration worked closely with that group.

To show its appreciation after the triumphant Senate floor vote, the White House invited in about thirty of the most active coalition members for what one aide called a "Thank You, Keep on Trucking" session. Eizenstat, Kahn, and Goldschmidt were all there to commend the group for its efforts. President Carter was scheduled to drop in as well—"to emphasize the importance of the measure," as a staff memo requesting his presence explained. But the day beforehand proved one of crisis when the attempt to rescue the fifty-two American hostages in Iran ended in disaster, and the president's appearance was cancelled.

The administration worked primarily through the coalition to reach corporate executives and other influential supporters of trucking reform. But the White House contacted some corporate leaders directly to mobilize their support, or, in the case of General Motors, to question their opposition. (Shortly after GM representatives spoke out in favor of the ATA's position on antitrust immunity, a White House aide reported the news to Eizenstat for his information "in case (GM president) Murphy asks you for any more help on 'excessive government regulation.' ")

13. Neustadt, pp. 34–35.

14. If an Oval Office meeting on trucking in the midst of the Iran hostage crisis symbolizes the use of heavy artillery, then another incident illustrates the attention to detail. Throughout the day that the Senate debated and voted on S. 2245, the administration kept a team of DOT and White House staffers in the Capitol, ready to answer questions or track down information. When Will Ris, the Senate Commerce Committee counsel, pointed out the Hollings amendment on food and said he thought it was flawed, the administration team members went to work. Within twenty minutes, they confirmed Ris's suspicion, giving Cannon and Packwood powerful new ammunition to use in winning the critical vote of the day.

15. Ron Lewis, deputy director, Council on Wage and Price Stability, personal interview, September 15, 1980.

16. Under any circumstances, Goldschmidt's testimony represented an unusual step for a president to take against a member of his own party in Congress. White House aide Ron Lewis described how it was handled. "We told Howard we would criticize his bill ahead of time. . . . We did it more nicely than we said we would, and Howard was grateful to us for that. But he knew we were serious then." Lewis interview.

17. For example, prior to a meeting between White House officials and key committee staffers, DPS member Rick Neustadt gave Stuart Eizenstat the following advice: "If they press us on whether we are threatening a veto, I urge you *not* to get into a discussion of which items are indispensable. It is too early to spell out veto threats or lock ourselves in. On the other hand, the House staffers must understand that we are going to be tough. The trick is to let them know their bill is unacceptable without threatening them." Memorandum, February 20, 1980.

18. The following account draws largely from a series of memos from Rick Neustadt and Ron Lewis to Stuart Eizenstat, written during late April and May of 1980.

19. Memorandum from Rick Neustadt to Stuart Eizenstat, October 23, 1979.

20. Undated memorandum from Stuart Eizenstat and Alfred Kahn to President Carter. The memo, written in late December 1979, was never sent.

21. Memorandum from Rick Neustadt to Bernie Aronson, February 27, 1980.

22. Memorandum from Rick Neustadt to Stuart Eizenstat, March 7, 1980.

23. Ibid., April 14, 1980.

24. Schelling, pp. 22–23.

25. This section draws heavily on informal conversations as well as formal interviews with the following: Mark Aron, Ron Lewis, Rick Neustadt, and James Voytko.

26. Nancy Drabble, staff attorney, Congress Watch, personal interview, October 8, 1980.

27. This section draws heavily on informal conversations as well as formal interviews with the following: Ron Lewis, Rick Neustadt, B. Kent Burton, George Mead, Will Ris, and Jay Steptoe.

28. This section draws heavily on informal conversations as well as formal interviews with the following: William Diefenderfer, Cindy Douglass, Will Ris, and Matt Scocozza.

29. This section draws heavily on informal conversations as well as formal interviews with the following: Ron Lewis and Jay Steptoe.

30. This section draws heavily on informal conversations as well as formal interviews with the following: B. Kent Burton, Jack Fryer, Pamela Garvey, George Mead, Jack Schenendorf, and Richard Sullivan.

31. Transcript of proceedings, ATA executive committee meeting, May 28, 1980, pp. 22–23.

32. This section draws heavily on informal conversations as well as formal interviews with the following ATA representatives: B. Kent Burton, Martin Cromartie, Stanley Hamilton, Allan Jones, George Mead, and Don Tepper.

33. Transcript of proceedings, ATA executive committee meeting, February 20, 1980, p. 84.

34. Ibid., October 19, 1976, p. 105.

35. Ibid., June 18, 1975, p. 44.

36. This same reasoning is responsive to an economic critique of the industry's historical "bargaining" stance. That critique says that carriers and Teamsters were myopic in being so fiercely protectionist, because the result was to drive business into the unregulated sector—primarily private carriage. Granted, private carriage had become a significant threat to the regulated industry by the late 1970s, but it's not certain that the loss of business due to protectionism more than offset the monopoly profits that ICC controls produced.

37. Transcript of proceedings, ATA executive committee meeting, June 17, 1976, p. 62.

Chapter Eight

1. Arthur M. Okun, "Consensus and Controversy in Political Economy," in Ryan C. Amacher, Robert D. Tollison, and Thomas D. Willett (eds.), *The Economic Approach to Public Policy: Selected Readings* (Ithaca: Cornell University Press, 1976), p. 44.

2. Darius W. Gaskins, Jr., "Some Implications of Recent Reforms in Surface Transportation Regulation," paper delivered to a symposium at the School of Business Administration, University of California, Berkeley, March 2, 1981, p. 3.

3. Ibid., p. 4.

4. As of 1983, nearly one-fourth of all active federal judges had attended a two-week seminar in law and economics sponsored by Emory University. Henry G. Manne, director, Law and Economics Center, Emory University, telephone conversation, April 20, 1983.

5. Hugh Heclo, "Issue Networks and the Executive Establishment," in Anthony King (ed.), *The New American Political System* (Washington, D.C.: American Enterprise Institute, 1978), pp. 87–124.

6. John Maynard Keynes, *The General Theory of Employment, Interest, and Money* (New York: Harcourt, Brace and Co., 1936), p. 283.

7. James Q. Wilson (ed.), *The Politics of Regulation* (New York: Basic Books, 1980), p. 379.

8. Michael Pertschuk, *Revolt against Regulation: The Rise and Pause of the Consumer Movement* (Berkeley: University of California Press, 1982), p. 57.

9. For much the same reasons, deregulation served the political needs of various elected and appointed officials, and the competition between them for credit was extremely important in promoting the issue. Kennedy's attempt to get jurisdiction pressured Cannon to act on both the airline and trucking issues, and both senators were a goad to Carter. In that respect, the fragmentation of our political system, and of Congress in particular—a structural feature that is generally thought to work to the benefit of client groups—did just the opposite in this instance. Martha Derthick and Paul Quirk, moreover, conclude that this phenomenon may be characteristic rather than atypical of what some have called the "new American political system," in which fragmentation is greater than ever: "The current political system encourages rival credit claiming and competition for proprietary sponsorship of promising issues, and this means that few issues with potential for successful action are likely to be ignored."

More generally, Derthick and Quirk conclude that the current condition of our political system is notable for the resources and rewards it offers for overcoming particularism: "Responsive to mass sentiment almost since its founding, the political system seems to be more so than ever today, when mass education and communication and new technologies make it possible for such sentiment to be formed, expressed, and measured with unprecedented speed. At the same time, expert analysis, oriented toward broad conceptions of the public interest, is more thoroughly institutionalized in and addressed to the national government than ever before. This creates an unprecedented potential for linking the forces of expert analysis and mass sentiment as the basis for action—and political leaders who by luck or skill manage to achieve that union have a good chance of defeating narrow, particularistic interests." Martha Derthick and Paul J. Quirk, *The Politics of Deregulation* (Washington, D.C.: The Brookings Institution, 1985), pp. 255; 257–58.

10. Airline deregulation is illustrative. The airline industry succumbed to a divide-and-conquer tactic; the trucking industry did not. And while some accounts of

the airline contest attribute victory to that, no less important were several other factors: economists' evidence from unregulated markets, the guarantee of "essential air service" to small communities, and pressure from the Carter White House.

11. To see this, consider again the nature of the problem examined in chapter 1. Most important, the group that benefits is organized around the issue whereas whose who pay (diffusely) for it are not. Mobilization of a coalition representing consumers and other payer groups is the most direct response to that tactical advantage. Chief-executive support is also necessary because, as we've seen, the major contribution of even a strong coalition is largely symbolic and hence insufficient to offset the bargaining advantage of a powerful client group.

Even in the politically easier case where the aim is to block the initiation of a client policy, success would likely require both activity by a coalition of players who stand to lose and executive leverage. The harder case—trying to terminate an existing client policy—calls for yet more: A strong case on the merits is necessary to overcome the Do-No-Direct-Harm rule of our political system as well as to reduce legislators' fear of the devil unknown. Transitional policy mechanisms such as delay and ambiguity also serve to lessen uncertainty and/or to reduce the perceived and real economic loss to client-group members.

12. John Mendeloff, *Regulating Safety: An Economical and Political Analysis of Occupational Safety and Health Policy* (Cambridge: MIT Press, 1979), p. x.

13. Graham T. Allison, *Essence of Decision: Explaining the Cuban Missile Crisis* (Boston: Little, Brown and Co., 1971), p. 68.

14. The definitive work on this general subject is still Murray Edelman, *The Symbolic Uses of Politics* (Urbana: University of Illinois Press, 1964).

15. Robert D. Behn, "Policy Analysis and Policy Politics," *Policy Analysis,* Spring 1981, p. 223.

16. Ibid., p. 215.

17. Ibid., p. 224.

18. George J. Stigler, "The Theory of Economic Regulation," *Bell Journal of Economics* 2 (Spring 1971); Richard A. Posner, "Theories of Economic Regulation," *Bell Journal of Economics* 5 (Autumn 1974); Sam Peltzman, "Toward a More General Theory of Regulation," *The Journal of Law and Economics,* August 1976.

19. In the course of explaining why economic theories of regulation had failed to account for certain kinds of regulatory behavior, James Q. Wilson implicitly criticized their excessive tidiness: ". . . politics differs from economics in that it manages conflict by forming heterogeneous coalitions out of persons with changeable and incommensurable preferences in order to make binding decisions for everyone. Political science is an effort to make statements about the formation of preferences and nonmarket methods of managing conflict among those preferences; as a discipline, it will be as inelegant, disorderly, and changeable as its subject matter." One reviewer of Wilson responded as follows: "Inelegance, disorder, and the absence of theoretical commitment are not scientific ideals." Wilson, p. 363. Review of Wilson's *The Politics of Regulation,* by Kenneth A. Shepsle, *Journal of Political Economy,* February 1982, p. 220.

20. Wilson, p. 394.

21. Both quotes are from Gaskins, pp. 9-10; 11.

Index